IN ASSOCIATION WITH

SQA

**HODDER GIBSON**

# Model Papers

## WITH ANSWERS

**PLUS:** Official SQA 2014 & 2015 Past Papers With Answers

# National 5
# English

Model Papers, 2014 & 2015 Exams

**HODDER GIBSON**

AN HACHETTE UK COMPANY

This book contains the official SQA 2014 and 2015 Exams for National 5 English, with associated SQA approved answers modified from the official marking instructions that accompany the paper.

In addition the book contains model papers, together with answers, plus study skills advice. These papers, some of which may include a limited number of previously published SQA questions, have been specially commissioned by Hodder Gibson, and have been written by experienced senior teachers and examiners in line with the new National 5 syllabus and assessment outlines, Spring 2013. This is not SQA material but has been devised to provide further practice for National 5 examinations in 2014 and beyond.

Hodder Gibson is grateful to the copyright holders, as credited on the final page of the Answer Section, for permission to use their material. Every effort has been made to trace the copyright holders and to obtain their permission for the use of copyright material. Hodder Gibson will be happy to receive information allowing us to rectify any error or omission in future editions.

Hachette UK's policy is to use papers that are natural, renewable and recyclable products and made from wood grown in sustainable forests. The logging and manufacturing processes are expected to conform to the environmental regulations of the country of origin.

Orders: please contact Bookpoint Ltd, 130 Park Drive, Milton Park, Abingdon, Oxon OX14 4SE. Telephone: (44) 01235 827720. Fax: (44) 01235 400454. Lines are open 9.00–5.00, Monday to Saturday, with a 24-hour message answering service. Visit our website at www.hoddereducation.co.uk. Hodder Gibson can be contacted direct on: Tel: 0141 848 1609; Fax: 0141 889 6315; email: hoddergibson@hodder.co.uk

This collection first published in 2015 by
Hodder Gibson, an imprint of Hodder Education,
An Hachette UK Company
2a Christie Street
Paisley PA1 1NB

Typeset by Aptara, Inc.

Printed in the UK

A catalogue record for this title is available from the British Library

ISBN: 978-1-4718-6056-0

3 2 1

2016 2015

# Introduction

## Study Skills – what you need to know to pass exams!

### Pause for thought

Many students might skip quickly through a page like this. After all, we all know how to revise. Do you really though?

### Think about this:

"IF YOU ALWAYS DO WHAT YOU ALWAYS DO, YOU WILL ALWAYS GET WHAT YOU HAVE ALWAYS GOT."

Do you like the grades you get? Do you want to do better? If you get full marks in your assessment, then that's great! Change nothing! This section is just to help you get that little bit better than you already are.

There are two main parts to the advice on offer here. The first part highlights fairly obvious things but which are also very important. The second part makes suggestions about revision that you might not have thought about but which WILL help you.

### Part 1

DOH! It's so obvious but …

### Start revising in good time

Don't leave it until the last minute – this will make you panic.

Make a revision timetable that sets out work time AND play time.

### Sleep and eat!

Obvious really, and very helpful. Avoid arguments or stressful things too – even games that wind you up. You need to be fit, awake and focused!

### Know your place!

Make sure you know exactly **WHEN and WHERE** your exams are.

### Know your enemy!

**Make sure you know what to expect in the exam.**

How is the paper structured?

How much time is there for each question?

What types of question are involved?

Which topics seem to come up time and time again?

Which topics are your strongest and which are your weakest?

Are all topics compulsory or are there choices?

### Learn by DOING!

There is no substitute for past papers and practice papers – they are simply essential! Tackling this collection of papers and answers is exactly the right thing to be doing as your exams approach.

### Part 2

People learn in different ways. Some like low light, some bright. Some like early morning, some like evening / night. Some prefer warm, some prefer cold. But everyone uses their BRAIN and the brain works when it is active. Passive learning – sitting gazing at notes – is the most INEFFICIENT way to learn anything. Below you will find tips and ideas for making your revision more effective and maybe even more enjoyable. What follows gets your brain active, and active learning works!

### Activity 1 – Stop and review

#### Step 1

When you have done no more than 5 minutes of revision reading STOP!

#### Step 2

Write a heading in your own words which sums up the topic you have been revising.

#### Step 3

Write a summary of what you have revised in no more than two sentences. Don't fool yourself by saying, "I know it, but I cannot put it into words". That just means you don't know it well enough. If you cannot write your summary, revise that section again, knowing that you must write a summary at the end of it. Many of you will have notebooks full of blue/black ink writing. Many of the pages will not be especially attractive or memorable so try to liven them up a bit with colour as you are reviewing and rewriting. **This is a great memory aid, and memory is the most important thing.**

## Activity 2 – Use technology!

Why should everything be written down? Have you thought about "mental" maps, diagrams, cartoons and colour to help you learn? And rather than write down notes, why not record your revision material?

What about having a text message revision session with friends? Keep in touch with them to find out how and what they are revising and share ideas and questions.

Why not make a video diary where you tell the camera what you are doing, what you think you have learned and what you still have to do? No one has to see or hear it, but the process of having to organise your thoughts in a formal way to explain something is a very important learning practice.

Be sure to make use of electronic files. You could begin to summarise your class notes. Your typing might be slow, but it will get faster and the typed notes will be easier to read than the scribbles in your class notes. Try to add different fonts and colours to make your work stand out. You can easily Google relevant pictures, cartoons and diagrams which you can copy and paste to make your work more attractive and **MEMORABLE**.

## Activity 3 – This is it. Do this and you will know lots!

### Step 1

In this task you must be very honest with yourself! Find the SQA syllabus for your subject (www.sqa.org.uk). Look at how it is broken down into main topics called MANDATORY knowledge. That means stuff you MUST know.

### Step 2

BEFORE you do ANY revision on this topic, write a list of everything that you already know about the subject. It might be quite a long list but you only need to write it once. It shows you all the information that is already in your long-term memory so you know what parts you do not need to revise!

### Step 3

Pick a chapter or section from your book or revision notes. Choose a fairly large section or a whole chapter to get the most out of this activity.

With a buddy, use Skype, Facetime, Twitter or any other communication you have, to play the game "If this is the answer, what is the question?". For example, if you are revising Geography and the answer you provide is "meander", your buddy would have to make up a question like "What is the word that describes a feature of a river where it flows slowly and bends often from side to side?".

Make up 10 "answers" based on the content of the chapter or section you are using. Give this to your buddy to solve while you solve theirs.

### Step 4

Construct a wordsearch of at least 10 × 10 squares. You can make it as big as you like but keep it realistic. Work together with a group of friends. Many apps allow you to make wordsearch puzzles online. The words and phrases can go in any direction and phrases can be split. Your puzzle must only contain facts linked to the topic you are revising. Your task is to find 10 bits of information to hide in your puzzle, but you must not repeat information that you used in Step 3. DO NOT show where the words are. Fill up empty squares with random letters. Remember to keep a note of where your answers are hidden but do not show your friends. When you have a complete puzzle, exchange it with a friend to solve each other's puzzle.

### Step 5

Now make up 10 questions (not "answers" this time) based on the same chapter used in the previous two tasks. Again, you must find NEW information that you have not yet used. Now it's getting hard to find that new information! Again, give your questions to a friend to answer.

### Step 6

As you have been doing the puzzles, your brain has been actively searching for new information. Now write a NEW LIST that contains only the new information you have discovered when doing the puzzles. Your new list is the one to look at repeatedly for short bursts over the next few days. Try to remember more and more of it without looking at it. After a few days, you should be able to add words from your second list to your first list as you increase the information in your long-term memory.

## FINALLY! Be inspired...

Make a list of different revision ideas and beside each one write **THINGS I HAVE** tried, **THINGS I WILL** try and **THINGS I MIGHT** try. Don't be scared of trying something new.

And remember – "FAIL TO PREPARE AND PREPARE TO FAIL!"

# English

## The course

The National 5 English course aims to enable you to develop the ability to:

- Listen, talk, read and write, as appropriate to purpose, audience and context
- Understand, analyse and evaluate texts, including Scottish texts, as appropriate to purpose and audience in the contexts of literature, language and media
- Create and produce texts, as appropriate to purpose, audience and context
- Apply knowledge and understanding of language.

### How the course is graded

The grade you finally get for National 5 English depends on three things:

- The two internal Unit Assessments you do in school or college: "Analysis and Evaluation" and "Creation and Production"; these don't count towards the final grade, but you must have passed them before you can get a final grade
- Your Portfolio of Writing – this is submitted in April for marking by SQA and counts for 30% of your final grade
- The two exams you sit in May – that's what this book is all about.

## The exams

### Reading for Understanding, Analysis and Evaluation

- Exam time: 1 hour
- Total marks: 30
- Weighting in final grade: 30%
- What you have to do: read a passage and answer questions about it.

### Critical Reading

- Exam time: 1 hour 30 minutes
- Total marks: 40 (20 for each section)
- Weighting in final grade: 40%
- What you have to do: Section 1: read an extract from one of the Scottish Texts which are set for National 5 and answer questions about it; Section 2: write an essay about a work of literature you have studied during your course.

## Reading for Understanding, Analysis and Evaluation

### Three important tips to start with

- Since there will usually be a question asking you to summarise some or all of the passage, it is really important to read the whole passage before you even look at the questions. Doing this will give you a chance to get a rough idea of the main ideas in the passage, and you can add to this as you work your way through the questions.
- Pay close attention to the number of marks available for each question and make sure your answer is appropriate to the number of marks. In most questions, you will get 1 mark for each correct point.
- Some questions tell you to "use your own words". This means you mustn't just copy chunks from the passage – you have to show that you understand what it means by rephrasing it in your own words.

### Questions which ask for understanding

- Keep your answers fairly short and pay attention to the number of marks available.

### Questions about language features

- This type of question will ask you to comment on features such as Word Choice, Imagery, Sentence Structure and Tone.
- You should pick out a relevant language feature and make a valid comment about its impact. Try to make your comments as specific as possible and avoid vague comments (like "It is a good word to use because it gives me a clear picture of what the writer is saying"). Some hints:

  - **Word Choice:** always try to pick a single word and then give its connotations, i.e. what it **suggests**
  - **Sentence Structure:** don't just name the feature – try to explain what effect it achieves **in that particular sentence**
  - **Imagery:** try to explain what the image means **literally** and then go on to explain what the writer is **suggesting** by using that image

- **Tone**      this is always difficult – a good tip is to imagine the sentence or paragraph being read out loud and try to spot how the words or the structure give it a particular tone.

## Summary questions

- Make sure you follow the instruction about what it is you are to summarise (the question will be as helpful as possible).
- Stick to the main ideas; avoid unimportant points and never include examples.
- Make sure you earn all the marks available for the question.

# Critical Reading

## Section 1 – Scottish Text

The most important thing to remember here is that there are two very different types of question to be answered:

- Three or four questions (for a total of 12 marks) which focus entirely on the extract
- One question (for 8 marks) which requires knowledge of the whole text (or of another poem or short story by the same writer).

The first type of question will often ask you to use the same type of close textual analysis skills you used in the Reading part of your Analysis and Evaluation Unit. There can also be a question asking for the type of summary skills you're used to in the Reading part of the exam. The golden rule is to read each question very carefully and do exactly as instructed.

The last question for 8 marks can be answered **either** in bullet points **or** as a "mini-essay". Choose whichever approach you are more comfortable with. Make as many relevant points as you can. If you look at the Marking Guide which is used for this type of question (see page 163), you'll get an idea of how this question is marked and this should help you in your approach.

Final bit of advice for the Scottish Text question: when you see the extract in the exam paper, don't get too confident just because you recognise it (you certainly should recognise it if you've studied properly!) And even if you've answered questions on it before, remember that the questions in the exam are likely to be different, so stay alert.

## Section 2 – Critical Essay

A common mistake is to rely too heavily on whole paragraphs you have used in practice essays and try to use them for the question you have chosen in the exam. The trick is to come to the exam with lots of ideas and thoughts about at least one of the texts you have studied and use these to tackle the question you choose from the exam paper. You mustn't use the exam question as an excuse to trot out an answer you've prepared in advance.

## Structure

Every good essay has a structure, but there is no "correct" structure, no magic formula that the examiners are looking for. It's **your** essay, so structure it the way **you** want. As long as you're answering the question all the way through, then you'll be fine.

## Relevance

Be relevant to the question **all the time** – not just in the first and last paragraphs.

## Central Concerns

Try to make sure your essay shows that you have thought about and understood the central concerns of the text, i.e. what it's "about" – the ideas and themes the writer is exploring in the text.

## Quotations

In poetry and drama essays, you're expected to quote from the text, but never fall into the trap of learning a handful of quotations and forcing them all into the essay regardless of the question you're answering. In prose essays, quotation is much less important, and you can show your knowledge much more effectively by referring in detail to what happens in key sections of the novel or the short story.

## Techniques

You are expected to show some understanding of how various literary techniques work within a text, but simply naming them will not get you marks, and structuring your essay around techniques rather than around relevant ideas in the text is not a good idea.

# Good luck!

Remember that the rewards for passing National 5 English are well worth it! Your pass will help you get the future you want for yourself. In the exam, be confident in your own ability. If you're not sure how to answer a question, trust your instincts and just give it a go anyway – keep calm and don't panic! GOOD LUCK!

NATIONAL 5

# Model Paper 1

Whilst this Model Paper has been specially commissioned by Hodder Gibson for use as practice for the National 5 exams, the key reference documents remain the SQA Specimen Paper 2013 and the SQA Past Papers 2014 and 2015.

HODDER GIBSON
LEARN MORE

# National Qualifications
## MODEL PAPER 1

# English
# Reading for Understanding, Analysis and Evaluation

Duration — 1 hour

**Total marks — 30**

When you are told to do so, open the booklet, read the passage and attempt all the questions, using your own words as far as possible.

**Before attempting the questions you must check that your answer booklet is for the same subject and level as this question paper.**

On the answer booklet, you must clearly identify the question number you are attempting.

Use **blue** or **black** ink.

Before leaving the examination room you must give your answer booklet to the Invigilator.
If you do not, you may lose all the marks for this paper.

## SUPERSTITION

*In this passage, the writer explores how superstition can both help and hinder us.*

Tennis players are a funny bunch. Have you noticed how they always ask for three balls instead of two; how they bounce the ball the same number of times before serving, as if any deviation from their routine might bring the world collapsing on their heads?

5 But the superstitions and rituals so beloved by the world's top players are not confined to the court. They take even more bizarre twists when the poor dears get home after their matches. Goran Ivanisevic got it into his head that if he won a match he had to repeat everything he did the previous day, such as eating the same food at the same restaurant, talking to the same people and watching the same TV programmes. One year this meant that he had to watch Teletubbies every morning during his Wimbledon campaign. "Sometimes it got very boring," he 10 said.

Could it be that these multifarious superstitions tell us something of deeper importance not only about humanity but about other species on the planet?

The answer, I think, is to be found in the world of pigeon. Yes, really. These feathered fellows, you see, are the tennis players of the bird world. Don't take my word for it: that was the 15 opinion of B. F. Skinner, the man widely regarded as the father of modern psychology.

Skinner's view was based on a groundbreaking experiment that he carried out in 1947 in which he placed some hungry pigeons in a cage attached to an automatic mechanism that delivered food "at regular intervals with no reference whatsoever to the bird's behaviour". He discovered that the pigeons associated the delivery of the food with whatever chance actions they happened to be 20 performing at the moment it was first delivered. So what did the pigeons do? They kept performing the same actions, even though they had no effect whatsoever on the release of food.

I know, I know. This is nothing compared with the weird behaviour that goes on at Wimbledon, but do you see the connection? The pigeons were acting as if they could influence the mechanism delivering the Trill in just the same way that Ivanisevic thought that he could 25 influence the outcome of his next match by watching Teletubbies. To put it a tad formally, they both witnessed a random connection between a particular kind of behaviour and a desired outcome, and then (wrongly) inferred that one caused the other.

But did Ivanisevic really believe that his superstitions were effective or was he just having us on? Well, let's hear from the man himself — this is what he said when asked if he had ever 30 abandoned a ritual when it stopped working: "I didn't. They do work. I won Wimbledon." So, he really did believe. And what of the pigeons? They were, unfortunately, unavailable for interview.

Even cricketers, perhaps the brightest and most sensible sportsmen of all (well, that's what they tell us), are not immune to superstition. Jack Russell, the former England wicketkeeper, was among the most notorious, refusing to change his hat or wicketkeeping pads throughout his 35 career, even though they became threadbare and smelly, something that really got up the noses of his team-mates.

But this raises another, deeper question: why do so many of us maintain rituals of various kinds when they have no real connection with the desired outcome? Or, to put it another way, why is superstitious behaviour so widespread, not just within our species but beyond, when it seems to 40 confer no tangible benefits? It's here that things get really interesting (and just a little complex). And, as with most interesting things, the answer is to be found in deep evolutionary history.

Imagine a caveman going to pick some berries from some bushes near his rocky abode. He hears some rustling in the bushes and wrongly infers that there is a lion lurking in there and scarpers.
45  He even gets a little superstitious about those bushes and gives them a wide berth in future. Is this superstition a problem to our caveman? Well, not if there are plenty other berry-bearing bushes from which to get his five-a-day.

But suppose that there really is a lion living in those bushes. The caveman's behaviour now looks not only sensible but life-saving. So, a tendency to perceive connections that do not actually
50  exist can confer huge evolutionary benefits, providing a cocoon of safety in a turbulent and dangerous world. The only proviso (according to some devilishly complicated mathematics known as game theory) is this: your superstitions must not impose too much of a burden on those occasions when they are without foundation.

And this is almost precisely what superstitions look like in the modern world. Some believe in
55  horoscopes, but few allow them to dictate their behaviour; some like to wear the same lucky shoes to every job interview, but it is not as if wearing a different pair would improve their chances of success; some like to bounce the ball precisely seven times before serving at tennis, but although they are wrong to suppose that this ball-bouncing is implicated in their success, it does not harm their prospects.

60  It is only when a superstition begins to compromise our deeper goals and aspirations that we have moved along the spectrum of irrationality far enough to risk a diagnosis of obsessive compulsive disorder. Take Kolo Touré, the former Arsenal defender who insists on being the last player to leave the dressing room after the half-time break. No real problem, you might think, except that when William Gallas, his team-mate, was injured and needed treatment at half-time
65  during a match, Touré stayed in the dressing room until Gallas had been treated, forcing Arsenal to start the second half with only nine players.

When a superstition that is supposed to help you actually hinders you, it is probably time to kick the ritual into touch. With a rabbit's foot, obviously.

*Adapted from an article by Matthew Syed in The Times.*

MARKS

**Questions**

1. In line 14, the writer says that pigeons "are the tennis players of the bird world". Referring to key ideas in lines 1–27, explain what he means by this.    4

2. Look at lines 28–36.

   (a) What impression does the writer create of Goran Ivanisevic in these lines?    2

   (b) How does the writer convey surprise at the behaviour of Jack Russell?    2

3. Explain **in your own words** what key points the writer is illustrating by referring to the caveman (lines 43–53).    4

4. Describe the key features of the **sentence structure** in lines 54–59 and explain how it helps to convey the writer's main point.    4

5. Look at lines 60–68.

   (a) Explain how effective you find the word "spectrum" (line 61) as an **image** or **metaphor** to illustrate people's "irrationality".    2

   (b) Why does the writer include the anecdote about the footballer Kolo Touré (lines 62–66)?    2

   (c) How effective do you find the tone of the last paragraph (lines 67–68) as a conclusion to the passage?    2

6. A common feature of the writer's style in this passage is to use words or expressions which are unexpected in order to create a light-hearted tone. Find **two** examples of this from lines 1–47 and explain what is unexpected about each.    4

7. Referring to the whole article, list **in your own words** the key points the writer makes about superstitions.    4

**[END OF MODEL PAPER]**

# National
# Qualifications
# MODEL PAPER 1

## English
## Critical Reading

Duration — 1 hour and 30 minutes

**Total marks — 40**

**SECTION 1 — Scottish Text — 20 marks**

Read an extract from a Scottish text you have previously studied and attempt the questions.

Choose ONE text from either

Part A — Drama        Pages 2–7

or

Part B — Prose        Pages 8–17

or

Part C — Poetry       Pages 18–25

Attempt ALL the questions for your chosen text.

**SECTION 2 — Critical Essay — 20 marks**

Write ONE critical essay on previously studied text from Drama, Prose, Poetry, Film and Television Drama, or Language.

Your answer must be on a different genre from that chosen in Section 1.

You should spend approximately 45 minutes on each Section.

**Before attempting the questions you must check that your answer booklet is for the same subject and level as this question paper.**

On the answer booklet, you must clearly identify the question number you are attempting.

Use **blue** or **black** ink.

Before leaving the examination room you must give your answer booklet to the Invigilator. If you do not you may lose all the marks for this paper.

**HODDER**
GIBSON
LEARN MORE

## SECTION 1 — SCOTTISH TEXT — 20 marks

### PART A — SCOTTISH TEXT — DRAMA

**Text 1 — Drama**

If you choose this text you may not attempt a question on Drama in Section 2.

Read the extract below and then attempt the following questions.

**Bold Girls** by Rona Munro

*This extract is from Act One.*

*Deirdre appears in Marie's house for the first time.*

*Deirdre comes into the room. She stands uncertain in the centre of the room.*

*Marie enters behind her*

*The three older women just stare at Deirdre.*

DEIRDRE:   Can I stay here till I'm dry, Mrs? They won't let me up the road.

5 *There is a pause then Marie finally stirs*

MARIE:      You better sit down by the fire *(She switches on the TV)*

*Deirdre sits by the fire*

*Nora, Marie and Cassie slowly sit as well, watching her*

NORA:       I don't know your face.

10 *Deirdre says nothing. She doesn't look up from the fire*

Well where are you from?

*Deirdre jerks her head without turning*

Where?

DEIRDRE:   *(sullen, quietly)* Back of the school there.

15 NORA:       What's that?

DEIRDRE:   *(loudly)* Back of the school there.

NORA:       Those houses next the off-licence?

*Deirdre nods*

I know where you are. So what happened to you then?

20 *Deirdre shrugs. She looks up and catches Cassie's eye*

*Cassie turns quickly to look at the TV*

MARIE:      Will you take a cup of tea, love?

*Deirdre nods*

*Marie goes to make it*

25 *Nora stares at Deirdre a while longer, then turns to Cassie*

NORA:       So Cassie, looks like that wee brother of yours will miss his tea altogether?

CASSIE:     *(with her eyes on the TV)* Looks like he might.

NORA:       I hope he's the sense to stay in town.

MARKS

CASSIE:     Sure he'll phone next door, let us know what's happening.

30 NORA:       Aye he's a good boy.

*There is a pause while everyone watches the TV in an uncomfortable silence*

*Marie brings Deirdre the tea and some biscuits.  Deirdre takes it without saying anything, starts to eat and drink furtively and ravenously.  Cassie and Marie exchange glances over her head*

35 MARIE:      Turn the sound up on that will you, Nora?

## Questions

1. By referring to the whole extract, identify **four** ways in which Deirdre's behaviour makes her appear strange.                                                                                          4

2. Describe the way each of the three older women treats Deirdre.  Support your answers with reference to the text.                                                                                          6

3. Why do you think Marie asks Nora to turn up the sound on the TV? (line 35)                     2

4. By referring to this extract and to the play as a whole, discuss the role of Deirdre in the play.                                                                                                                      8

OR

**Text 2 — Drama**

If you choose this text you may not attempt a question on Drama in Section 2.

Read the extract below and then attempt the following questions.

*Sailmaker* **by Alan Spence**

*This extract is from the closing moments of Act One.*

(DAVIE *and* BILLY *enter, opposite sides of stage*)

BILLY:      What's up wi your face?

(DAVIE *shakes head*)

            What's the matter?

5  DAVIE:     Ah just got ma jotters.  Week's notice.

BILLY:      Jesus Christ!  What for?

DAVIE:     Ach!  They're saying the book's a dead loss.  They're gonnae shut it awthegether.  Put the sheriff's officers on tae the folk that still owe money.

BILLY:      Bastards.

10  DAVIE:     Getting that doin just finished it.  Losin the money an the ledgers an everythin.

BILLY:      But that wasnae your fault!

DAVIE:     Try tellin *them* that!  So that's me.  Scrubbed.  Again.  Laid off.  Redundant.  Services no longer required.  Just like that.  Ah don't know.  Work aw yer days an what've ye got tae show for it?  Turn roon an kick ye in the teeth.  Ah mean, what *have* ye got when ye come right down tae it.  Nothin.

15

BILLY:      Ah might be able to get ye a start in our place.  Cannae promise mind ye.  An if there was anything it wouldnae be much.  Maybe doin yer sweeper up or that.

DAVIE:     Anythin's better than nothin.

BILLY:      An once yer in the place, ye never know.  Somethin better might come up.

20  DAVIE:     (*Dead*) Aye.

BILLY:      Likes ae a storeman's job or that.

DAVIE:     Aye.

BILLY:      We never died a winter yet, eh?

(DAVIE *nods.*  BILLY *exits*)

25  DAVIE:     Scrubbed.  Get yer jacket on.  Pick up yer cards.  On yer way pal!  Out the door.

(ALEC *is playing with yacht, positions fid like bowsprit, bow like mast, tries to make 'sail' with cellophane, can't hold all the separate bits, drops them.  DAVIE comes in behind him*)

DAVIE:     Bit of bad news son.

(*Pause*)

30          Ah've lost ma job.  They gave me ma books.

ALEC:      What'll we dae?

MARKS

DAVIE:    Billy says he might be able to fix me up wi something.  Wouldnae be much.  (*Shrugs*) Better than nothing.  Ach, that was a lousy job anyway.  Ah'm better off out ae it.  Whatever happens.

35          Place is a right mess eh.  Amazin how it gets on top of ye.

ALEC:    Ah'll shove this in the Glory Hole.  Out the road.

(*Folds up cellophane, puts tools in bag and picks up bow, yacht, carries the lot and exits*)

DAVIE:    Ach aye.  No to worry.  Never died a winter yet.

**Questions**

5.  Summarise what is said between Davie and Billy in lines 1–23.  Make at least **four** key points.                                                                                                     4

6.  Explain how the sentence structure of lines 12–15 help the audience to understand how Davie is feeling.                                                                                        2

7.  Explain how the dialogue in lines 16–23 emphasises the difference between the two characters.                                                                                                         2

8.  Explain in detail what is revealed about Davie's personality in lines 32–38.                4

9.  By referring to this extract and to elsewhere in the play, show how the playwright presents the character of Davie.                                                                                        8

OR

### Text 3 — Drama

If you choose this text you may not attempt a question on Drama in Section 2.

Read the extract below and then attempt the following questions.

*Tally's Blood* **by Ann Marie di Mambro**

*This extract is from Act One, Scene Two.  It is 1939.  Lucia is five years old.*

| | |
|---|---|
| MASSIMO: | Listen, Rosie, I thought you went to Glasgow to buy yourself a new coat. |
| ROSINELLA: | Oh, but see when I saw that wee dress I just had to get her it. My heart's breaking for that wee lassie these days. |
| MASSIMO: | She's just a wean. She'll no understand. |

5 ROSINELLA: But she's lovely in it, isn't she?

MASSIMO: Don't get me wrong. I don't grudge the wean a frock. God forbid. It's just you I'm worried about. Last year when I gave you money for a coat you bought jumpers to send to Italy.

ROSINELLA: So?

10 *Massimo smiles with great affection, squeezes her cheek between his thumb and forefinger.*

MASSIMO: So what have I to do with you, you daft wee besom, you?

*Lucia comes back carrying her schoolbag: Massimo takes it from her.*

MASSIMO: Oh, is this what I got? Let me see. Oh, that's great, so it is. Just what I was needing for bringing home the tatties. Oh here, it's awfy wee. You better just take
15 it, Lucia.

*He pretends to put it on: Lucia giggles.*

LUCIA: Uncle Massimo, you're awful silly.

ROSINELLA: Now away you go, Lucia, and take off your lovely dress.

LUCIA: *(Mood changing/petulant)* I want to keep it on.

20 ROSINELLA: *(Coaxing)* You need to take it off, love.

LUCIA: No.

MASSIMO: Keep it nice for something special.

LUCIA: No.

ROSINELLA: If you take it off now I'll let you wear it to mass this Sunday.

25 LUCIA: I want to keep it on.

ROSINELLA: Come on, hen.

LUCIA: I'm keeping it on, I says.

MASSIMO: You better no let her away with that.

ROSINELLA: Come on, darling, we'll get you changed.

30 LUCIA: *(Starting to shout)* No, no, no.

ROSINELLA: *(Voice raised but pleading)* Now Lucia!

*Massimo glances over shoulder in direction of front shop.*

**MARKS**

LUCIA:    I don't want to. I don't want to.

35  MASSIMO:    Sshh! You two. I've got customers out there. *(To Lucia)* Do what your Auntie Rosinella tells you, darling, there's a good girl.

*Rosinella takes Lucia's arm to lead her away.*

ROSINELLA:    Come on, Lucia.

*Lucia starts to scream and pull back.*

LUCIA:    No, no, no, leave me alone, I want to keep it on. I want to keep it on.
40       No – no – no –

*Rosinella and Massimo look helplessly at each other. Massimo also keeps glancing in direction of shop, anxious to get back.*

ROSINELLA:    *(Appealing)* Massimo.

MASSIMO:    Maybe you're being too hard on her.

45  ROSINELLA:    Me?

MASSIMO:    Why no let her keep it on for a wee while, eh?

ROSINELLA:    Just a wee while, then, OK.

*Lucia controls her sobs (she's won).*

LUCIA:    Okay.

## Questions

10.  Summarise what happens in this extract.  Make at least three key points.    **3**

11.  What does the audience learn about Rosinella's character from lines 1–9?    **2**

12.  By referring in detail to lines 19–49, explain how the playwright makes Lucia's behaviour typical of a young child.    **4**

13.  At this stage in the play the characters have only been in Scotland for three years, but their speech shows clear signs of Scottish words and phrases.  Quote three examples of this from anywhere in the extract.    **3**

14.  The extract looks at the relationship between Lucia and her aunt and uncle.  With close reference to this extract and elsewhere in the play, explain how their relationship is portrayed.    **8**

## PART B — SCOTTISH TEXT — PROSE

### Text 1 — Prose

If you choose this text you may not attempt a question on Prose in Section 2.

Read the extract below and then attempt the following questions.

### *The Cone-Gatherers* by Robin Jenkins

*This extract is from Chapter 11. Calum and Neil are in a tree when a storm begins and they climb down to seek shelter.*

The brothers crept slowly downward. Every time lightning flashed and thunder crashed they thought their tree had been shattered, and clung, helpless as woodlice, waiting to be hurled to the ground with the fragments. The tree itself seemed to be terrified; every branch, every twig, heaved and slithered. At times it seemed to have torn its roots in its terror and to be dangling in
5  the air.

At last they reached the ground. At once Neil flung his bag of cones down and snatched up his knapsack. He shouted to Calum to do likewise.

"We'd never get to the hut alive," he gasped. "We'd get killed among the trees. Forby, it's too far away. We're going to the beach hut."

10  "But we're not allowed, Neil."

Neil clutched his brother and spoke to him as calmly as he could.

"I ken it's not allowed, Calum," he said. "I ken we gave our promise to Mr. Tulloch not to get into any more trouble. But look at the rain. We're soaked already. I've got rheumatics, and you ken your chest is weak. If we shelter under a tree it might get struck by lightning and we'd
15  be killed. In three minutes we can reach the beach hut."

"But we promised, Neil. The lady will be angry again."

"Do you want me then to be a useless cripple for the rest of my days? What if she is angry? All she can do is tell us to leave her wood, and I'll be glad to go. I don't want you to do what you think is wrong, Calum; but sometimes we've got to choose between two things, neither of them
20  to our liking. We'll do no harm. We'll leave the place as we find it. Nobody will ever ken we've been in it. What do you say then?"

Calum nodded unhappily.

"I think maybe we should go," he said.

"All right then. We'd better run for it. But didn't I tell you to drop your cone bag?"

25  "They'll get all wet, Neil."

Neil stood gaping; he saw the rain streaming down the green grime on his brother's face; beyond Calum was the wood shrouded in wet.

"They'll get wet," he heard himself repeating.

"Aye, that's right, Neil. Mind what Mr. Tulloch said, if they get wet they're spoiled."

30  It was no use being bitter or angry or sarcastic.

"Is there never to be any sun again then," cried Neil, "to dry them?"

Calum looked up at the sky.

"I think so, Neil," he murmured.

**MARKS**

Questions

15. Explain **two** ways in which the writer's use of language in lines 1–5 conveys the violence of the storm.    4

16. Look at lines 6–10.  Show how the writer's word choice makes clear how impatient Neil is.  Refer to **two** examples.    2

17. Using your own words as far as possible, summarise the key points in Neil's argument to persuade Calum to go to the beach hut (lines 12–21).  Make at least **four** key points.    4

18. How does the writer make Calum seem childlike in lines 25–34?    2

19. By referring to this extract and to elsewhere in the novel, discuss the relationship between Calum and Neil.    8

**OR**

### Text 2 – Prose

If you choose this text you may not attempt a question on Prose in Section 2.

Read the extract below and then attempt the following questions.

### *The Testament of Gideon Mack* by James Robertson

*This extract is from Chapter 25. Gideon is visiting Catherine Craigie for the first time. He has rung the bell twice, but nothing has happened...*

"Just come in, for heaven's sake. It's not locked."

I leaned forward to open the door and noticed a handwritten card taped to wall of the vestibule: *Please ring and enter. If locked go away.*

"Can't you read?" the voice said as I let myself in.

5   "Sorry," I said, "I only just saw it. I'm sorry if I've interrupted you."

"You shouldn't have rung the bell if you didn't want to interrupt me," Miss Craigie said. "I don't sit around waiting for visitors all day, you know. Oh, it's you."

She said these last words not apologetically but with added distaste. It was dark in the hallway, and I could not make out the expression on her face, but the tone of voice told
10   me all I needed to know. I'd been well warned by various members of my flock: Catherine Craigie thought that the Kirk, by and large, had been, was and always would be a scabrous outbreak on the flesh of Scotland.

I was wearing my dog collar – I was planning to make some other calls that evening – and assumed that this was the cause of her aggravation. I tapped it with my forefinger.

15   "It doesn't make you a bad person," I said.

"Hmph," she retorted. "It doesn't make you a good one either. What do you want?"

"I've come to say hello, Miss Craigie. I've been here nearly four years and I feel we should have met by now." This didn't seem to impress her. "And I want to ask you some questions about the standing stones. I've been reading your book."

20   "Well, it's all in there, so I don't see why you need to come bothering me if you haven't taken the trouble to read it properly."

"Supplementary questions," I said. "Arising out of what I've read."

"I know what a supplementary question is," she said. "Such as?"

I'd had the forethought to compose something beforehand.

25   "Well, it seems to me, in all this debate about pre-Christian and Christianised Picts, that we forget that they were under pressure from two rival Christianities, the Celtic and the Roman – the Scots in the west and the Northumbrians in the south. And I wondered what bearing that might have had on the symbols on the stones."

During this speech her head inclined toward me like a bird's listening for danger, or for a
30   worm. Later, I realised that this stance was in part due to her illness, which prevented her from moving her neck very much. She was standing halfway down the hallway, holding on to a tall wooden plant-stand positioned in the middle of a large rug. There was no plant on the plant-stand and it took me a moment to understand the reason for its location: the lay-out of the hall, from the front door to the foot of the stairs and on towards the back
35   lobby, was a kind of domestic rock-face, with hand-holds and rest points along the way, some pre-existing and some strategically placed: the plant-stand, a chair, a table, a stool, a shelf, the banister end, radiators. This horizontal climbing-wall was how Miss Craigie managed to get around her house.

**MARKS**

Questions

20. By referring closely to lines 1–12, show how the writer presents Miss Craigie as an intimidating character. **4**

21. Show how the dialogue in lines 13–23 conveys the friction between Gideon and Miss Craigie. **4**

22. Show how the writer's **sentence structure** and **imagery** help to describe the layout of Miss Craigie's hallway in lines 31–38. **4**

23. By referring to the extract and to elsewhere in the novel, discuss the relationship between Gideon and Miss Craigie. **8**

OR

### Text 3 — Prose

If you choose this text you may not attempt a question on Prose in Section 2.

Read the extract below and then attempt the following questions.

### *Kidnapped* by Robert Louis Stevenson

*This extract is from Chapter 19 - "The House of Fear".  David and Alan arrive at the home of James Stewart of the Glens.*

At last, about half-past ten of the clock, we came to the top of a brae, and saw lights below us. It seemed a house door stood open and let out a beam of fire and candle-light; and all round the house and steading five or six persons were moving hurriedly about, each carrying a lighted brand.

5   "James must have tint his wits," said Alan. "If this was the soldiers instead of you and me, he would be in a bonny mess. But I dare say he'll have a sentry on the road, and he would ken well enough no soldiers would find the way that we came."

Hereupon he whistled three times, in a particular manner. It was strange to see how, at the first sound of it, all the moving torches came to a stand, as if the bearers were affrighted; and
10   how, at the third, the bustle began again as before.

Having thus set folks' minds at rest, we came down the brae, and were met at the yard gate (for this place was like a well-doing farm) by a tall, handsome man of more than fifty, who cried out to Alan in the Gaelic.

"James Stewart," said Alan, "I will ask ye to speak in Scotch, for here is a young gentleman
15   with me that has nane of the other. This is him," he added, putting his arm through mine, "a young gentleman of the Lowlands, and a laird in his country too, but I am thinking it will be the better for his health if we give his name the go-by."

James of the Glens turned to me for a moment, and greeted me courteously enough; the next he had turned to Alan.

20   "This has been a dreadful accident," he cried. "It will bring trouble on the country." And he wrung his hands.

"Hoots!" said Alan, "ye must take the sour with the sweet, man. Colin Roy is dead, and be thankful for that!"

"Ay," said James, "and by my troth, I wish he was alive again! It's all very fine to blow and
25   boast beforehand; but now it's done, Alan; and who's to bear the wyte of it? The accident fell out in Appin – mind ye that, Alan; it's Appin that must pay; and I am a man that has a family."

While this was going on I looked about me at the servants. Some were on ladders, digging in the thatch of the house or the farm buildings, from which they brought out guns, swords, and
30   different weapons of war; others carried them away; and by the sound of mattock blows from somewhere farther down the brae, I suppose they buried them. Though they were all so busy, there prevailed no kind of order in their efforts; men struggled together for the same gun and ran into each other with their burning torches; and James was continually turning about from his talk with Alan, to cry out orders which were apparently never understood.
35   The faces in the torchlight were like those of people overborne with hurry and panic; and though none spoke above his breath, their speech sounded both anxious and angry.

**MARKS**

Questions

24. Look at lines 1–7.

    Why does Alan think that "James must have tint his wits"?                     2

25. What impression of David is Alan trying to create when he introduces him to James Stewart? Support your answer with reference to lines 14–17.     2

26. By referring to lines 20–27, explain in your own words the differing reactions of Alan and James to the "accident".                                    4

27. Show how the writer creates a sense of panic in lines 28–36.                 4

28. With reference to this extract and to elsewhere in the novel, discuss the characterisation of Alan Breck.                                                      8

OR

## Text 4 — Prose

If you choose this text you may not attempt a question on Prose in Section 2.

Read the extract below and then attempt the following questions.

### *Mother and Son* by Iain Crichton Smith

In the bed was a woman. She was sleeping, her mouth tightly shut and prim and anaemic. There was a bitter smile on her lips as if fixed there; just as you sometimes see the insurance man coming to the door with the same smile each day, the same brilliant smile which never falls away till he's gone into the anonymity of the streets. The forehead was
5  not very high and not low, though its wrinkles gave it an expression of concentration as if the woman were wrestling with some terrible witch's idea in dreams.

The man looked at her for a moment, then fumbled for his matches again and began to light a fire. The sticks fell out of place and he cursed vindictively and helplessly. For a moment he sat squatting on his haunches staring into the fire, as if he were thinking of
10  some state of innocence, some state to which he could not return: a reminiscent smile dimpled his cheeks and showed in eyes which immediately became still and dangerous again.

The clock struck five wheezingly and, at the first chime, the woman woke up. She started as she saw the figure crouched over the fire and then subsided: "It's only you." There was
15  relief in the voice, but there was a curious hint of contempt or acceptance. He still sat staring into the fire and answered dully: "Yes, it's only me!" He couldn't be said to speak the words: they fell away from him as sometimes happens when one is in a deep reverie where every question is met by its answer almost instinctively.

"Well, what's the matter with you!" she snapped pettishly, "sitting there moping with the
20  tea to be made. I sometimes don't know why we christened you John" – with a sigh. "My father was never like you. He was a man who knew his business."

"All right, *all* right," he said despairingly. "Can't you get a new record for your gramophone. I've heard all that before," as if he were conscious of the inadequacy of this familiar retort – he added: "hundreds of times." But she wasn't to be stopped.

25  "I can't understand what has come over you lately. You keep mooning about the house, pacing up and down with your hands in your pockets. Do you know what's going to happen to you, you'll be taken to the asylum. That's where you'll go. Your father's people had something wrong with their heads, it was in your family but not in ours."

MARKS

**Questions**

29. Explain two ways the writer creates an unpleasant impression of the mother in lines 1–6.  **4**

30. Show how the man's reaction is made clear in lines 7–12.  **2**

31. Look at lines 13–18. Describe in your own words the way the son replies to his mother's comment.  **2**

32. By referring closely to lines 19–28, show how the hostility between mother and son is made clear to the reader.  **4**

33. By referring to this story and to at least one other by Iain Crichton Smith, discuss how he explores conflict between characters.  **8**

OR

**Text 5 — Prose**

If you choose this text you may not attempt a question on Prose in Section 2.

Read the extract below and then attempt the following questions.

*Zimmerobics* **by Anne Donovan**

And there's this constant feeling of awareness in every part of my body; jaggy pains in my elbows and knees, vertebrae grinding against one another, bits that used to fit together smoothly now clicking and clunking like the central heating boiler starting up. I did once try to explain it to Catherine.

5 "It's like the shows, those games where you get a circle on a stick and you have to feed it along a twisted wire, very carefully without touching it and, if you touch the wire a bell rings."

"Uh-huh." She is busy rearranging ornaments on the mantelpiece.

"It's like that. I have to do everything really slowly and carefully, otherwise it hurts."

10 Catherine gave me one of her looks and said I should take more interest in things. She knows I can't knit any more and reading tires me but she's always trying to get me to put photographs in albums or watch the TV.

"*Top Hat*'s on TV this afternoon," she said as she was getting ready to leave. "Fred Astaire and Ginger Rogers."

15 "Oh, is it?"

"It starts at two-thirty and it's all set for you. I'm away for the two o'clock bus. See you on Friday."

I didn't watch the film. I'd rather sit and daydream out of the window, lost inside my own head. Catherine can't understand as it's not in her nature to daydream or dawdle or drift.
20 She's like an office stapler, precisely snapping shut, securing papers in the correct order forever. She never lets anything go. When she returned on Friday the first thing she said to me was:

"Did you enjoy the film?"

I was caught off my guard.

25 "The film?"

"*Top Hat* – you didn't watch it, did you? I knew you wouldn't. I don't know why I bother. You've no interest in anything outside yourself. You never even bother to go along to the dayroom. There's three ladies sitting there now, having a wee chat. You could go and meet people."

30 Catherine always pronounces "meet" as if it were printed in capital letters. This was one of her favourite monologues, that I should MEET people in the dayroom. I knew I could shuffle along there with my Zimmer but I could never be bothered. There was bingo on Mondays and a drink on Saturday nights but I never went to either. She thinks I'm a snob, that I think I'm better that these women but it's not that; it's just, I'd rather sit here.

MARKS

**Questions**

34. Look at lines 1–4. By referring to two examples of the writer's use of language, show how she conveys the narrator's physical discomfort.    **4**

35. What impressions of Catherine's personality can be seen in lines 5–17? Support your points with textual reference.    **4**

36. Show how, in lines 18–34, the writer conveys the contrast between the narrator and her niece.    **4**

37. By referring to this story and to **at least one other story** by Anne Donovan, discuss the way she explores conflict between characters.    **8**

**PART C — SCOTTISH TEXT — POETRY**

**Text 1 — Poetry**

If you choose this text you may not attempt a question on Poetry in Section 2.

Read the poem below and then attempt the following questions.

*Originally* **by Carol Ann Duffy**

We came from our own country in a red room
which fell through the fields, our mother singing
our father's name to the turn of the wheels.
My brothers cried, one of them bawling *Home*,
5   *Home*, as the miles rushed back to the city,
the street, the house, the vacant rooms
where we didn't live any more. I stared
at the eyes of a blind toy, holding its paw.

All childhood is an emigration. Some are slow,
10   leaving you standing, resigned, up an avenue
where no one you know stays. Others are sudden.
Your accent wrong. Corners, which seem familiar,
leading to unimagined, pebble-dashed estates, big boys
eating worms and shouting words you don't understand.
15   My parents' anxiety stirred like a loose tooth
in my head. *I want our own country*, I said.

But then you forget, or don't recall, or change,
and, seeing your brother swallow a slug, feel only
a skelf of shame. I remember my tongue
20   shedding its skin like a snake, my voice
in the classroom sounding just like the rest. Do I only think
I lost a river, culture, speech, sense of first space
and the right place? Now, *Where do you come from?*
strangers ask. *Originally?* And I hesitate.

MARKS

Questions

38. Summarise the key things that happen to the speaker of this poem.  Make at least **three** points.

3

39. "All childhood is an emigration." (line 9)

    (a) Explain briefly what the poet means by this.

    1

    (b) Referring closely to lines 9–14, show how the poet's use of language makes a clear distinction between "slow" and "sudden" emigration.

    4

40. By referring closely to lines 17–24, show how the poet conveys the speaker's feelings of uncertainty.

4

41. By referring to **at least one** other poem by Carol Ann Duffy, discuss in what ways *Originally* is similar and/or dissimilar to other poetry by her.  You may refer to language and/or ideas in your answer.

8

OR

**Text 2 — Poetry**

If you choose this text you may not attempt a question on Poetry in Section 2.

Read the extract below and then attempt the following questions.

*Hyena* **by Edwin Morgan**

I am waiting for you.
I have been travelling all morning through the bush
and not eaten.
I am lying at the edge of the bush
5  on a dusty path that leads from the burnt-out kraal.
I am panting, it is midday, I found no water-hole.
I am very fierce without food and although my eyes
are screwed to slits against the sun
you must believe I am prepared to spring.

10  What do you think of me?
I have a rough coat like Africa.
I am crafty with dark spots
like the bush-tufted plains of Africa.
I sprawl as a shaggy bundle of gathered energy
15  like Africa sprawling in its waters.
I trot, I lope, I slaver, I am a ranger.
I hunch my shoulders. I eat the dead.

Do you like my song?
When the moon pours hard and cold on the veldt
20  I sing, and I am the slave of darkness.
Over the stone walls and the mud walls and the ruined places
and the owls, the moonlight falls.
I sniff a broken drum.  I bristle.  My pelt is silver.
I howl my song to the moon – up it goes.
25  Would you meet me there in the waste places?

**MARKS**

Questions

42. Look at lines 1–9. By referring to two poetic techniques, show how the poet makes the hyena sound threating in these lines.    4

43. Look at lines 10–17.

   (a) All the similes in these lines refer to "Africa". Why do you think the poet does this?    2

   (b) Show how the sentence structure in lines 16–17 enhances the poet's description of the hyena.    2

44. Explain in detail how the poet conveys the harshness of the hyena's world in lines 18–25.    4

45. By referring to this poem and to **at least one** other poem by Edwin Morgan, discuss the view he presents of the natural world.    8

OR

## Text 3 — Poetry

If you choose this text you may not attempt a question on Poetry in Section 2.

Read the poem below and then attempt the following questions.

### *Assisi* by Norman MacCaig

The dwarf with his hands on backwards
sat, slumped like a half-filled sack
on tiny twisted legs from which
sawdust might run,
5  outside the three tiers of churches built
in honour of St Francis, brother
of the poor, talker with birds, over whom
he had the advantage
of not being dead yet.

10  A priest explained
how clever it was of Giotto
to make his frescoes tell stories
that would reveal to the illiterate the goodness
of God and the suffering
15  of His Son.  I understood
the explanation and
the cleverness.

A rush of tourists, clucking contentedly,
fluttered after him as he scattered
20  the grain of the Word.  It was they who had passed
the ruined temple outside, whose eyes
wept pus, whose back was higher
than his head, whose lopsided mouth
said *Grazie* in a voice as sweet
25  as a child's when she speaks to her mother
or a bird's when it spoke
to St Francis.

**Questions**

46. For each of the following, show how any one example of the poet's use of language contributes to his description of:

    (a)  the dwarf

    (b)  the church

    (c)  the tourists                                                                                 6

47. What is the poet's attitude to the priest?  Justify your answer with close reference to lines 10–20.                                                                                 3

48. Look at lines 24–27.  Do you think this is an effective way to end the poem?  Justify your answer by referring to these lines and to the poem as a whole.                    3

49. Referring to this poem and to **at least one** other poem by Norman MacCaig, discuss how he creates feelings of sympathy in the reader.                                        8

OR

**Text 4 — Poetry**

If you choose this text you may not attempt a question on Poetry in Section 2.

Read the extract below and then attempt the following questions.

**My Grandmother's Houses** by Jackie Kay

By the time I am seven we are almost the same height.
She still walks faster, rushing me down the High Street
till we get to her cleaning house.  The hall is huge.
Rooms lead off like an octopus's arms.
5   I sit in a room with a grand piano, top open –
a one-winged creature, whilst my gran polishes
for hours.  Finally bored I start to pick some notes,
oh can you wash a sailor's shirt oh can you wash and clean
till my gran comes running, duster in hand.
10   I told you don't touch anything.  The woman comes too;
the posh one all smiles that make goosepimples
run up my arms.  Would you like to sing me a song?
Someone's crying my Lord Kumbaya.  Lovely, she says,
beautiful child, skin the colour of café au lait.
15   "Café oh what?  Hope she's not being any bother."
Not at all.  Not at all.  You just get back to your work.
On the way back to her high rise I see her
like the hunchback of Notre Dame.  Everytime I crouch
over a comic she slaps me.  Sit up straight.

MARKS

Questions

50. Identify **four** aspects of the grandmother's personality that emerge from the extract.    4

51. Choose **one** example of imagery from lines 4–7 and explain what it suggests about what is being described.    2

52. By referring closely to lines 10–16, describe how the poet conveys the personality of "the woman".    6

53. By referring to *My Grandmother's Houses* and to **at least one** other poem by Jackie Kay, discuss how she creates vivid impressions of people.    8

[END OF SECTION 1]

## SECTION 2 — CRITICAL ESSAY — 20 marks

**Attempt ONE question from this section of the paper from ONE of the Parts A-E.**

**You may use a Scottish text but not the one used in Section 1.**

**Your essay should be on a different genre to the one used in Section 1.**

**Write the number of your chosen question in the margin of your answer.**

**You should spend about 45 minutes on the essay.**

### DRAMA

*Answers to questions in this part should refer to the text and to such relevant features as characterisation, key scene(s), structure, climax, theme, plot, conflict, setting . . .*

1. Choose a play in which there is conflict between two characters in a family **or** a group.

   Show how the conflict occurs and then, by referring to appropriate techniques, explain how it affects the characters and the events of the play.

2. Choose a play in which a main character's actions have a significant effect on the rest of the play.

   By referring to appropriate techniques, show how this character's actions have affected the other characters **and/or** the outcome of the play.

### PROSE

*Answers to questions in this part should refer to the text and to such relevant features as characterisation, setting, language, key incident(s), climax, turning point, plot, structure, narrative technique, theme, ideas, description . . .*

3. Choose a novel **or** short story in which you feel sympathy with one of the main characters because of the difficulties or injustice or hardships she or he has to face.

   Describe the problems the character faces and, by referring to appropriate techniques, show how you are made to feel sympathy for her or him.

4. Choose a novel **or** a short story **or** a work of non-fiction in which the writer uses a memorable style/voice/narrative technique.

   By referring to appropriate techniques, explain in detail how features of the writing style/voice/narrative technique contribute to the effectiveness of the text.

## POETRY

*Answers to questions in this part should refer to the text and to such relevant features as word choice, tone, imagery, structure, content, rhythm, rhyme, theme, sound, ideas . . .*

5. Choose a poem which describes a person's experience.

   By referring to appropriate techniques, explain how the description of the experience makes the poem more interesting.

6. Choose a poem which has as one of its central concerns a personal, social or religious issue.

   By referring to appropriate techniques, show how the poem increases your understanding of the issue.

## FILM AND TV DRAMA

*Answers to questions in this part should refer to the text and to such relevant features as use of camera, key sequence, characterisation, mise-en-scène, editing, setting, music/ sound, special effects, plot, dialogue . . .*

7. Choose a film or TV drama* which has a character who could be described as a hero or as a villain.

   By referring to appropriate techniques, explain how the character is introduced and then developed throughout the film or TV drama.

8. Choose a sequence from a film which is important both to the atmosphere and to the plot of the film.

   By referring to appropriate techniques, show how atmosphere is created in the sequence and go on to show how the sequence and the atmosphere are important to the film as a whole.

* "TV drama" includes a single play, a series or a serial.

## LANGUAGE STUDY

*Answers to questions in this part should refer to the text and to such relevant features as register, accent, dialect, slang, jargon, vocabulary, tone, abbreviation . . .*

9. Consider the differences between written language and an aspect of spoken language which you have studied.

   By referring to specific examples and to appropriate features of language, explain the similarities and differences between the two forms of language you have studied.

10. Consider the language of advertising.

    In any one advertisement identify the ways in which language is used successfully.  By referring to specific examples and to appropriate features of language, explain what it is about these usages which make them effective.

[END OF SECTION 2]

[END OF MODEL PAPER]

*Page three*

# Model Paper 2

Whilst this Model Paper has been specially commissioned by Hodder Gibson for use as practice for the National 5 exams, the key reference documents remain the SQA Specimen Paper 2013 and the SQA Past Papers 2014 and 2015.

HODDER
GIBSON
LEARN MORE

National
Qualifications
MODEL PAPER 2

# English
# Reading for Understanding,
# Analysis and Evaluation

Duration — 1 hour

**Total marks — 30**

When you are told to do so, open the booklet, read the passage and attempt all the questions, using your own words as far as possible.

**Before attempting the questions you must check that your answer booklet is for the same subject and level as this question paper.**

On the answer booklet, you must clearly identify the question number you are attempting.

Use **blue** or **black** ink.

Before leaving the examination room you must give your answer booklet to the Invigilator. If you do not, you may lose all the marks for this paper.

## The gr8 db8

Recently, a newspaper article headed "I h8 txt msgs: how texting is wrecking our language" argued that texters are "vandals who are doing to our language what Genghis Khan did to his neighbours 800 years ago. They are destroying it: pillaging our punctuation; savaging our sentences."

As a new variety of language, texting has been condemned as "textese", "slanguage", a "digital
5  virus, "bleak, bald, sad shorthand", "drab shrinktalk which masks dyslexia, poor spelling and mental laziness".

Ever since the arrival of printing — thought to be the invention of the devil because it would put false opinions into people's minds — people have been arguing that new   technology   would   have disastrous consequences for language.  Scares accompanied the introduction of the telegraph, the
10  telephone, and broadcasting.  But has there ever been a linguistic phenomenon that has aroused such curiosity, suspicion, fear, confusion, antagonism, fascination, excitement and enthusiasm all at once as texting?

People think that the written language seen on mobile phone screens is new and alien, but all the popular beliefs about texting are wrong.  Its distinctiveness is not a new phenomenon, nor is
15  its use restricted to the young.  There is increasing evidence that it helps rather than hinders literacy.  Texting has added a new dimension to language use, but its long-term impact is negligible.

Research has made it clear that the early media hysteria about the novelty (and thus the dangers) of text messaging was misplaced.  People seem to have swallowed whole the stories
20  that youngsters use nothing but abbreviations when they text, such as the reports that a teenager had written an essay so full of textspeak that her teacher was unable to understand it. An extract was posted online, and quoted incessantly, but, as no one was ever able to track down the entire essay, it was probably a hoax.

There are several distinctive features of the way texts are written that combine to give the
25  impression of novelty, but people have been initialising common phrases for ages. IOU is known from 1618.  There is no real difference between a modern kid's "lol" ("laughing out loud") and an earlier generation's "SWALK" ("sealed with a loving kiss").

English has had abbreviated words ever since it began to be written down.  Words such as exam, vet, fridge and bus are so familiar that they have effectively become new words.  When some of
30  these abbreviated forms first came into use, they also attracted criticism.  In 1711, for example, Joseph Addison complained about the way words were being "miserably curtailed" — he mentioned pos (itive) and incog (nito).

Texters use deviant spellings — and they know they are deviant.  But they are by no means the first to use such nonstandard forms as "cos" for "because" or "wot" for "what".  Several of
35  these are so much part of English literary tradition that they have been given entries in the Oxford English Dictionary.  "Cos" is there from 1828 and "wot" from 1829.  Many can be found in the way dialect is written by such writers as Charles Dickens, Mark Twain, Walter Scott and D.H. Lawrence.

Sending a message on a mobile phone is not the most natural of ways to communicate.  The
40  keypad isn't linguistically sensible.  No one took letter-frequency considerations into account when designing it.  For example, key 7 on my mobile contains four symbols, pqrs.  It takes four key-presses to access the letter s, and yet s is one of the most frequently occurring letters in English.  It is twice as easy to input q, which is one of the least frequently occurring letters.  It should be the other way round.  So any strategy that reduces the time and awkwardness of
45  inputting graphic symbols is bound to be attractive.

Abbreviations were used as a natural, intuitive response to a technological problem. And they appeared in next to no time.  Texters simply transferred (and then embellished) what they had encountered in other settings.  We have all left notes in which we have replaced "and" with "&", "three" with "3", and so on.

0    But the need to save time and energy is by no means the whole story of texting. When we look at some texts, they are linguistically quite complex.  There are an extraordinary number of ways in which people play with language — creating riddles, solving crosswords, playing Scrabble, inventing new words.  Professional writers do the same — providing catchy copy for advertising slogans, thinking up puns in newspaper headlines, and writing poems, novels and plays.  Children
5    quickly learn that one of the most enjoyable things you can do with language is to play with its sounds, words, grammar — and spelling.

An extraordinary number of doom-laden prophecies have been made about the supposed linguistic evils unleashed by texting.  Sadly, its creative potential has been virtually ignored.  But children could not be good at texting if they had not already developed considerable literacy
0    awareness.  Before you can write and play with abbreviated forms, you need to have a sense of how the sounds of your language relate to the letters.  You need to know that there are such things as alternative spellings.  If you are aware that your texting behaviour is different, you must have already realized that there is such a thing as a standard.

Some people dislike texting.  Some are bemused by it.  But it is merely the latest manifestation
5    of the human ability to be linguistically creative and to adapt language to suit the demands of diverse settings.  There is no disaster pending.  We will not see a new generation of adults growing up unable to write proper English.  The language as a whole will not decline.  In texting what we are seeing, in a small way, is language in evolution.

*Adapted from an article by David Crystal in The Guardian.*

MARKS

### Questions

1. Choose any **two** examples of the language used to criticise texting in lines 1–6 and explain why each is effective in conveying disapproval.    4

2. Look at lines 7–12.

   (a) What difference does the writer identify between the reaction to texting and the reaction to other new technologies?    2

   (b) Explain one way in which the writer's use of language in these lines conveys his surprise at the reaction to texting.    2

3. In lines 13–14 the writer says: "… all the popular beliefs about texting are wrong". **Explain in your own words** the evidence he provides for this in the rest of the paragraph.    3

4. Show how any **two** examples of the writer's word choice in lines 18–23 make clear his belief that the critics of texting are in the wrong.    4

5. Explain briefly how, in lines 24–38, the writer makes texting appear respectable.    3

6. Explain the function of each of the three dashes used in lines 50–56.    3

7. Show how any **two** examples of the writer's use of language in the last paragraph (lines 64–68) create a reassuring tone.    4

8. Referring to lines 24–63, summarise **in your own words** the key reasons not to worry about texting.    5

**[END OF MODEL PAPER]**

**National Qualifications MODEL PAPER 2**

# English
# Critical Reading

Duration — 1 hour and 30 minutes

**Total marks — 40**

**SECTION 1 — Scottish Text — 20 marks**

Read an extract from a Scottish text you have previously studied and attempt the questions.

Choose ONE text from either

Part A — Drama          Pages 2–9

or

Part B — Prose          Pages 10–19

or

Part C — Poetry          Pages 20–26

Attempt ALL the questions for your chosen text.

**SECTION 2 — Critical Essay — 20 marks**

Write ONE critical essay on previously studied text from Drama, Prose, Poetry, Film and Television Drama, or Language.

Your answer must be on a different genre from that chosen in Section 1.

You should spend approximately 45 minutes on each Section.

**Before attempting the questions you must check that your answer booklet is for the same subject and level as this question paper.**

On the answer booklet, you must clearly identify the question number you are attempting.

Use **blue** or **black** ink.

Before leaving the examination room you must give your answer booklet to the Invigilator. If you do not you may lose all the marks for this paper.

**HODDER GIBSON**
LEARN MORE

## SECTION 1 — SCOTTISH TEXT — 20 marks

### PART A — SCOTTISH TEXT — DRAMA

### Text 1 — Drama

If you choose this text you may not attempt a question on Drama in Section 2.

Read the extract below and then attempt the following questions.

*Tally's Blood* by Ann Marie di Mambro

*This extract is from Act Two, Scene Two, in the back shop.*

|  | ROSINELLA: | You like Silvio Palombo, don't you? |
|---|---|---|
|  | LUCIA: | He's okay. |
|  | ROSINELLA: | Nice looking boy too. |
|  | LUCIA: | He's okay. |
| 5 | ROSINELLA: | Oh, come on, Lucia, you can't kid me on. I know you're daft for him. But I like the way you kind of stand back a bit – don't let him see you're too keen. Italian boys like that. Don't want him to get fed up waiting. |
|  | LUCIA: | Auntie Rosinella...? |
| 10 | ROSINELLA: | He cannae keep his eyes off you. And if he's who you want, then it's not for me to stand in your way. But I told his mother. I made sure I told her. 'Mrs Palombo', I said, 'our Lucia's a lady. She's not been brought up to work in a shop, running after some man'. I tell you, Lucia, she liked me for that. They've got class that family. |
|  | LUCIA: | Auntie Rosinella...? |
| 15 | ROSINELLA: | I hear them all the time. 'Ma lassie's an awfy good worker' – 'Ma lassie cleaned four chickens' – I promised myself – my Lucia's to marry a man that really loves HER – no to put her in a shop and make her work. How much you got there? |
|  | LUCIA: | Three pounds, seven and tenpence ha'penny. |
| 20 | ROSINELLA: | That's what I want for you – a good life – with a good Italian man – here. |
|  | LUCIA: | Auntie Rosinella...? |
|  | ROSINELLA: | You see the way the Italians are getting on now, eh? Beginning to make a wee bit money? Because they're prepared to WORK that's why. I don't know anybody works so hard as the Italian men. |
| 25 |  | *Hughie in with pail and mop.* |
|  | HUGHIE: | That's the tables cleared and the front shop mopped, Mrs Pedreschi, and the chip pan cleaned out. Is the milk boiled? |
|  | ROSINELLA: | Should be. |
| 30 |  | *She turns attention back to Lucia, Hughie lifts pot from stove and pours contents into two pails; he covers them and sets them aside, working like a Trojan.* |
|  | ROSINELLA: | And the way they love their families. Nobody loves their families like the Italians! You want to stay for a wee bit pasta, Hughie? It's your favourite – Rigatoni. |

*Page two*

| 35 | HUGHIE: | No thanks, Mrs Pedreschi. I better get up the road. Bridget's going out and I don't like my mammy left on her own. |
| | ROSINELLA: | Bridget's going out is she? Don't tell me she's winching? |
| | HUGHIE: | No. Her and Davie are going up to Charmaine's the night – to go over all the arrangements. My mammy's no up to it. |
| 40 | ROSINELLA: | That's right. When's the wedding now? |
| | HUGHIE: | Saturday. |
| | ROSINELLA: | Is he no getting married a wee bit quick, your brother? |

*Hughie shrugs, a bit embarrassed: Lucia mortified at Rosinella.*

| | ROSINELLA: | And where are they going to stay? |
| 45 | HUGHIE: | At Charmaine's. |
| | ROSINELLA: | It's funny that, isn't it? But that's the way they do it here. In Italy, the girl must go to her husband's house. That's why you must have land if you've got sons. |

*Massimo in.*

| 50 | | So that'll be your mammy left with her eldest and her youngest, eh? I don't see your Bridget ever marrying, do you? You see, Lucia, there's a lot of women Bridget's age no' married. The war killed that many young men. I'm right there, aren't I, Massimo? |
| | MASSIMO: | You got those pails ready, son? |
| 55 | HUGHIE: | I'll bring them through. |
| | MASSIMO: | And give's a hand to put these shutters up before you go. |

*Hughie and Massimo out: Rosinella watches him go.*

| | ROSINELLA: | I'm right about that Davie, amn't I, Lucia? Give it five or six months, Hughie'll be telling us he's an uncle again. Mind you, I suppose |
| 60 | | his mother must feel it, right enough. Can you find me a wee envelope hen, a wee poke or something? What was I saying... ah, yes... See what I mean about Italian men? Just take that brother of Hughie's. Getting married on a Saturday. Give him two or three days and he'll be out DRINKING with his pals. |

| 65 | | *Rosinella shushes up when Hughie comes in, followed by Massimo: all locked up. Massimo takes off his apron, reaches for a bottle of wine.* |

| | MASSIMO: | Thanks, Hughie, son. You want a wee glass of wine? |
| | HUGHIE: | I better not, Mr Pedreschi. I better get up the road. |

MARKS

Questions

1. Read lines 1–19.

   (a) Show how the playwright makes the audience aware of **two** aspects of Rosinella's character.                4

   (b) How is the audience made aware of Lucia's lack of interest in what her aunt is saying?                2


2. In lines 20–68 Rosinella displays a number of prejudices.  Explain how the playwright makes the audience aware of how silly her prejudices are.  Refer to at least three different prejudices.                6


3. Referring to the extract and elsewhere in the play, discuss the role of Hughie in the play as a whole.                8

**OR**

**Text 2 — Drama**

If you choose this text you may not attempt a question on Drama in Section 2.

Read the extract below and then attempt the following questions.

*Bold Girls* **by Rona Munro**

*This extract is from Scene 2 in the Club.  Cassie is dancing alone, and Nora persuades Marie to join her.*

> *Marie crosses over and joins Cassie, who beams, applauding her.  Marie starts shuffling cautiously from foot to foot.*

CASSIE:     I'm telling you this is a great diet Marie, you really feel the benefit of the gin.

MARIE:     Well maybe you should go easy now Cassie.

5  CASSIE:     Oh I'm a long way from being lockjawed

> *Nora is beckoning at them frantically.*

MARIE:     Your mummy's asking us to come and sit down.

CASSIE:     The song's just started.

> *Marie glances round nervously.*

10             What?  Are they all watching us?

MARIE:     They are.

CASSIE:     Let them.

MARIE:     (*with a shaky laugh*):  Feel a bit like the last meat pie in the shop out here, Cassie.

CASSIE:     Well let them stay hungry.  They can just look and think what they like.

15  MARIE:     Cassie, what's wrong?

CASSIE:     Oh, I'm just bad, Marie, didn't you know?

MARIE:     No. I never knew that.

CASSIE:     You remember that wee girl in Turf Lodge, the one Martin couldn't get enough of?  She was a decent wee girl.  She's bad now.  Ask my mummy.

20  MARIE:     Have you had words?

CASSIE:     He's out in less than a year, Marie.

*Page five*

**MARKS**

MARIE:     *Martin!?*

CASSIE:    Joe.

MARIE:     I know.  It'll be all right Cassie.

25              *They stop dancing, they look at each other.*

MARIE:     It'll be all right, Cassie.

CASSIE:    I tell you Marie I can't stand the *smell* of him.  The greasy, grinning, beer bellied smell of him.  And he's winking away about all he's been dreaming of, wriggling his fat fingers over me like I'm a poke of chips – I
30              don't want him in the house in my *bed*, Marie.

MARIE:     You'll cope.

CASSIE:    Oh I'm just bad.  I am.

MARIE:     Don't.  Don't say that about yourself.

CASSIE:    I'll go crazy.

35  MARIE:     I won't let you.  You won't get a chance Cassie, I'll just be across the road, I won't let you go crazy.  You just see what you'll get if you try it.

                *Slowly Cassie smiles at her.*

                (*Putting a hand on Cassie's arm*)  Now will you come and sit down?

## Questions

4.  Show how the playwright contrasts the characters of Marie and Cassie through their language and their actions in lines 1–14.                                                  **4**

5.  Explain how the dialogue in lines 15–38 reveals aspects of the relationship between Marie and Cassie.                                                                              **4**

6.  Referring closely to the language of lines 27–30 show how Cassie reveals her attitude to Joe.                                                                                        **4**

7.  Referring to the extract and elsewhere in the play, discuss the relationship between Marie and Cassie.                                                                               **8**

**OR**

## Text 3 — Drama

If you choose this text you may not attempt a question on Drama in Section 2.

Read the extract below and then attempt the following questions.

### *Sailmaker* by Alan Spence

*This extract is from Act One.*

        (*Enter DAVIE and BILLY, talking as they walk*)

| | | |
|---|---|---|
| | DAVIE: | Eh, Billy … that coupla quid ah tapped off ye.  Could it wait till next week? |
| | BILLY: | Aye sure. |
| | DAVIE: | Things are still a wee bit tight. |
| 5 | BILLY: | What's the score? |
| | DAVIE: | Eh? |
| | BILLY: | Ye shouldnae be this skint.  What is it? |
| | DAVIE: | Ah told ye.  It's the job.  Just hasnae been so great.  No sellin enough.  No collectin enough.  No getting much over the basic. |
| 10 | BILLY: | Aye, but ye should be able tae get by.  Just the two ae ye. |
| | DAVIE: | It's no easy. |
| | BILLY: | Ye bevvyin? |
| | DAVIE: | Just a wee half when ah finish ma work.  An by Christ ah need it. |
| 15 | BILLY: | Ye bettin too heavy?  Is that it? |
| | DAVIE: | (*Hesitates then decides to tell him*) It started a coupla months ago.  Backed a favourite.  Absolutely surefire certainty.  Couldnae lose.  But it was even money, so ah had tae put quite a whack on it.  (*Slightly shamefaced*) Best part ae a week's wages. |
| 20 | BILLY: | An it got beat? |
| | DAVIE: | Out the park.  So ah made it up by borrowin off the bookie.  He does his moneylender on the side.  Charges interest. |
| | BILLY: | An every week ye miss the interest it goes up. |
| 25 | DAVIE: | This is it.  Now when ah pay him ah'm just clearing the interest.  Ah'm no even touchin the original amount ah borrowed.  Ah must have paid him back two or three times over, an ah still owe him the full whack. |
| | BILLY: | Bastard, eh?  Sicken ye.  And he's a pape. |

        (*DAVIE laughs*)

|   | DAVIE: | Still, aw ah need's a wee turn.  Ah mean ma luck's got tae change sometime hasn't it?  Law of averages. |
|---|---|---|
| 30 | | |

BILLY:    Whatever that is.

DAVIE:    Thing's have got tae get better.

BILLY:    It's a mug's game.  The punter canny win.

DAVIE:    Got tae keep trying.

35    BILLY:    Flingin it away!

Look, don't get me wrong.  Ah don't mind helping ye out, but I'm no exactly rollin in it maself.

DAVIE:    Ye'll get yer money back.

BILLY:    That's no what ah mean!

40    DAVIE:    What am ah supposed tae dae?  Get a job as a company director or something!  Ah'll go doon tae the broo in the morning!

BILLY:    There must be some way tae get this bookie aff yer back for a start.

DAVIE:    Aye sure!

BILLY:    Ah mean, you've paid him.

45    DAVIE:    Ah knew his terms.

BILLY:    It's no even legal.

DAVIE:    Neither is getting his heavies tae kick folk's heids in.

BILLY:    So maybe he's no the only wan that knows a few hard men.

DAVIE:    (*Sighs*) Whit a carry on, eh?

MARKS

## Questions

8. Referring to the whole extract, explain why Davie is having money problems. Make at least four key points.    **4**

9. What does the audience learn in lines 1–14 about the character of Billy?    **2**

10. Why does Davie laugh (line 28)?    **2**

11. Look closely at lines 29–49. Referring closely to the text, explain how this dialogue shows clearly the difference in outlook between Davie and Billy.    **4**

12. Money problems and ways to escape them are an important theme in *Sailmaker*. With reference to the extract and to elsewhere in the play, disuss how this theme is explored.    **8**

**PART B — SCOTTISH TEXT — PROSE**

## Text 1 — Prose

If you choose this text you may not attempt a question on Prose in Section 2.

Read the extract below and then attempt the following questions.

### *In Church* by Iain Crichton Smith

"At the age of eighteen I was forced into the army to fight for what they call one's country. I did not know what this was since my gaze was always directed inward and not outward. I was put among men whom I despised and feared – they fornicated and drank and spat and lived filthily. Yet they were my comrades in arms.

5    "I was being shot at by strangers. I was up to my knees in green slime. I was harassed by rats. I entered trenches to find the dead buried in the walls. Once, however, on a clear starry night at Christmas time we had a truce. This lasted into the following day. We – Germans and English – showed each other our photographs, though I had none. We, that is, the others, played football. At the end of it a German officer came up to us and said:

10    'You had better get back to your dugouts: we are starting a barrage at 13.00 hours.' He consulted his watch and we went back to our trenches after he had shaken hands with each other.

"One day I could bear no more of the killing and I ran away. And I came here, Lord. And now I should like to say something to you, Lord. I was never foolish enough to think that

15    I understood your ways. Nevertheless I thought you were on the side of the good and the innocent. Now I no longer believe so. You may strike me dead with your lightning – I invite you to do so – but I think that will not happen. All these years, Lord, you have cheated me. You in your immense absence." He paused a moment as if savouring the phrase. "Your immense absence. As for me, I have been silent for a year without love,

20    without hope. I have lived like an animal, I who was willing to give my all to you. Lord, do you know what it is to be alone? For in order to live we need language and human beings.

"I think, Lord, that I hate you. I hate you for inventing the world and then abandoning it. I hate you because you have not intervened to save the world.

25    "I hate you because you are as indifferent as the generals. I hate you because of my weakness.

"I hate you, God, because of what you have done to mankind."

He stopped and looked at Colin as if he were asking him, Am I a good preacher or not?

"You have said," said Colin after a long time, "exactly what I would have said. "I have no

30    wish to ..."

"Betray me? But you are an officer. It is your duty. What else can you do?"

MARKS

## Questions

13. Explain briefly what has led up to this moment in the story, and say what happens immediately after it.    **4**

14. How do any **two** examples of the writer's use of language in lines 1–4 make clear the speaker's dislike for the army?    **2**

15. Explain one way in which the writer uses contrast in lines 5–12 to emphasise the strangeness of the Christmas truce.    **2**

16. Explain your own words why the speaker is angry at God.    **4**

17. Referring to the extract and to **at least one** other story by Iain Crichton Smith, discuss how he makes the reader aware of the personality of a main character.    **8**

OR

Text 2 — Prose

If you choose this text you may not write a critical essay on Prose in Section 2.

Read the extract below and then attempt the following questions.

### *Away in a Manger* by Anne Donovan

They turned the corner and the cauld evaporated.  The square shimmerin wi light, brightness sharp against the gloomy street.  Trees frosted wi light.  Lights shaped intae circles and flowers, like the plastic jewellery sets wee lassies love.  Lights switchin on and off in a mad rhythm ae their ain, tryin tae look like bells ringin and snow fallin.  Reindeer
5  and Santas, holly, ivy, robins, all bleezin wi light.  Amy gazed at them, eyes shinin.

"Haud ma haund tae get across this road.  There's lots of motors here." Sandra pulled Amy close tae her.  "They're lovely aren't they?"

"Uh huh." Amy nodded.  "Can we walk right round the square?"

A tape of Christmas carols was playin on the sound system, fillin the air like a cracklin
10  heavenly choir.  Sandra and Amy joined the other faimlies wanderin round.

"Look at they reindeer, Mark!"

"There's a star, Daddy!"

"Check the size a that tree!"

Amy stopped in front of the big Christmas tree in the square.

15  "Can we sit doon tae look at it, Mammy?"

"Naw, just keep walkin', pet.  It's too cauld."

Anyway, nearly every bench was occupied.  Newspapers neatly smoothed oot like bedclothes.  Some folk were huddled under auld coats, tryin tae sleep their way intae oblivion while others sat upright, hauf-empty cans in their haunds, starin at passers-by.
20  Sandra minded when she was wee and her mammy'd brought her tae see the lights.  There were folk on benches then, down-and-outs, faces shrunk wi drink and neglect, an auld cap lyin hauf-heartedly by their sides.  But now the people who slept in the square werenae just auld drunks and it was hard tae pick them oot fae everyone else.  That couple ower there wi their bags roond them, were they just havin a rest fae their Christmas shoppin,
25  watchin the lights?  But who in their right minds would be sittin on a bench in George Square on this freezing cauld night if they had a hame tae go tae?

Amy tugged at her airm.  "Ah know that song."

"Whit song?"

"That one." Amy pointed upwards.  "Silent Night, Holy Night."

30  "Do you?"

"We learned it at school.  Mrs Anderson was telling us aboot the baby Jesus and how there was nae room at the inn so he was born in a stable."

"Oh."

"It's no ma favourite, but."

35  "What's no your favourite?"

"Silent Night.  Guess what ma favourite is?"

MARKS

"Don't know."

"Guess, Mammy, you have tae guess."

40 Sandra couldnae be bothered guessin but she knew there'd be nae peace tae she'd made some attempt and anyway, Amy'd get bored wi the "Guess what?" game quick enough.

"Little donkey?"

"Naw."

"O Little Town of Bethlehem?"

45 "Naw.  Gie in?"

"OK."

"Away in a Manger.  Ah've won!" Amy jumped up and doon.  "Mammy, what's a manger?"


**Questions**

18. Show how the writer creates a mood of excitement in lines 1–10.  **4**

19. Why do you think lines 11–13 are included in the story at this point?  **2**

20. What difference does Sandra notice between the square now and what it was like when she went with her mother?  **2**

21. It what ways are lines 27–48 typical of an exchange between an excited child and a parent?  **4**

22. Referring to the extract and to **at least one** other story by Anne Donovan, discuss the way she explores parent/child relationships.  **8**

OR

**Text 3 — Prose**

If you choose this text you may not write a critical essay on Prose in Section 2.

Read the extract below and then attempt the following questions.

### *The Cone-Gatherers* by Robin Jenkins

*This extract is from Chapter Five. Calum and Neil are high in a tree; they hear Duror starting to climb towards them.*

They heard the scrapes and thumps of his nailed boots on the rungs and then on the branches. A branch cracked suddenly. He exclaimed as if in anger, and paused for a full minute. When he resumed he climbed even more slowly than before. Soon he stopped. He was still a long way below.

5    They waited, but he did not start to climb again. For three or four minutes they waited. Still he remained motionless and silent. One of the dogs barked unhappily.

They thought that he must have climbed as high as he wished and now was admiring the view of the loch. After all, the tree was not private just because they happened to be in it; the ladder, too, belonged to the estate. At the same time Neil felt curiously
10    embarrassed and could not think to start gathering cones again. Calum kept shivering.

They were far from guessing the truth, that Duror had ceased to climb because of fear; that weak and dizzy and full of shame, he was clinging with ignominious tightness; that the dread of the descent was making him sick; and that he had almost forgotten his purpose in ascending to them.

15    At last Neil had to end the suspense.

"Hello, Mr Duror," he called. "It's a grand day, isn't it?"

No reply came.

Neil tried again.

"Do you want to talk to us about something?" he shouted

20    This time, after another long delay, there was a reply. They were surprised by the mildness of his voice. It was so faint too they had to strain to hear it.

"I've got a message for you," he said.

"A message? Is it from Mr. Tulloch?"

There was a pause. "Aye, from him."

25    "Have we to go back home, to Ardmore?" cried Neil hopefully.

"You know these woods belong to Lady Runcie-Campbell?"

"We know that."

"She wants you as beaters in a deer drive this afternoon."

Neil was shocked.

30    "But we're here to gather cones," he yelled. "She can't order us about. She's not our mistress."

"She telephoned Tulloch. He said you've to work for her this afternoon."

"How could he? Didn't he tell us we'd to gather every cone we could? Didn't he ask us to work as much overtime as we liked? What's the good of all that if we're
35  to be taken away for deer drives." Neil's voice grew hoarse with indignation. "My brother's never asked to take part in deer hunts," he shouted. "Mr. Tulloch knows that. I don't believe he knows anything about this. It's just a trick to get us to work for the lady."

Duror was silent. His triumph was become a handful of withered leaves. When he
40  had seen the ladder, he had thought how gratifying it would be to deliver the deadly message to them in the eyrie where they fancied themselves safe. He had not anticipated this lightheadedness, this heaving of the stationary tree, this sickening of his very will to hate. He had never dreamed that he would not be able to do once only what the hunchback did several times a day. It seemed to him that
45  he must therefore be far more ill and decayed than he had thought. He was like a tree still straight, still showing green leaves; but underground death was creeping along the roots.

**Questions**

23. Summarise what happens in this extract. Make at least four key points.          **4**

24. Show how the writer creates a tense mood in lines 1–6.          **2**

25. Look carefully at what Neil says in lines 16–38. Referring closely to the text, show how his attitude to Duror goes through at least two changes.          **4**

26. Explain what the image in the final sentence tells you about Duror.          **2**

27. Referring to the extract and to elsewhere in the novel, discuss the conflict between Duror and the cone-gatherers.          **8**

OR

**Text 4 — Prose**

If you choose this text you may not attempt a question on Prose in Section 2.

Read the extract below and then attempt the following questions.

*The Testament of Gideon Mack* by James Robertson

*This extract is from Chapter 7.*

Another few minutes must have gone by. I forgot where I was and what day it was. The sound was louder than I'd intended. I was only a foot away from the screen, finger hovering near the off switch, and maybe that was why I failed to hear my father's footsteps in the hall. By the time the door opened and his voice filled the room – "Agnes?
5   I thought I heard somebody ..." – there was no point in even bothering to switch the television off. I did, though, and jumped to my feet in a flush of shame and fury.

He closed the door behind him. I stood between him and the television set as if to protect it, as if to say it was not to blame. I could see the wee flames in his cheeks. I bowed my head, fixing my eye on a crack in the skirting board. I heard him say, "Put it back on."

10   "No, no, it doesn't matter, I'm sorry," I mumbled. Entirely the wrong thing. He cut me off, his voice shaking.

"It doesn't *matter*?" he said "Do you dare to disobey me? Put it back on."

I turned and reached for the switch. The television, being warm, came on at once. If my father understood that, he made no allowance for it.

15   "I see you have become very skilled at operating that thing," he said quietly, almost admiringly. "How often have you done this?"

"Never," I said. It was true that I'd not touched the set before on a Sunday. "I promise this is the first time."

"It will be the last," he said. "Come here."

20   He pointed beside him and I went and stood there. His huge right hand descended on my neck and the thumb and fingers gripped it so that I cried out. He increased the pressure. I thought my head would snap off. His breathing was like that of some monstrous creature in its den. The blood in  his fingers pulsed furiously against my neck.

Thus we stood in front of the television together, father and son, for the remaining ten
25   minutes of the programme. It felt like an hour. If I squirmed to try and ease the pain, his grip tightened. I hated him then, hated what he was doing to me and hated my own helplessness. *ZAP! BLAM! POW!* I hated the screen with its cartoon punches and I hated the way the parlour echoed with screeching tyres and wisecracks delivered in American accents. I saw it as if through his eyes – cheap, tawdry, meaningless rubbish – and I
30   longed for it to end.

He pushed me from him as the credits rolled and the inane theme music played. "Turn it off," he said. I did as I was told, rubbing my neck and wiping away the tears that he had squeezed out of me.

"What ... is ... that?" he said, dropping the words methodically into the silence.

35   "*Batman*," I said.

"Bat ... man," he said.

"Yes," I said. And then again, "I'm sorry." But I don't think he heard that.

"It is not bat ... man," he said, and I could not stop myself, I was trying to explain, I said, "It *is*."

**MARKS**

40   "Do not interrupt me," he said.  His voice grew louder and louder.  "Do not contradict me.  It is not bat … man, whatever that means.  I'll tell you what it is. It is drivel.  It is the most unutterable garbage I have ever witnessed.  Garbage from the land of garbage."

## Questions

**28.** Summarise what happens in this extract.  Make **three** key points.    3

**29.** How is the reader made aware, in lines 1–11, of Gideon's nervousness after he hears his father's voice?    2

**30.** Explain how the writer conveys the aggressiveness of Gideon's father in lines 12–33.    4

**31.** Show how the father's contempt for American culture is conveyed in lines 34–42.    3

**32.** Referring to the extract and to elsewhere in the novel, discuss the relationship between Gideon and his father.    8

OR

## Text 5 — Prose

If you choose this text you may not attempt a question on Prose in Section 2.

Read the extract below and then attempt the following questions.

### *Kidnapped* by Robert Louis Stevenson

*This extract is from Chapter 10 – "The Siege of the Roundhouse".*

The sea had gone down, and the wind was steady and kept the sails quiet; so that there was a great stillness in the ship, in which I made sure I heard the sound of muttering voices. A little after, and there came a clash of steel upon the deck, by which I knew they were dealing out the cutlasses and one had been let fall; and after that, silence again.

5   I do not know if I was what you call afraid; but my heart beat like a bird's, both quick and little; and there was a dimness came before my eyes which I continually rubbed away, and which continually returned. As for hope, I had none; but only a darkness of despair and a sort of anger against all the world that made me long to sell my life as dear as I was able. I tried to pray, I remember, but that same hurry of my mind, like a man running, would not
10   suffer me to think upon the words; and my chief wish was to have the thing begin and be done with it.

It came all of a sudden when it did, with a rush of feet and a roar, and then a shout from Alan, and a sound of blows and some one crying out as if hurt. I looked back over my shoulder, and saw Mr. Shuan in the doorway, crossing blades with Alan.

15   "That's him that killed the boy!" I cried.

"Look to your window!" said Alan; and as I turned back to my place, I saw him pass his sword through the mate's body.

It was none too soon for me to look to my own part; for my head was scarce back at the window, before five men, carrying a spare yard for a battering-ram, ran past me and took
20   post to drive the door in. I had never fired with a pistol in my life, and not often with a gun; far less against a fellow-creature. But it was now or never; and just as they swang the yard, I cried out: "Take that!" and shot into their midst.

I must have hit one of them, for he sang out and gave back a step, and the rest stopped as if a little disconcerted. Before they had time to recover, I sent another ball over their heads;
25   and at my third shot (which went as wide as the second) the whole party threw down the yard and ran for it.

Then I looked round again into the deck-house. The whole place was full of the smoke of my own firing, just as my ears seemed to be burst with the noise of the shots. But there was Alan, standing as before; only now his sword was running blood to the hilt, and
30   himself so swelled with triumph and fallen into so fine an attitude, that he looked to be invincible. Right before him on the floor was Mr. Shuan, on his hands and knees; the blood was pouring from his mouth, and he was sinking slowly lower, with a terrible, white face; and just as I looked, some of those from behind caught hold of him by the heels and dragged him bodily out of the round-house. I believe he died as they were doing it.

35   "There's one of your Whigs for ye!" cried Alan; and then turning to me, he asked if I had done much execution.

I told him I had winged one, and thought it was the captain.

"And I've settled two," says he. "No, there's not enough blood let; they'll be back again. To your watch, David. This was but a dram before meat."

MARKS

**Questions**

33. Show how Stevenson creates a tense atmosphere in lines 1–4.                    3

34. What mixed emotions does David feel in lines 5–11?                              2

35. Explain briefly **three** ways by which Stevenson makes the events in lines 12–26 dramatic and exciting.                                                         3

36. What impressions is the reader given of Alan Breck in lines 27–39?             2

37. "This was but a dram before meat" (line 39).  Explain in your own words what Alan means by this.                                                              2

38. Referring to the extract and to elsewhere in the novel, discuss the relationship between David and Alan Breck.                                                  8

MARKS

## PART C — SCOTTISH TEXT — POETRY

### Text 1 — Poetry

If you choose this text you may not write a critical essay on Poetry in Section 2.

Read the extract below and then attempt the following questions.

#### *Anne Hathaway* by Carol Ann Duffy

The bed we loved in was a spinning world
of forests, castles, torchlight, clifftops, seas
where he would dive for pearls. My lover's words
were shooting stars which fell to earth as kisses
5  on these lips; my body now a softer rhyme
to his, now echo, assonance; his touch
a verb dancing in the centre of a noun.
Some nights, I dreamed he'd written me, the bed
a page beneath his writer's hands. Romance
10  and drama played by touch, by scent, by taste.
In the other bed, the best, our guests dozed on,
dribbling their prose. My living laughing love –
I hold him in the casket of my widow's head
as he held me upon that next best bed.

### Questions

**39.** Referring to the section "The bed …" to "… these lips" (lines 1–5), show how the poet conveys a sense of joy and happiness.    4

**40.** In lines 5–10, there are many references to writing poetry and plays.  Choose any two examples of this and explain how each one adds to your understanding of the speaker's feelings.    4

**41.** Look at the last four lines (lines 11–14).

  (a) How does the poet makes clear how different the guests are from the speaker and her lover?    2

  (b) What feelings does the speaker show for her lover at the end of the poem?    2

**42.** With close textural reference to this poem and to **at least one** other poem by Carol Ann Duffy, discuss how she explores the theme of love.    8

**OR**

## Text 2 — Poetry

If you choose this text you may not attempt a question on Poetry in Section 2.

Read the poem below and then attempt the following questions.

### *Lucozade* by Jackie Kay

My mum is on a high bed next to sad chrysanthemums.
'Don't bring flowers, they only wilt and die.'
I am scared my mum is going to die
on the bed next to the sad chrysanthemums.

5   She nods off and her eyes go back in her head.
Next to her bed is a bottle of Lucozade.
'Orange nostalgia, that's what that is,' she says.
'Don't bring Lucozade either,' then fades.

'The whole day was a blur, a swarm of eyes.
10   Those doctors with their white lies.
Did you think you could cheer me up with a *Woman's Own*?
Don't bring magazines, too much about size.'

My mum wakes up, groggy and low.
'What I want to know,' she says, 'is this:
15   where's the big brandy, the generous gin, the Bloody Mary,
the biscuit tin, the chocolate gingers, the dirty big meringue?'

I am sixteen; I've never tasted a Bloody Mary.
'Tell your father to bring a luxury,' says she.
'Grapes have no imagination, they're just green.
20   Tell him: stop the neighbours coming.'

I clear her cupboard in Ward 10B, Stobhill Hospital.
I leave, bags full, Lucozade, grapes, oranges,
sad chrysanthemums under my arms,
weighted down. I turn round, wave with her flowers.

25   My mother, on her high hospital bed, waves back.
Her face is light and radiant, dandelion hours.
Her sheets billow and whirl. She is beautiful.
Next to her the empty table is divine.

I carry the orange nostalgia home singing an old song.

**MARKS**

Questions

**43.** The poet twice refers to Lucozade as "orange nostalgia".  What does she mean by this?    **2**

**44.** Briefly describe the mother's mood in lines 1–12.    **2**

**45.** Explain fully how the poet contrasts "grapes" with the "luxury" the mother asks for.    **4**

**46.** Describe the speaker's mood in lines 21–29 and explain how it is conveyed.    **4**

**47.** With close textural reference to this poem and to **at least one** other poem by Jackie Kay, discuss how she explores relationships between generations.    **8**

MARKS

OR

## Text 3 — Poetry

If you choose this text you may not attempt a question on Poetry in Section 2.

Read the poem below and then attempt the following questions.

### *Trio* by Edwin Morgan

Coming up Buchanan Street, quickly, on a sharp winter evening
a young man and two girls, under the Christmas lights –
The young man carries a new guitar in his arms,
the girl on the inside carries a very young baby,
5  and the girl on the outside carries a chihuahua.
And the three of them are laughing, their breath rises
in a cloud of happiness, and as they pass
the boy says, "Wait till he sees this but!"
The chihuahua has a tiny Royal Stewart tartan coat like a teapot-
10       holder,
the baby in its white shawl is all bright eyes and mouth like favours
       in a fresh sweet cake,
the guitar swells out under its milky plastic cover, tied at the neck
       with silver tinsel tape and a brisk sprig of mistletoe.
15 Orphean sprig! Melting baby! Warm chihuahua!
The vale of tears is powerless before you.
Whether Christ is born, or is not born, you
put paid to fate, it abdicates
        under the Christmas lights.
20 Monsters of the year
go blank, are scattered back,
can't bear this march of three.

– And the three have passed, vanished in the crowd
(yet not vanished, for in their arms they wind
25 the life of men and beasts, and music,
laughter ringing them round like a guard)
at the end of this winter's day.

MARKS

**Questions**

48. Explain briefly how the poet establishes a happy mood in lines 1–8.    2

49. Look at the descriptions in lines 9–14 of the chihuahua, the baby, and the guitar.  Choose any **two** of these and explain how the poet's use of language creates an effective description.    4

50. In lines 15–22 the poet gives his thoughts about what he has just seen.  In your own words, explain what he says.    4

51. Describe the poet's mood in the final stanza (lines 23–27).    2

52. With close textual reference to this poem and to **at least one** other poem by Edwin Morgan, discuss how he takes an everyday, ordinary situation and transforms it into something special and thought provoking.    8

OR

## Text 4 — Poetry

If you choose this text you may not attempt a question on Poetry in Section 2.

Read the poem below and then attempt the following questions.

### *Visiting Hour* by Norman MacCaig

The hospital smell
combs my nostrils
as they go bobbing along
green and yellow corridors.

5   What seems a corpse
is trundled into a lift and vanishes
heavenward.

I will not feel, I will not
feel, until
10  I have to.

Nurses walk lightly, swiftly,
here and up and down and there,
their slender waists miraculously
carrying their burden
15  of so much pain, so
many deaths, their eyes
still clear after
so many farewells.

Ward 7.
20  She lies
in a white cave of forgetfulness.
A withered hand
trembles on its stalk.  Eyes move
behind eyelids too heavy
25  to raise.  Into an arm wasted
of colour a glass fang is fixed,
not guzzling but giving.
And between her and me
distance shrinks till there is none left
30  but the distance of pain that neither she nor I
can cross.

**MARKS**

She smiles a little at this
black figure in her white cave
who clumsily rises
35  in the round swimming waves of a bell
and dizzily goes off, growing fainter,
not smaller, leaving behind only
books that will not be read
and fruitless fruits.

**Questions**

**53.** Explain how the speaker's sense of discomfort is conveyed in lines 1–10.    4

**54.** What is the speaker's attitude to the nurses (lines 11–18)?  Refer to the text to support your answer.    2

**55.** Choose **two** examples of imagery from lines 19–31 and explain how each one adds to your understanding of the poem.    4

**56.** "...leaving behind only
books that will not be read
and fruitless fruits."

Do you think this is a good way to end the poem?  Justify your answer.    2

**57.** With close textual reference to this poem and to **at least one** other poem by Norman MacCaig, discuss how he explores powerful emotions.    8

**[END OF SECTION 1]**

## SECTION 2 — CRITICAL ESSAY — 20 marks

Attempt ONE question from this section of the paper from ONE of the Parts A–E.

You may use a Scottish text but <u>not</u> the one used in Section 1.

Your essay should be on a different <u>genre</u> to the one used in Section 1.

Write the number of your chosen question in the margin of your answer.

You should spend about 45 minutes on the essay.

### DRAMA

> *Answers to questions in this part should refer to the text and to such relevant features as characterisation, key scene(s), structure, climax, theme, plot, conflict, setting . . .*

1. Choose a play in which there is a character who suffers from a human weakness such as ambition, selfishness, lack of self-knowledge, jealousy, pride, lust . . .

   By referring to appropriate techniques, show how the weakness is revealed, and then explain how this weakness affects both the characters and the events of the play.

2. Choose a play which you feel has a dramatic final scene.

   Describe briefly what happens in the final scene and then, by referring to appropriate techniques, explain how effective the ending is in bringing to a conclusion the central concerns of the text.

### PROSE

> *Answers to questions in this part should refer to the text and to such relevant features as characterisation, setting, language, key incident(s), climax, turning point, plot, structure, narrative technique, theme, ideas, description . . .*

3. Choose a novel **or** short story with an ending which you find satisfactory.

   By referring to appropriate techniques, explain why you find the ending satisfactory in bringing to a conclusion the main concerns of the text as a whole.

4. Choose a novel **or** a short story **or** a work of non-fiction which deals with an important human issue (such as the abuse of power, conflict between good and evil, loss of freedom or hatred between individuals or groups).

   By referring to appropriate techniques, show how the author reveals the issue through the portrayal of people and events throughout the text, and show how your understanding of the issue has deepened.

## POETRY

> *Answers to questions in this part should refer to the text and to such relevant features as word choice, tone, imagery, structure, content, rhythm, rhyme, theme, sound, ideas . . .*

5. Choose a poem in which the poet creates a particular mood or atmosphere.

    By referring to appropriate techniques, show how the poet creates this mood **or** atmosphere.

6. Choose a poem which could be considered as having a powerful message.

    By referring to appropriate techniques, show how the poet effectively conveys this message.

## FILM AND TV DRAMA

> *Answers to questions in this part should refer to the text and to such relevant features as use of camera, key sequence, characterisation, mise-en-scène, editing, setting, music/ sound, special effects, plot, dialogue . . .*

7. Choose a film **or** TV drama* which creates suspense or tension either in a particular scene **or** throughout the whole film or TV drama.

    By referring to appropriate techniques, show how the suspense or tension is created and how it affects your enjoyment of the film or TV drama as a whole.

8. Choose a film **or** TV drama* which both entertains and helps to raise awareness of social issues.

    By referring to appropriate techniques, show how the film or TV drama you have chosen succeeds in both these aspects.

* "TV drama" includes a single play, a series or a serial.

## LANGUAGE STUDY

> *Answers to questions in this part should refer to the text and to such relevant features as register, accent, dialect, slang, jargon, vocabulary, tone, abbreviation . . .*

9. Consider the specialist language used by any group of people to talk about a particular interest, for example, a sport, a job, a hobby . . .

    By referring to specific examples and to appropriate features of language, show how the specialist language used by the group is effective in communicating ideas clearly.

10. Consider how TV programmes aimed at young audiences have an effect on the language young people use.

    Identify any recent changes in vocabulary or accent that you are aware of and, by referring to specific examples and to appropriate features of language, explain whether you feel the new words/accents are more effective in communicating than those which they have replaced.

[END OF SECTION 2]

[END OF MODEL PAPER]

# Model Paper 3

Whilst this Model Paper has been specially commissioned by Hodder Gibson for use as practice for the National 5 exams, the key reference documents remain the SQA Specimen Paper 2013 and the SQA Past Papers 2014 and 2015.

For reasons of space and copyright, Model Paper 3 does not include Section 1 of the Critical Reading paper.

National
Qualifications
MODEL PAPER 3

# English
# Reading for Understanding,
# Analysis and Evaluation

Duration — 1 hour

**Total marks — 30**

When you are told to do so, open the booklet, read the passage and attempt all the questions, using your own words as far as possible.

**Before attempting the questions you must check that your answer booklet is for the same subject and level as this question paper.**

On the answer booklet, you must clearly identify the question number you are attempting.

Use **blue** or **black** ink.

Before leaving the examination room you must give your answer booklet to the Invigilator.
If you do not, you may lose all the marks for this paper.

**HODDER**
GIBSON
LEARN MORE

## Why Dickens was the hero of Soweto

*In this passage, the writer informs us about the effect that books by Charles Dickens, a 19th-century English writer, had on black South African children during the time of racial segregation ("apartheid") in South Africa. "Afrikaans" is the language which was spoken in South Africa by the white rulers before the arrival of democracy in that country.*

Hector Pieterson was 12 when he died. Today a museum bearing his name commemorates his death — and hundreds of others — which occurred some 30 years ago at a place whose name has come to symbolise uprising against oppression: Soweto.

Hector was one of thousands of black children who took to the streets on June 16, 1976, in
5 protest about schooling under the apartheid regime in South Africa. When police opened fire on the march it brought the word Soweto to the attention of the world. But less well known is the role that Charles Dickens played in events.

The march was in protest at a government edict making Afrikaans compulsory in schools. From January 1976, half of all subjects were to be taught in it, including ones in which difficulties of
10 translation were often an issue.

To pupils accustomed to being educated in English, the Afrikaans policy was the last of a line insults delivered in the name of "Bantu" or "negative education". They thought being taught in Afrikaans, the language of a regime that had tried to "unpeople" them, would cost them their last remaining freedom — that of thinking for themselves, using their minds.

15 That is where Dickens came in. Many books were banned under apartheid but not the classics of English literature. Pupils arriving hungry at school every day were captivated by the story of a frail but courageous boy named Oliver Twist.

The book was a revelation. Systemised oppression of children happened in England too! They were not alone. Slave labour, thin rations and cruel taunts were part of a child's life in the
20 world outside as well.

One former pupil, now in his forties, says of Dickens: "Four or five of us would be together and discuss the stories. And to think he wasn't banned! The authorities didn't know what was in these books, how they helped us to be strong, to think that we were  not forgotten."

Not being forgotten was particularly crucial. The apartheid regime had tried to "vanish" black
25 people. Feeling abandoned and isolated, people turned to Dickens as someone who understood their plight.

But there were not enough books to go round. Few of the crateloads of Shakespeare,  Hardy and Dickens shipped from Britain reached the townships. Instead, they came to Soweto in parcels from charities. They were read by candlelight, often out loud, shared in a circle, or passed from
30 hand to hand.

At Morrris Isaacson School, one of the moving forces behind the Soweto protest, which produced two of its leaders, Murphy Morobe, "Shakespeare's best friend in Africa", and Tsietsi Mashinini, there were 1,500 pupils and three copies of *Oliver Twist* in 1976. The former pupils recall waiting months for their turn, with a similar wait for *Nicholas Nickleby*.

35 But it was Oliver that they took to heart: students at one of the country's leading black colleges, Lovedale, formed a committee to ask for more.

Calling it the Board, after Dickens' Board of Guardians, they asked for more lessons, more food — and more and better books.  Their reward was to be charged with public violence.  All 152 "board" members were expelled from the college and some were jailed.

40 They felt that Dickens was obviously on their side.  Descriptions of Gamfield's "ugly leer" and Bumble's "repulsive countenance" and Oliver being beaten by Mrs Sowerberry and shoved "but nothing daunted" into the dust-cellar were evidence that this English author understood the plight of black South Africans.

Dickens' compassion for the poor linked the people of Soweto to a worldwide literature of tremendous importance.

45 The veteran South African trumpeter Hugh Masekela later chose *Nicholas Nickleby* as his favourite book on a popular radio programme, *Desert Island Discs*, telling the presenter what its author did for people in the townships:  "He taught us suffering is the same everywhere."

The love of books that enabled an author dead for more than 100 years to inspire thousands of schoolchildren came mainly from grandmothers who had educated their  families orally, then 50 urged them to read widely and learn all that they could.

It also came from people such as the activist Steve Biko, whose own mentor, the Brazilian educator Paulo Freire, spent a lifetime working with forest people who had no formal education, teaching them to "name the world their own way".

That is what the youth of Soweto wanted — a future in their own words.  And they got it. By the 55 following year, Afrikaans had been withdrawn from classrooms as unworkable. And so, thanks to the influence of a long-dead British author, the sacrifices of Hector Pieterson and many other Africans have proved to be not entirely in vain — which Dickens himself would surely applaud.

*Adapted from an article by Carol Lee in The Times.*

MARKS

## Questions

1. Explain fully any **two** ways in which the writer makes the opening paragraph dramatic.

    4

2. Referring to lines 1–14, explain **in your own words** why Sowetans were protesting.

    3

3. Why, according to the writer in lines 15–26, was the story of Oliver Twist so popular among young Sowetans?

    4

4. Show how any **two** examples of the writer's word choice in lines 15–20 create sympathy for the character Oliver Twist.

    4

5. Explain the function of the colon in line 35.

    2

6. Referring to lines 27–47, summarise **in your own words** the key evidence the writer uses to show Dickens' popularity among black South Africans.

    4

7. What does the paragraph in lines 37–39 suggest about the Government in South Africa at the time?

    2

8. Look at lines 48–57.

    (a) Explain briefly how each paragraph shows the importance various groups of people attach to education.

    3

    (b) Show how any **two** examples of the writers' use of language in these lines create a very positive and inspiring conclusion to the passage.

    4

**[END OF MODEL PAPER]**

## SECTION 2 — Critical Essay — 20 marks

Write ONE critical essay on a previously studied text from Drama, Prose, Poetry, Film and Television Drama or Language.

Your answer must be on a different genre from that chosen in Section 1.

You should spend approximately 45 minutes on each Section.

**Before attempting the questions you must check that your answer booklet is for the same subject and level as this question paper.**

On the answer booklet, you must clearly identify the question number you are attempting.

Use **blue** or **black** ink.

Before leaving the examination room you must give your answer booklet to the Invigilator. If you do not you may lose all the marks for this paper.

## SECTION 2 — CRITICAL ESSAY — 20 marks

Attempt ONE question from this section of the paper from ONE of the Parts A-E.

You may use a Scottish text but <u>not</u> the one used in Section 1.

Your essay should be on a different <u>genre</u> to the one used in Section 1.

Write the number of your chosen question in the margin of your answer.

You should spend about 45 minutes on the essay.

### DRAMA

*Answers to questions in this part should refer to the text and to such relevant features as characterisation, key scene(s), structure, climax, theme, plot, conflict, setting . . .*

1. Choose a play in which one of the main concerns is love **or** jealousy **or** betrayal **or** reconciliation.

   Explain what the concern is, and by referring to appropriate techniques show how it is explored throughout the play.

2. Choose a scene from a play in which suspense or tension is built up.

   By referring to appropriate techniques, show how this suspense or tension is built up and what effect this scene has on the play as a whole.

### PROSE

*Answers to questions in this part should refer to the text and to such relevant features as characterisation, setting, language, key incident(s), climax, turning point, plot, structure, narrative technique, theme, ideas, description . . .*

3. Choose a novel **or** a short story in which a character is in conflict with his or her friends or relatives or society.

   By referring to appropriate techniques, show how the conflict arises and what effect it has on the character's fate in the novel or short story as a whole.

4. Choose a novel **or** a short story **or** a work of non-fiction in which setting is an important feature.

   By referring to appropriate techniques, explain how the writer creates the setting, and then go on to show how this feature contributes to your understanding of the text as a whole.

## POETRY

> Answers to questions in this part should refer to the text and to such relevant features as word choice, tone, imagery, structure, content, rhythm, rhyme, theme, sound, ideas . . .

5. Choose a poem which reflects on an aspect of human behaviour in such a way as to deepen your understanding of human nature.

   Describe the aspect of human behaviour which you have identified and, by referring to appropriate techniques, show how the poem brought you to a deeper understanding of human nature.

6. Choose a poem which portrays an interesting character.

   By referring to appropriate techniques, show how the poet makes the character interesting.

## FILM AND TV DRAMA

> Answers to questions in this part should refer to the text and to such relevant features as use of camera, key sequence, characterisation, mise-en-scène, editing, setting, music/sound, special effects, plot, dialogue . . .

7. Choose a film **or** TV drama* in which the main character is an individual for whom we feel sympathy.

   By referring to appropriate techniques, show how the character is portrayed in such a way that we feel sympathy.

8. Choose an opening sequence from a film which effectively holds your interest and makes you want to watch the rest of the film.

   By referring to appropriate techniques, show what elements of the opening sequence have this effect, and how they relate to the film as a whole.

* "TV drama" includes a single play, a series or a serial.

## LANGUAGE STUDY

> Answers to questions in this part should refer to the text and to such relevant features as register, accent, dialect, slang, jargon, vocabulary, tone, abbreviation . . .

9. Consider the ways that young people use the internet to communicate and socialise, for example: social networking sites, instant messaging, chat rooms, blogs . . .

   By referring to specific examples and to appropriate features of language, explain how such communication differs from formal English, and what its attractions are for young people.

10. Consider a text which you find to be persuasive, for example: an advertisement, a speech, a newspaper article . . .

    By referring to specific examples and to appropriate features of language, show how persuasive techniques have been used to convince you.

### [END OF SECTION 2]

### [END OF MODEL PAPER]

*Page three*

National
Qualifications
2014

X724/75/01

English
Reading for Understanding,
Analysis and Evaluation

WEDNESDAY, 30 APRIL
1:00 PM – 2:00 PM

**Total marks — 30**

Attempt ALL questions.

Write your answers clearly in the answer booklet provided. In the answer booklet you must clearly identify the question number you are attempting.

Use **blue** or **black** ink.

Before leaving the examination room you must give your answer booklet to the Invigilator; if you do not you may lose all the marks for this paper.

**Hey, parents, leave those kids alone.**

In many ways, nothing changes. We love our children. We want our children to grow up to be competent, decent human beings fit for adult purpose. These are the main things, and in these we have, I think we are all agreed, not done too badly. Our children, and I'll generalise here, are not serial axe murderers or kitten drowners. Our children do make
5 an effort — at least on special occasions anyway — to repay the enormous investment of time, energy, money and emotion we have poured into them. Children are programmed to please, to be loved, and to love us back.

So we are not here to examine our children. What we should do is try to find out where we have gone so terribly wrong. Before we come to the wretchedly indulgent state of
10 modern parenting, though, I suppose I'd better set out my stall. Inevitably, when one becomes a parent, one can't help revisiting one's own childhood to make comparisons.

When I was little, we were given no choices — about what we ate, what we wore, what we did, where we went to school, when we went to bed etc. I could only choose what to read.

15 There was not so much stuff (many of my son's 15-year-old friends have iPods, iPads, MacBooks, unlimited access to their parents' credit cards, Pay Pal, eBay and iTunes accounts — and not just iPhones, but BlackBerrys too), so we made our own fun.

Our parents provided us with the essentials, then got on with their own lives. Which makes me realise that my parents were brilliant, not for what they did, but more for
20 what they didn't do.

So we were fed, we were clothed, we were loved, and we had all the books we could read. But there was not the expectation of having every wish granted, as there is now, and that is the best thing that my parents could ever have given us.

I remember only once going to a restaurant in the UK. It was a motorway café on the
25 A303. My father told us, wincing as he looked at the laminated text, with its stomach-churning pictograms, that we could have the spag bol. From the children's menu.

We had a TV, but as we lived in Belgium there was nothing to watch apart from two American sitcoms, which came on only once a week.

My parents were so hard up that when we went to England for holidays on the family farm
30 on Exmoor — mainly spent "wooding" for winter fuel on rainswept hillsides — my father would invariably book cheap overnight ferry crossings from the Continent. He would never shell out for a cabin, despite the 1am or 3am departure slots. Instead, he would tell us to go to sleep in the back of the car, parked in the lower deck, where we would eventually pass out from suffocation or diesel fumes.

35 We never had friends round for "playdates". Keeping children busy and happy was not a parental priority. If we were bored, that was our own fault. In fact, there was nothing to do for weeks on end except rake leaves (my father once made us spend a whole half-term raking leaves) and read on our beds. Occasionally my mother would shout up the stairs: "Stop reading!" Imagine that now, when children are on their laptops in their rooms,
40 looking at . . . I don't even want to imagine.

As for school, well, reports were read, not dwelt upon, as they were not parents' business, but ours. As for parental involvement, all I can tell you is that my father's proudest boast as a parent is that he never, once, attended a parent-teacher meeting at any one of our schools.

45 It never did me any harm, but still, I can't repeat this sensible, caring regime of character-building, toughening, benign neglect for my own children . . . and nor, it appears, can anyone else. Now examples of "wet parenting" abound.

We also live in a world where a manic mum calls herself a Tiger Mother and writes a bestselling book by the same name about how to produce straight-A violin-playing
50  tennis-champ superkids, and where pushy, anxious helicopter parents hover over every school.  A friend reports that when her son was due to visit the Brecon Beacons on a school camping trip this summer, three mothers pulled out their sons because the weather forecast was "rainy".

University dons are also complaining of a traumatic level of parental over-involvement
55  just at the exact moment that mummies and daddies are supposed to be letting go.

It was the complete opposite in my day.  When I was on my gap year, I called my father from Israel in September and told him I'd decided not to take up my place at university.  I announced that I wanted to stay in Galilee with a handsome local shepherd.  For ever.

My father didn't miss a beat.  "Great scheme!" he cried, astutely divining that if he
60  approved the plan, I would never carry it out.

In my lifetime, parenthood has undergone a terrifying transition.  Becoming a mother or father is no longer something you just are.  It is something you do, like becoming a vet — complete with training courses, parenting vouchers, government targets and guidelines, and a host of academics and caring professionals (as well as their websites,
65  and telephone helplines) on hand 24/7 to guide you through what to expect when your twentysomethings return home.

Parenting has become subsidised and professionalised, even though anyone can (and, frankly, does) have a baby, after which they become parents.

I love being a parent, most of the time anyway, but we should immediately
70  de-professionalise it, on the grounds that:  one, it's unpaid; and two, thanks to the economy, lack of housing and jobs etc, you never get to retire.

*Rachel Johnson, in The Times*

MARKS

1.  Look at line 9, where the writer gives the view that, nowadays, parents "have gone . . . terribly wrong".

    Explain **in your own words** what the writer goes on to say has gone wrong.    2

2.  Explain any way in which the sentences in lines 12 – 14 help to provide a link between ideas at this point in the passage.    2

3.  Look at lines 24 – 40, where the writer develops the idea of her family being "hard up".

    Show fully how examples of the writer's use of such features of language as **word choice** or **sentence structure** helps to convey her ideas effectively.    4

4.  Look at lines 45 – 47.

    Explain what is meant by the expression "benign neglect", and explain what is surprising about this expression.    3

5.  Look at lines 48 – 55.

    With reference to **three** examples of the writer's **word choice** from these lines, show fully how she makes clear her disapproval of what she calls "wet parenting".    6

6.  In the expression "straight-A violin-playing tennis-champ superkids" the writer tries to achieve a humorous, mocking tone.

    Explain with reference to her use of language how successful you think she has been in achieving this tone.    2

7.  Look at lines 59 – 60.

    Show fully how the writer conveys her father's **apparent** attitude, and his **actual attitude**, to her plan.    4

8.  Look at lines 61 – 66, and then explain **as far as possible in your own words** what similarities the writer sees between "Becoming a mother or father" and "becoming a vet".    2

9.  In this article, the writer points out several differences between parenting and childhood when she was little and parenting and childhood now (she refers to "a terrifying transition", line 61).

    **As far as possible in your own words**, summarise what some main differences are.    5

**[END OF QUESTION PAPER]**

# National Qualifications 2014

**X724/75/02**

**English Critical Reading**

WEDNESDAY, 30 APRIL
2:20 PM – 3:50 PM

**Total marks — 40**

**SECTION 1 — Scottish Text — 20 marks**

Read an extract from a Scottish text you have previously studied.

Choose ONE text from either

Part A — Drama      Pages 2–7
or
Part B — Prose      Pages 8–17
or
Part C — Poetry      Pages 18–25

Attempt ALL the questions for your chosen text.

**SECTION 2 — Critical Essay — 20 marks**

Attempt ONE question from the following genres — Drama, Prose, Poetry, Film and Television Drama, or Language.

Your answer must be on a different genre from that chosen in Section 1.

You should spend approximately 45 minutes on each Section.

Write your answers clearly in the answer booklet provided. In the answer booklet you must clearly identify the question number you are attempting.

Use **blue** or **black** ink.

Before leaving the examination room you must give your answer booklet to the Invigilator; if you do not you may lose all the marks for this paper.

**SECTION 1 — SCOTTISH TEXT — 20 marks**

**PART A — SCOTTISH TEXT — DRAMA**

**Text 1 — Drama**

If you choose this text you may not attempt a question on Drama in Section 2.

Read the extract below and then attempt the following questions.

***Bold Girls by Rona Munro***

*Marie's house.  Belfast.  Late afternoon.  Present day*

*It is irons and ironing boards and piles of clothes waiting to be smoothed, socks and pegs and damp sheets waiting for a break in the Belfast drizzle for the line; it's toys in pieces and toys that are just cardboard boxes and toys that are new and gleaming and flashing*
5 *with lights and have swallowed up the year's savings.  It's pots and pans and steam and the kettle always hot for tea; it's furniture that's bald with age and a hearth in front of the coal fire that's gleaming clean.*

*At the moment it's empty, an unnatural, expectant emptiness that suggests this room is never deserted; it's too stuffed with human bits and pieces, all the clutter of housework*
10 *and life.*

*There is a small picture of the virgin on one wall, a large grainy blow-up photo of a smiling young man on the other.  He has a seventies haircut and moustache.*

*Deirdre is not in this room, she is crouching on all fours on her own talking out of darkness in which only her face is visible.  She is wary, young.*

15 DEIRDRE:   (*moving from all fours*) The sun is going down behind the hills, the sky is grey. There's hills at the back there, green.  I can't hardly see them because the stones between here and there are grey, the street is grey.  Somewhere a bird is singing and falling in the sky.  I hear the ice cream van and the traffic and the helicopter overhead.

*Black-out; after a few minutes Lights come up on Marie's house.*

20 *Marie bursts into the room with her arms laden with four packets of crisps, two of Silk Cut and a packet of chocolate biscuits.  She is cheerful, efficient, young.  She drops one of the crisps, tuts in exasperation, and looks at it*

MARIE:      (*shouting back out the door*) Mickey! Mickey were you wanting smoky bacon?... Well this is salt and vinegar . . . Well, why did you not say?  Away you and swap this . . .
25 Catch now.  (*She hurls the bag*) No you cannot . . . No . . . because you'll not eat your tea if you do! (*At the doorway*) Mickey, pick up those crisps and don't be so bold.

*Marie comes back into the room and starts two jobs simultaneously.  First she puts the crisps etc away, then she fills a pan with water and throws it on the stove.  She starts sorting her dry washing into what needs ironing and what doesn't; she sorts a few items*
30 *then starts peeling potatoes; all her movements have a frenetic efficiency.*

**MARKS**

Questions

1.  Look at the description of Marie's house.  By referring to word choice and/or sentence structure, explain what impression this creates of Marie's daily life.

    4

2.  With close reference to the text, explain what Deirdre's **actions** and **speech** tell us about her relationship to her surroundings.  You could consider: word choice, tone, the use of imagery etc . . .

    4

3.  The playwright introduces Marie.  What do we find out about:

    (*a*)  her attitude towards Mickey;

    2

    (*b*)  her attitude towards her daily routine?

    2

4.  The play goes on to develop our understanding of how challenging life is in many respects for the "bold girls".  By referring to this extract and at least one other example from the play, discuss what these challenges are.

    8

[Turn over

**OR**

**Text 2 — Drama**

If you choose this text you may not attempt a question on Drama in Section 2.

Read the extract below and then attempt the following questions.

*Sailmaker* **by Alan Spence**

*Extract from Act Two*

|  |  |  |
|---|---|---|
| ALEC: | Look at the state ae us. We're livin like bloody Steptoe and Son! Nae light. Place is like a midden. When did we last gie it a good clean? Needs gutted. | |

Look at it!

| DAVIE: | It's hard son. It's no easy on yer own. |
|---|---|
| 5 ALEC: | So ye go an get bevvied. Forget it all. |
| DAVIE: | Ye'd think ah came in steamin every night! |

Christ ah need a wee break once in a while. Like the night. Nae harm in it. Good company. Wee sing song. Right gents, a wee bit order there. One singer one song. That lassie's a rare singer. Sang Honky Tonk Angels.

10    She's the one ah told ye about.

| ALEC: | (*Sarcastic*) The really nice person. |
|---|---|
| DAVIE: | She wis. |
| ALEC: | Who was that lady I saw you with last night? |
| DAVIE: | That was no lady, that was a really nice person. |

15    Nae harm in it.

| ALEC: | It's always the same. Every time ye meet a wumman she's a really really really nice person. |
|---|---|

Why don't ye just admit that ye fancy her?

(DAVIE *slaps him, exits*)

20    Ach aye, yirra good boy son. Wallop!

Bad. Bad. Bad.

(*Pause*)

Wallop.

(*Darkness. Spotlight on* ALEC)

25    I keep goin back.

What is it I'm tryin to remember?

What is it I'm tryin to say?

There's somethin I've lost. Something I've forgotten.

Sometimes in the middle of the night . . .

30    What is it I'm looking for?

God knows.

MARKS

**Questions**

5. **In your own words**, summarise what happens in this part of the play. Make **two** key points.    **2**

6. Think about how Alec and Davie are feeling during their dialogue with one another (lines 1—19).

   (a) Show how Alec's language reflects his feelings.    **2**

   (b) Although he does not say very much, Davie experiences a range of emotions during his dialogue with his son. With close reference to the text, explain what **at least two** of these are.    **4**

7. Alec is left alone at the end of this extract.

   With reference to word-choice and sentence structure, explain clearly his state of mind at this stage in the play.    **4**

8. By referring to this extract, and to elsewhere in the play, explain how the character of Alec develops and changes as he grows older.    **8**

[Turn over

**OR**

**Text 3 — Drama**

If you choose this text you may not attempt a question on Drama in Section 2.

Read the extract below and then attempt the following questions.

***Tally's Blood* by Ann Marie di Mambro**

*This scene takes place in the back of the Pedreschi's shop.*

ROSINELLA:     You see the way Italians are getting on now, eh?  Beginning to make a wee bit money?  Because they're prepared to WORK that's why.  I don't know anybody who works so hard as the Italian men.

*Hughie in: with pail and mop.*

5   HUGHIE:        That's the tables cleared and the front shop mopped, Mrs Pedreschi, and the chip pan cleaned out.  Is the milk boiled?

ROSINELLA:     Should be.

*She turns attention back to Lucia, Hughie lifts pot from stove and pours contents into two pails:  he covers them and sets them aside, working like a trojan.*

10  ROSINELLA:     And the way they love their families.  Nobody loves their families like the Italians.  You want to stay for a wee bit pasta, Hughie?  It's your favourite.  Rigatoni.

HUGHIE:        No thanks, Mrs Pedreschi.  I better get up the road.  Bridget's going out and I don't like my mammy left on her own.

15  ROSINELLA:     Bridget's going out is she?  Don't tell me she's winching?

HUGHIE:        No.  Her and Davie are going up to Charmaine's the night — to go over all the arrangements.  My mammy's no up to it.

ROSINELLA:     That's right.  When's the wedding now?

*Hughie and Lucia exchange glances: he makes gesture of "go ahead" to her.  Lucia shakes*
20  *head.*

Hughie:        Saturday.

ROSINELLA:     And where are they going to stay?

HUGHIE:        At Charmaine's.

ROSINELLA:     It's funny that, isn't it, but that's the way they do it here.  In Italy a girl
25               must go to her husband's house.  That's why you must have land if you've got sons.

*Massimo in.*

ROSINELLA:     So that'll be your mammy left with her eldest and her youngest, eh?  I don't see your Bridget ever marrying, do you?  You see, Lucia, there's a lot
30               of women Bridget's age no married.  The war killed that many young men. I'm right there, amn't I Massimo?

MASSIMO:       You got those pails ready, son?

HUGHIE:        I'll bring them through.

MARKS

|       |         |                                                                                                                                                                                                                                                                                                                                                                                                                                                                                                  |
| ----- | ------- | --- |

MASSIMO:    And give's a hand to put these shutters up before you go.

35 *Hughie and Massimo out: Rosinella watches him go.*

ROSINELLA:    I'm right about that Davie, amn't I Lucia?  Give it five or six months, Hughie'll be telling us he's an uncle again.  Mind you, I suppose his mother must feel it, right enough.  Can you find me a wee envelope hen, a wee poke or something?  What was I saying . . . ah yes . . . See what I mean
40                about Italian men.  Just take that brother of Hughie's.  Getting married on Saturday, give him two or three days and he'll be out DRINKING with his pals.

*Rosinella shooshes up when Hughie comes in, followed by Massimo:  all locked up. Massimo takes off his apron, reaches for a bottle of wine.*

45 MASSIMO:    Thanks, Hughie son.  You want a wee glass of wine?

HUGHIE:    I better not, Mr Pedreschi.  I better get up the road.

ROSINELLA:    Hang on a minute, son.  (She has slipped a couple of notes into the poke, gives it to Hughie) Here, give this to your brother from me.  Instead of a present.  Help them out a wee bit, eh?  (Hughie hangs back, embarrassed)
50                . . . Take it.

## Questions

9.  (a)  Rosinella makes stereotypical statements about Italians and/or Scots which are shown to be false in this extract.  Identify **two** statements and explain how the playwright shows they are false.    **4**

    (b)  Explain how you think the audience would react to this falseness.    **2**

10.  Think about the character Rosinella.

     (a)  How is Rosinella shown to be kind or caring in this extract?    **2**

     (b)  How is Rosinella shown to be unkind or unpleasant in this extract?    **2**

11.  Identify **two** examples of colloquial or conversational language from the extract.    **2**

12.  This extract deals with racial stereotypes.  With close reference to this extract and elsewhere in the play explain how the issue of racism is explored.    **8**

[Turn over

## PART B — SCOTTISH TEXT — PROSE

**Text 1 — Prose**

If you choose this text you may not attempt a question on Prose in Section 2.

Read the extract below and then attempt the following questions.

**The Cone-Gatherers by Robin Jenkins.**

*In this extract, a deer hunt, at which Neil and Calum have been told to help out, is coming to its violent end.*

The drive was nearly over.  Only a hundred or so yards away were the waiting guns. Frightened by the noises approaching them from the rear, and apprehensive of the human silence ahead, the five roe deer were halted, their heads high in nervous alertness.  When Calum saw them, his cry was of delight and friendship, and then of terrified warning as
5  the dogs too, and Duror, caught sight of them and rushed in pursuit.  Silently, with marvellous grace and agility over such rough ground, the deer flew for the doom ahead. Their white behinds were like moving glints of sunlight; without them their tawny hides might not have been seen in the autumnal wood.

Calum no longer was one of the beaters; he too was a deer hunted by remorseless men.
10  Moaning and gasping, he fled after them, with no hope of saving them from slaughter but with the impulse to share it with them.  He could not, however, be so swift or sure of foot.  He fell and rose again; he avoided one tree only to collide with another close to it; and all the time he felt, as the deer must have, the indifference of all nature; of the trees, of tall withered stalks of willow herb, of the patches of blue sky, of bushes, of piles
15  of cut scrubwood, of birds lurking in branches, and of the sunlight: presences which might have been expected to help or at least sympathise.

The dogs barked fiercely.  Duror fired his gun in warning to those waiting in the ride.  Neil, seeing his brother rush into danger, roared to him to come back.  All the beaters, except Charlie far in the rear, joined in the commotion; the wood resounded with their exultant
20  shouts.   Realising this must be the finish or kill, Graham, recuperating on the road, hopped back over the fence into the wood and bellowed loudest of all.

As Duror bawled to his dogs to stop lest they interfered with the shooting, and as the deer hesitated before making the dash across the ride, Calum was quite close to them as silent, desperate, and heroic, they sprang forward to die or escape.  When the guns
25  banged he did not, as Neil had vehemently warned him to do, fall flat on the ground and put his fingers in his ears.  Instead, with wails of lament, he dashed on at demented speed and shot out onto the broad green ride to hear a deer screaming and see it, wounded in the breast and forelegs, scrabbling about on its hindquarters.  Captain Forgan was feverishly reloading his guns to fire again.  Calum saw no one else, not even the lady
30  or Mr Tulloch, who was standing by himself about twenty yards away.

Screaming in sympathy, heedless of the danger of being shot, Calum flung himself upon the deer, clasped it around the neck and tried to comfort it.  Terrified more than ever, it dragged him about with it in its mortal agony.  Its blood came off onto his face and hands.

While Captain Forgan, Young Roderick, and Lady Runcie-Campbell stood petrified by this
35  sight, Duror followed by his dogs came leaping out of the wood.  He seemed to be laughing in some kind of berserk joy.

Questions

13. Look at the first paragraph and describe the changing emotions Calum experiences when he sees the deer.    2

14. In lines 5—8 how does the writer emphasise the sadness of what is about to happen to the deer?    2

15. Identify two examples of how the writer's language in lines 9—16 convey Calum's clumsy panic as he tries to help the hunted animals.    2

16. Look again at lines 24—33.  Show how the writer conveys the chaos of the moment when Calum reaches and tries to help the wounded deer.    4

17. How unusual do you find Duror's reaction in lines 34—36 to Calum ruining the deer drive?    2

18. Discuss how Duror is portrayed in this extract and elsewhere in the novel.    8

[Turn over

OR

## Text 2 — Prose

If you choose this text you may not attempt a question on Prose in Section 2.

Read the extract below and then attempt the following questions.

### *The Testament of Gideon Mack* by James Robertson

I went running every second or third day.  I ran not as a member of a club, not in training for competitions (although I have run marathons for charity), not even to keep fit (although it had that effect), but because I enjoyed it.  Yes, running filled me with joy, contentment, as nothing else did.  It took me out of myself.  Also, it was how I released
5 the energy inside me: as if the fire blazing away in there was my fuel.  If I went four days without a run, I grew hot and tense and felt as if my chest was about to explode.  I *needed* to run.  It was how I got the heat out of my system.

Running made me aware both of the countryside in which I lived and of my physical self.  When I set off through the streets of Monimaskit, I could feel the disapproval of some of
10 my parishioners boring into the back of my neck — there was something just *no richt* about a minister in shorts, and sweating.  But once out of the town I left all that behind me.  I avoided traffic-heavy main roads and ran on narrow, deserted unclassifieds, farm tracks, paths that led me through woods and alongside fields and over burns.  I ran along the shore, I ran up into the low hills, I ran beside the crashing of the sea on sand and
15 shingle and I ran above the roaring of the Keldo Water as it fought through the Black Jaws on its way to that sea.  I loved the idea of myself — was this vanity? — running among the shadows of trees, against the backdrop of hills, in the echo of birdsong and bellowing cows.  I could run for a couple of hours at a time if I chose, barely pausing at gates or stiles, sensitive to the different noises my trainers made when I went up or down a hill, or
20 when I moved from hard road to soft path or grass.  Usually I ran in the late afternoon, the dead time between daytime appointments and evening visits and meetings, and I seldom met anybody else.  A woman walking her dog, perhaps, or a couple of lads on their bikes.  Sometimes the woman would recognise me and say hello.  Sometimes she'd recognise me but pretend not to, embarrassed by the ministerial knees.  If the boys had a
25 clue who I was, they never let on.

I loved that time of day in all seasons and all weathers, the bright hot stillness of summer and the dark moody dampness of winter.  I loved it for itself, but running made it more special still.  Running emptied my head of work, the Kirk, the world.  Difficult issues and awkward individuals were repelled by the force of my energy, and their ghosts faded into
30 the trees.  In Israel young fanatics with explosives strapped to their bodies were wiping themselves and busloads of hated strangers off the planet; insect species were being extinguished every five minutes in the Amazon forest; military coups were being bloodily launched in Africa; dams were being built in China, making tens of thousands homeless; but in Keldo Woods, alone and immune and having slipped his clerical collar, Gideon Mack
35 was running.  Sometimes a line from a song or a hymn got trapped in my head and I ran to its rhythm, half-enjoying it and half-annoyed by it.  Phrases from the Scriptures that became strange and mantra-like in the repetition: *Nec tamen consumebatur*; "The Lord is with thee, thou mighty man of valour"; MENE, MENE, TEKEL UPHARSIN.  Sometimes I heard my own voice in there, bits of poems I'd read, things I wished I'd said at the right
40 moment, heroic and true things I might say in the future — nothing, as it's turned out, remotely connected with what I would actually say.

MARKS

Sometimes I saw myself as I do now — as if in a film, splashing through puddles to a soundtrack by Vangelis:  *when I run I feel God's pleasure*. But that was somebody else: Eric Liddell, the Flying Scotsman, a missionary, a kind of saint.  *The loneliness of the*
45 *long-distance runner*:  phrases like that would enter my head and bounce around in there as I ran; but that was someone else again, a Borstal boy, a figure of fiction.  I was somewhere in between — an escapee from my professional hypocrisy, a minister off the leash, a creature neither wholly real nor wholly imagined, hurrying through an ancient landscape.  Yes, even then I suspected what I now know to be true: that life itself is not
50 wholly real.   Existence is one thing, life quite another:  it is the ghost that haunts existence, the spirit that animates it.  Running, whether in the rain or sun, felt like life.

### Questions

19. Using examples from this extract to support your points, explain the different reasons why Gideon Mack enjoys running.                                                4

20. What does this extract reveal about Mack's attitude to his job?  Give evidence from the extract to support your answer.                                                2

21. Look closely at the **language** used in this extract.

    (*a*) Show how **sentence structure** helps the reader understand how much Gideon Mack enjoys running.                                                3

    (*b*) Choose one example of **imagery** used to help the reader understand the importance of running to Gideon Mack and explain how it does so.                                                3

22. Discuss one aspect of Gideon Mack's character which features in this extract and is developed elsewhere in the novel.                                                8

[Turn over

OR

**Text 3 — Prose**

If you choose this text you may not attempt a question on Prose in Section 2.

Read the extract below and then attempt the following questions.

***Kidnapped* by Robert Louis Stevenson**

*In this extract, which is from Chapter 9 of the novel, David Balfour sees Alan Breck Stewart for the first time as he arrives on the* Covenant.

We had run down a boat in the fog, and she had parted in the midst and gone to the bottom with all her crew, but one.  This man (as I heard afterwards) had been sitting in the stern as a passenger, while the rest were on the benches rowing.  At the moment of the blow, the stern had been thrown into the air, and the man (having his hands free, and

5　for all he was encumbered with a frieze overcoat that came below his knees) had leaped up and caught hold of the brig's bowsprit.  It showed he had luck and much agility and unusual strength, that he should have thus saved himself from such a pass.  And yet, when the captain brought him into the round-house, and I set eyes on him for the first time, he looked as cool as I did.

10　He was smallish in stature, but well set and as nimble as a goat; his face was of a good open expression, but sunburnt very dark, and heavily freckled and pitted with the small-pox; his eyes were unusually light and had a kind of dancing madness in them, that was both engaging and alarming; and when he took off his great-coat, he laid a pair of fine silver-mounted pistols on the table, and I saw that he was belted with a great sword.

15　His manners, besides, were elegant, and he pledged the captain handsomely.  Altogether I thought of him, at the first sight, that here was a man I would rather call my friend than my enemy.

The captain, too, was taking his observations, but rather of the man's clothes than his person.  And to be sure, as soon as he had taken off the great-coat, he showed forth

20　mighty fine for the round-house of a merchant brig: having a hat with feathers, a red waistcoat, breeches of black plush, and a blue coat with silver buttons and handsome silver lace; costly clothes, though somewhat spoiled with the fog and being slept in.

"I'm vexed, sir, about the boat," says the captain.

"There are some pretty men gone to the bottom,"  said the stranger, " that I would

25　rather see on the dry land again than half a score of boats."

"Friends of yours?"  said Hoseason.

"You have none such friends in your country,"  was the reply.  "They would have died for me like dogs."

"Well, sir,"  said the captain, still watching him, "there are more men in the world than

30　boats to put them in."

"And that's true, too,"  cried the other, "and ye seem to be a gentleman of great penetration."

"I have been in France, sir," says the captain, so that it was plain he meant more by the words than showed upon the face of them.

35　"Well, sir," says the other, "and so has many a pretty man, for the matter of that."

MARKS

"No doubt, sir," says the captain, "and fine coats."

"Oho!" says the stranger, "is that how the wind sets?" And he laid his hand quickly on his pistols.

"Don't be hasty," said the captain.  "Don't do a mischief before ye see the need of it.
40 Ye've a French soldier's coat upon your back and a Scotch tongue in your head, to be sure; but so has many an honest fellow in these days, and I dare say none the worse of it."

## Questions

23.  Look at paragraph 1 (lines 1—9) and summarise the circumstances of how Alan Breck Stewart came to arrive on the Covenant.  You should make at least four key points.    **4**

24.  Look at paragraph 2 (lines 10—17).

  **In your own words**, explain what David Balfour's first impressions were of Alan Breck Stewart's physical appearance and character.    **4**

25.  Look at the conversation between Alan Breck Stewart and Captain Hoseason (lines 23—42).

  Show how any **two** examples of the writer's use of language contributes to the creation of tension in the dialogue.    **4**

26.  With reference to this extract and to elsewhere in the novel, discuss the development of David and Alan's relationship.    **8**

[Turn over

OR

Text 4 — Prose

If you choose this text you may not attempt a question on Prose in Section 2.

Read the extract below and then attempt the following questions.

*The Telegram* by Iain Crichton Smith

The elder had passed the Murrays.  The next house was her own.  She sat perfectly still.  Oh, pray God it wasn't hers.  And yet it must be hers.  Surely it must be hers.  She had dreamt of this happening, her son drowning in the Atlantic ocean, her own child whom she had reared, whom she had seen going to play football in his green jersey and white

5  shorts, whom she had seen running home from school.  She could see him drowning but she couldn't make out the name of the ship.  She had never seen a really big ship and what she imagined was more like the mailboat than a cruiser.  Her son couldn't drown out there for no reason that she could understand.  God couldn't do that to people.  It was impossible.  God was kinder than that.  God helped you in your sore trouble.  She began

10  to mutter a prayer over and over.  She said it quickly like the Catholics.  O God save my son O God save my son O God save my son.  She was ashamed of prattling in that way as if she was counting beads but she couldn't stop herself, and on top of that she would soon cry.  She knew it and she didn't want to cry in front of that woman, that foreigner.  It would be weakness.  She felt the arm of the thin woman around her shoulders, the thin

15  arm and it was like first love, it was like the time Murdo had taken her hand in his when they were coming home from the dance, such an innocent gesture, such a spontaneous gesture.  So unexpected, so strange, so much a gift.  She was crying and she couldn't look . . .

"He has passed your house," said the thin woman, in a distant firm voice, and she looked

20  up.  He was walking along and he had indeed passed her house.  She wanted to stand up and dance all around the kitchen, all fifteen stone of her, and shout and cry and sing a song but then she stopped.  She couldn't do that.  How could she do that when it must be the thin woman's son?  There was no other house.  The thin woman was looking out at the elder, her lips pressed closely together, white and bloodless.  Where had she learnt that

25  self control?  She wasn't crying or shaking.  She was looking out at something she had always dreaded but she wasn't going to cry or surrender or give herself away to anyone.

And at that moment the fat woman saw.  She saw the years of discipline, she remembered how thin and unfed and pale the thin woman had always looked, how sometimes she had had to borrow money, even a shilling to buy food.  She saw what it

30  must have been like to be a widow bringing up a son in a village not her own.  She saw it so clearly that she was astounded.  It was as if she had an extra vision, as if the air itself brought the past with all its details nearer.  The number of times the thin woman had been ill and people had said that she was weak and useless.  She looked down at the thin woman's arm.  It was so shrivelled, and dry.

35  And the elder walked on.

**MARKS**

Questions

27. Look closely at lines 1—18.

    How does the writer use language effectively to create tension?   4

28. Look closely at the description of the thin woman in lines 19—26.

    Show how the writer uses word choice to demonstrate:

    (a)  her fear;   2

    (b)  her self-control.   2

29. In your own words, summarise the main difficulties the thin woman has had to overcome in her life.  You should make at least four points.   4

30. By referring to this story, and to at least one other story by Iain Crichton Smith, show how he is successful in creating a character or characters we can feel sympathy for.   8

[Turn over

**OR**

**Text 5 — Prose**

If you choose this text you may not attempt a question on Prose in Section 2.

Read the extract below and then attempt the following questions.

***Away in a Manger* by Anne Donovan**

This year the nativity was bigger than life-sized.  The figures were bronze statues, staunin on a carpet of straw and surrounded by what looked like a hoose made of glass.  It was placed tae wan side of the square, inside a fence.  Sandra thought it was quite dull lookin.  Weans liked bright colours and these huge people were kind of scary.  She minded
5 the wee plastic figures of Mary and Joseph she used tae set carefully in place every Christmas, leavin the baby Jesus tae last.  They'd fitted intae the palm of her haund.  She'd need tae get a crib for Amy.  Sandra wisnae very religious, no religious at all, really, but still, it was nice for the wee ones tae have a crib.

"Is that a manger, Mammy?"  Amy pointed.

10 "That's right.  D'you know who all the people are?"

Amy sucked at her mitt and looked carefully at the figures.  "That's Mary and that's Joseph — and that's the baby Jesus.  And that's a shepherd wi his sheep.  But who's that, Mammy?"

"They're the three wise kings.  Look — they've got presents for the baby Jesus."

15 "But who's that, Mammy? Behind the cow."

Huddled in the straw, hidden in a corner behind the figure of a large beast, lay a man.  He was slightly built, dressed in auld jeans and a thin jaicket.  One of his feet stuck oot round the end of the statue and on it was a worn trainin shoe, the cheapest kind they sold in the store.  Sandra moved round tae get a better look at him.  He was quite young, wi a
20 pointed face and longish dark hair.  A stubbly growth covered his chin.  He seemed sound asleep.

"Is he an angel, Mammy?"

Sandra didnae answer.  She was lookin at the glass structure wonderin how on earth he'd got in.  One of the panels at the back looked a bit loose, but you'd think they'd have an
25 alarm on it.  Lucky for him they never — at least he'd be warm in there.  She was that intent on the glass panels that she'd nearly forgotten he wisnae a statue.  Suddenly he opened his eyes.  They were grey.

Amy grabbed her mother's arm and started jumpin up and down.

"Mammy, look, he's alive! Look Mammy.  He's an angel!"

MARKS

Questions

31. Using your own words as far as possible, summarise the main events in this extract. You should make at least two key points. 2

32. Look at lines 1—3. The writer uses a number of techniques to show how Amy tries to makes sense of the scene. Identify two techniques and explain their effects. 4

33. Look at lines 7—8 from "Sandra wisnae...". The writer creates the impression of Sandra thinking. Choose any one aspect of the writer's use of language and explain its effect. 2

34. Look at lines 16—20. The writer uses word choice to create a detailed picture of the man. Identify **two** separate examples of the writer's word choice from these lines and comment on their effects. 4

35. With reference to this story and at least one other story by Donovan, discuss how any one theme is explored. 8

[Turn over

**PART C — SCOTTISH TEXT — POETRY**

**Text 1 — Poetry**

If you choose this text you may not attempt a question on Poetry in Section 2.

Read the poem below and then attempt the following questions.

*War Photographer* **by Carol Ann Duffy**

In his darkroom he is finally alone
with spools of suffering set out in ordered rows.
The only light is red and softly glows,
as though this were a church and he
5  a priest preparing to intone a Mass.
Belfast. Beirut. Phnom Penh. All flesh is grass.

He has a job to do. Solutions slop in trays
beneath his hands, which did not tremble then
though seem to now. Rural England. Home again
10  to ordinary pain which simple weather can dispel,
to fields which don't explode beneath the feet
of running children in a nightmare heat.

Something is happening. A stranger's features
faintly start to twist before his eyes,
15  a half-formed ghost. He remembers the cries
of this man's wife, how he sought approval
without words to do what someone must
and how the blood stained into foreign dust.

A hundred agonies in black and white
20  from which his editor will pick out five or six
for Sunday's supplement. The reader's eyeballs prick
with tears between the bath and pre-lunch beers.
From the aeroplane he stares impassively at where
he earns his living and they do not care.

**MARKS**

Questions

36. As the photographer prepares to develop the film we learn important things about him.

Identify two important things we learn about him from stanza one.    **2**

37. Show how two examples of the poet's use of language in stanza two highlight the effect the photographer's work has had on the photographer.    **4**

38. Show how one example of the poet's use of language contributes to the dramatic effect of stanza three.    **2**

39. How effective do you find any two aspects of the final stanza as a conclusion to the poem?

Your answer might deal with ideas and/or language.    **4**

40. Using close textual reference, show how the presentation of the main character in this poem is similar or different to the presentation of the main character in another poem or poems by Duffy which you have read.    **8**

[Turn over

**OR**

**Text 2 — Poetry**

If you choose this text you may not attempt a question on Poetry in Section 2.

Read the poem below and then attempt the following questions.

*In the Snack-bar* **by Edwin Morgan**

A cup capsizes along the formica,

slithering with a dull clatter.

A few heads turn in the crowded evening snack-bar.

An old man is trying to get to his feet

5  from the low round stool fixed to the floor.

Slowly he levers himself up, his hands have no power.

He is up as far as he can get. The dismal hump

looming over him forces his head down.

He stands in his stained beltless gabardine

10  like a monstrous animal caught in a tent

in some story.  He sways slightly,

the face not seen, bent down

in shadow under his cap.

Even on his feet he is staring at the floor

15  or would be, if he could see.

I notice now his stick, once painted white

but scuffed and muddy, hanging from his right arm.

Long blind, hunchback born, half paralysed

he stands

20  fumbling with the stick

and speaks:

'I want – to go to the – toilet.'

It is down two flights of stairs but we go.

I take his arm. 'Give me – your arm – it's better,' he says.

25  Inch by inch we drift towards the stairs.

A few yards of floor are like a landscape

to be negotiated, in the slow setting out

time has almost stopped.  I concentrate

my life to his: crunch of spilt sugar,

30  slidy puddle from the night's umbrellas,

*Page twenty*

MARKS

table edges, people's feet,

hiss of the coffee-machine, voices and laughter,

smell of a cigar, hamburgers, wet coats steaming,

and the slow dangerous inches to the stairs.

## Questions

**41.** (*a*) Identify two of the poem's main ideas or central concerns that are introduced in this extract.

2

(*b*) Show how any two examples of the poet's use of language in stanza 1 help to make these concerns clear to readers.

4

**42.** Explain how the poet's own role in what is happening in the snack-bar changes from stanza 1 to stanza 2.

2

**43.** Look at lines 23—34. Show how the poet uses language to emphasise the difficulty of the start of the journey to the toilet.

4

**44.** By closely referring to the text of this and at least one other Morgan poem, show how Morgan uses language effectively to create interesting characters.

8

[Turn over

**OR**

**Text 3 — Poetry**

If you choose this text you may not attempt a question on Poetry in Section 2.

Read the poem below and then attempt the following questions.

***Basking Shark* by Norman MacCaig**

To stub an oar on a rock where none should be,
To have it rise with a slounge out of the sea
Is a thing that happened once (too often) to me.

But not too often—though enough  I count as gain
5   That once I met, on a sea tin-tacked with rain,
That roomsized monster with a matchbox brain.

He displaced more than water  He shoggled me
Centuries back—this decadent townee
Shook on a wrong branch of his family tree.

10   Swish up the dirt and, when it settles, a spring
Is all the clearer. I saw me, in one fling,
Emerging from the slime of everything.

So who's the monster? The thought made me grow pale
For twenty seconds while as, sail after sail,
15   The tall fin slid away, and then the tail.

MARKS

Questions

45. Look at stanza 1. What event is described in this stanza and how does MacCaig react? Refer to the poet's language in your answer.

3

46. Referring closely to stanza 2, show how MacCaig uses word choice to convey how he feels about the encounter.

4

47. "He displaced more than water". Explain what this line means and show how the poet in the rest of the stanza develops this idea further.

3

48. Choose an example of word choice in stanza 4 and explain how effective you find this example.

2

49. MacCaig often describes his personal experiences in his poetry, using these to explore wider themes. Referring closely to this poem and to at least one other poem by MacCaig, show how he uses personal experience to explore wider themes.

8

[Turn over

**OR**

**Text 4 — Poetry**

If you choose this text you may not attempt a question on Poetry in Section 2.

Read the poem below and then attempt the following questions.

*Lucozade* by Jackie Kay

My mum is on a high bed next to sad chrysanthemums.
"Don't bring flowers, they only wilt and die."
I am scared my mum is going to die
on the bed next to the sad chrysanthemums.

5  She nods off and her eyes go back in her head.
Next to her bed is a bottle of Lucozade.
"Orange nostalgia, that's what it is," she says.
"Don't bring Lucozade, either," then fades.

"The whole day was a blur, a swarm of eyes.
10  Those doctors with their white lies.
Did you think you could cheer me up with a Woman's Own?
Don't bring magazines, too much about size."

My mum wakes up, groggy and low.
"What I want to know," she says, "is this:
15  where's the big brandy, the generous gin, the Bloody Mary,
the biscuit tin, the chocolate gingers, the dirty big meringue?"

I am sixteen; I've never tasted a Bloody Mary.
"Tell your father to bring a luxury," says she.
"Grapes have no imagination, they're just green.
20  Tell him: stop the neighbours coming."

I clear her cupboard in Ward 10B, Stobhill Hospital.
I leave, bags full, Lucozade, grapes, oranges,
sad chrysanthemums under my arms,
weighted down.  I turn round, wave with her flowers.

25  My mother, on her high hospital bed, waves back.
Her face is light and radiant, dandelion hours.
Her sheets billow and whirl.  She is beautiful.
Next to her the empty table is divine.

I carry the orange nostalgia home singing an old song.

**Questions**

MARKS

**50.** Look at stanzas 1 and 2 (lines 1—8).

Why does the poet's mother not want her to bring flowers or Lucozade?

2

**51.** Referring to lines 9—20, show how the poet gives the reader a clear impression of the mother's character or personality.

4

**52.** Explain how the poet uses language in lines 21—29 to indicate a clear change in the girl's feelings.

6

**53.** Identify at least one theme from this poem. Using close textual reference, show how the theme (or themes) is explored in this poem, and in at least one other poem by Jackie Kay.

8

[END OF SECTION 1]

[Turn over

## SECTION 2 — CRITICAL ESSAY — 20 marks

Attempt ONE question from the following genres — Drama, Prose, Poetry, Film and Television Drama, or Language.

Your answer must be on a different genre from that chosen in Section 1.

You should spend approximately 45 minutes on this Section.

## DRAMA

*Answers to questions on Drama should refer to the text and to such relevant features as characterisation, key scene(s), structure, climax, theme, plot, conflict, setting . . .*

1. Choose a play in which there is a character who is important in relation to the theme of the play.

   Referring to appropriate techniques, explain how this character affects our understanding of this theme.

2. Choose a play in which there is a key scene.

   Briefly describe what happens in this scene then, by referring to dramatic techniques, go on to explain why the scene is important to the play as a whole.

## PROSE

*Answers to questions on Prose should refer to the text and to such relevant features as characterisation, setting, language, key incident(s), climax, turning point, plot, structure, narrative technique, theme, ideas, description . . .*

3. Choose a novel **or** short story **or** work of non-fiction which has a key incident.

   Give a brief account of the incident, and by referring to appropriate techniques, show how this incident is important to the text as a whole.

4. Choose a novel **or** short story in which there is a character involved in some form of conflict.

   By referring to appropriate techniques, show how the character comes to be involved in this conflict and how the conflict develops throughout the text.

## POETRY

*Answers to questions on Poetry should refer to the text and to such relevant features as word choice, tone, imagery, structure, content, rhythm, rhyme, theme, sound, ideas . . .*

5. Choose a poem which you find particularly thought-provoking.

   By referring to poetic techniques, explain how the poet makes this poem so thought-provoking.

6. Choose a poem which deals with human experience.

   By referring to poetic techniques, show how the poet makes this experience come alive and helps you appreciate the poem as a whole.

## FILM AND TELEVISION DRAMA

*Answers to questions on Film and Television Drama should refer to the text and to such relevant features as use of camera, key sequence, characterisation, mise-en-scène, editing, setting, music/sound, special effects, plot, dialogue . . .*

7. Choose the opening or closing scene or sequence from a film **or** television drama*.

   By referring to appropriate techniques, explain why you find it an effective opening or closing scene or sequence.

8. Choose a film or television drama* which has a character who either supports or threatens the main character.

   By referring to appropriate techniques, explain how this character plays an important role in the film/television drama as a whole.

* "television drama" includes a single play, a series or a serial.

[Turn over

## LANGUAGE

*Answers to questions on Language should refer to the text and to such relevant features as register, accent, dialect, slang, jargon, vocabulary, tone, abbreviation . . .*

9.  Choose two advertisements, and consider the language used.

    By referring to the language techniques used, explain how effective they are at persuading you.

10. Consider the differences in language between two groups of people – for example people who live in different areas, or who have different jobs.

    By referring to appropriate language techniques, explain the main differences in language use between the two groups.

[END OF SECTION 2]

[END OF QUESTION PAPER]

# National Qualifications 2015

X724/75/11

THURSDAY, 14 MAY
9:00 AM – 10:00 AM

**English
Reading for Understanding,
Analysis and Evaluation**

Total marks — 30

**Attempt ALL questions.**

Write your answers clearly in the answer booklet provided. In the answer booklet you must clearly identify the question number you are attempting.

Use **blue** or **black** ink.

Before leaving the examination room you must give your answer booklet to the Invigilator; if you do not you may lose all the marks for this paper.

## On the spot

If you throw a rat into the middle of a room full of humans, it will instinctively freeze. By becoming completely still, it is more likely to avoid detection. Then, it will dart into a corner of the room, hoping to flee danger. If cornered, however, it will fight. Ferociously.

5 Psychologists call it the fight-flight-freeze response, and it emerged very early in evolution. We know this because it is common to all vertebrates. The response starts in a part of the brain which reacts when an animal is confronted by a threat, and is controlled by the automatic nervous system. This is the same system that manages digestion and respiration, and is independent of conscious will.

10 At the World Cup finals, we were given a neat insight into this deeply ingrained response. The players who took penalties, and the former players who shared their experiences as pundits, talked about "the walk". This is the fearful, solitary journey from the halfway line to the penalty area in preparation for a single moment of truth: the spot-kick.

In the modern world, we rarely face danger head-on. It is not like the good old days
15 when the fight-flight-freeze response was regularly called upon to deal with predators (of both an animal and human kind). Instead, the danger we face today is artificially created: taking an exam, giving a speech, taking a penalty.

The psychological response, however, is the same. As footballers walk towards the spot, they are experiencing precisely the things you experience when put under pressure at
20 work. The threat is not to life or limb, but to ego and livelihood. We fear the consequences of messing up.

There is an acceleration of heart and lung function. There is paling and flushing. There is an inhibition of stomach action, such that digestion almost completely ceases. There is a constriction of blood vessels. There is a freeing up of metabolic energy sources (fat and
25 glycogen). There is a dilation of the pupils and a relaxation of the bladder. Perception narrows. Often, there is shaking.

All of these things are incredibly useful, in the right context. They prime the muscles; they massively increase body strength in preparation for fighting or running. The increased muscle flow and blood pressure means that you become hyper-vigilant. The
30 response is beautifully balanced for a simple reason: it helped our ancestors (and the ancestors of modern-day rats) to survive.

But there is a rather obvious problem. The fight-flight-freeze response is great for fighting, freezing or fleeing, but it is terrible if you have to do something complex, or subtle, or nuanced. When you are taking a penalty, or playing a piano concerto, or
35 marshalling the arguments necessary to pass a difficult interview, it is not helpful to have adrenalin pumping like crazy and perception obliterated by tunnel vision. You need to be calm and composed, but your body is taut, pumped and trembling.

Sports psychology can be thought of as helping performers to manage a response (ie fight, flight, freeze) that has outlived, to a large extent, its usefulness. The players standing in
40 the semi-circle holding hands are virtually motionless. It is a nice metaphor for the freeze response. The walk to the penalty spot is curiously self-conscious. You can almost hear the inner dialogue: "Get out of here, run away! 'But I can't run away. I have to take this thing!' "

How to deal with these responses? One way is with reflection. The next time you give a
45 speech or are doing a job interview, take note of how you feel. Gauge the curious feeling of dread, the desire to run away, the way your heart is beating out of your chest. But do not let this intimidate you; instead, reflect that these are normal reactions and everyone experiences them: even Michael Jordan (a marvel from the free-throw line) and Roger

Federer (who always looks unnaturally calm on Centre Court).

50   One of the most creative sports psychologists has found that simply discussing the fight-flight-freeze response has huge therapeutic benefit.  It takes the edge off.  It makes an otherwise bewildering reaction (what on earth is going on inside me?) into a comprehensible one.  To put it another way, the first stage of liberation from the tyranny of pressure is echoing the behaviour of our ancient selves.

55   This, I think, is what top athletes mean when they repeat that otherwise paradoxical saying: "Pressure is not a problem; it is a privilege".  Talk to David Beckham, Sebastian Coe or Sir Chris Hoy and they will be perfectly open about their nerves and fear.  But they also talk with great pride about facing up to them.  They didn't see these human responses as signs of weakness but as opportunities to grow.  They created mechanisms
60   (often highly personal ones) to help them through.  They seized every opportunity to face danger, and learnt from each experience.

So, here is a piece of (free) advice: if you are given an opportunity to take the equivalent of a penalty, whether at work or anywhere else, grab it.  Accept that you will feel uncomfortable, that your stomach will knot and that, at the moment of truth, you will
65   wish to be anywhere else in the world.  Think also, as you are about to perform, of the footballers at a World Cup who volunteered to step forward with the weight of a nation's expectations on their shoulders.

Because here is the most revelatory and paradoxical thing of all: if you miss, your life will not end.  If you fluff your lines, you won't die.  Instead, you will grow, learn and mature.
70   And isn't that what life – whether at home, on the football pitch, or in the office – is ultimately about?

*Matthew Syed*, in "The Times"

MARKS

Total marks — 30

Attempt ALL Questions

1. Explain fully why the first paragraph (lines 1—4) is an effective opening to the passage as a whole.

3

2. Look at lines 5—10, and then explain **in your own words** what the writer means when he calls the response "deeply ingrained".

2

3. Look at lines 14—21, and then explain **in your own words two** aspects of "danger" or "threat" we used to experience in the past, and **two** we face now.

4

4. Look at lines 22—37, and then summarise, **using your own words** as far as possible, some of the changes in the body which occur with the response.

You should make **five** key points in your answer.

5

5. Explain why the sentence "How to deal with these responses?" (line 44) provides an appropriate link at this point in the passage.

2

6. Look at lines 50—54, and then explain how **two** examples of the writer's **word choice** demonstrate the "benefit" of the response.

4

7. Look at lines 55—61. Explain what the attitude of top athletes is to pressure, and how **two** examples of the language used make this attitude clear.

5

8. Look at lines 62—67, and explain fully **using your own words** why the advice to "grab" the opportunity might at first seem strange.

3

9. Pick an expression from the final paragraph (lines 68—71), and show how it helps to contribute to an effective conclusion to the passage.

You should refer to an expression or idea from earlier in the article.

2

[END OF QUESTION PAPER]

[Open out for Questions]

**DO NOT WRITE ON THIS PAGE**

[BLANK PAGE]

DO NOT WRITE ON THIS PAGE

X724/75/12

**English**
**Critical Reading**

THURSDAY, 14 MAY

10:20 AM – 11:50 AM

Total marks — 40

**SECTION 1 — Scottish Text — 20 marks**

Read an extract from a Scottish text you have previously studied.

Choose ONE text from either

Part A — Drama          Pages 2–7
or
Part B — Prose          Pages 8–17
or
Part C — Poetry         Pages 18–25

Attempt ALL the questions for your chosen text.

**SECTION 2 — Critical Essay — 20 marks**

Attempt ONE question from the following genres — Drama, Prose, Poetry, Film and Television Drama, or Language.

Your answer must be on a different genre from that chosen in Section 1.

You should spend approximately 45 minutes on each Section.

Write your answers clearly in the answer booklet provided. In the answer booklet you must clearly identify the question number you are attempting.

Use **blue** or **black** ink.

Before leaving the examination room you must give your answer booklet to the Invigilator; if you do not, you may lose all the marks for this paper.

**SECTION 1 — SCOTTISH TEXT — 20 marks**

**PART A — SCOTTISH TEXT — DRAMA**

**Text 1 — Drama**

If you choose this text you may not attempt a question on Drama in Section 2.

Read the extract below and then attempt the following questions.

***Bold Girls* by Rona Munro**

*Cassie and Marie are on a piece of waste ground.   They are talking about their relationships with men . . .*

|   | MARIE: | I don't know how you coped with all Joe's carry on.  I don't.  You were the martyr there, Cassie. |
|---|---|---|
| 5 | CASSIE: | It gave me peace. |
|   | MARIE: | No but I couldn't have stood that, just the lying to you, the *lying* to you.  I used to say to Michael, "If you go with someone else it'll tear the heart out of me but tell me, just tell me the truth 'cause I'd want to know, I couldn't bear not to know."  He never did though.  So I never worried. |
| 10 | CASSIE: | No. |
|   | MARIE: | Do you know he was like my best friend.  Well, sure you're my best friend but if a man can be that kind of friend to you he was to me, could tell each other anything.  That's what I miss most.  The crack.  The *sharing*. |
|   | CASSIE: | Marie . . . |
| 15 | MARIE: | What? |
|   | CASSIE: | Aw Jesus I hate this place!  (She gets up, kicking the ground) |
|   | MARIE: | We'll get a weekend in Donegal again soon, the three of us and the kids.  Sure we could all do with a break. |
|   | CASSIE: | I'm leaving. |
| 20 | MARIE: | What? |
|   |   | *Cassie says nothing* |
|   |   | What do you mean you're leaving? |
|   | CASSIE: | Do you know she gives me a tenner before every visit to go up town and buy fruit for them.  "Poor Martin" and "poor Joe".  That's all she's allowed to give |
| 25 |   | them, all she can spoil them with, fruit, so she wants them to have grapes and melons and things you've never heard of and shapes you wouldn't know how to bite into.  I'll bring her home something that looks and smells like the Botanic Gardens and she'll sniff it and stroke it like it was her favourite son himself, 'stead of his dinner . . .  And I'll have three or four pounds in my |
| 30 |   | pocket, saved, sure she doesn't have a clue of the price of kiwi fruit.  (*Pause*) I've two hundred pounds saved.  I'm going, Marie. |

*Page two*

MARKS

MARIE:     Going where?

CASSIE:    It's desperate, isn't it?  Thirty-five years old and she's stealing from her
35         mummy's purse.  Well I thought about asking the broo for a relocation grant or
           something you know, but it seems to me all they can offer you is the straight
           swap of one hell hole for another.

MARIE:     You talking about a holiday?

CASSIE:    I'm talking about getting out of here.

MARIE:     Cassie, where could you go with two kids for two hundred pounds?

40         *Cassie says nothing for a moment*

**Questions**

1.  Using your own words as far as possible, summarise what happens in this extract.
    You should make **four** key points.                                                   4

2.  Referring closely to the extract, show how **two** aspects of Marie's attitude towards
    men are revealed by the playwright.                                                     4

3.  By referring closely to the extract, explain **two** aspects of Cassie's mood.  (You may
    refer to word choice, sentence structure and/or stage directions in your answer.)       4

4.  Gender is an important theme in this extract.  With reference to this extract and
    elsewhere in the play, explain how the theme of gender is explored.                     8

[Turn over

OR

**Text 2 — Drama**

If you choose this text you may not attempt a question on Drama in Section 2.

Read the extract below and then attempt the following questions.

*Sailmaker* **by Alan Spence**

*Extract from Act One*

|  |  |  |
|---|---|---|
| ALEC: | | Later on I opened the window and looked out across the back courts.  The breeze was warm.  Everything was the same.  It was very ordinary.  Nothing had changed.  I don't know what I had expected.  A sign.  Jesus to come walking across the back and tell me everything was all right.  A window in the sky to open and God to lean out and say my mother had arrived safe.  The sun shone on the grey tenements, on the railings and the middens, on the dustbins and the spilled ashes.  It glinted on windows and on bits of broken glass.  It was like something I remembered, something from a dream.  Across the back, a wee boy was standing, blowing on a mouth-organ, playing the same two notes over and over again. |

5

10

(*Two notes on mouth organ, repeated, continuing while he talks*)

My mother was dead.

My mother was dead.

The breeze touched my cheek.  It scattered the ashes round the midden.  It ruffled the clothes of the wee boy standing there, playing his two notes.

15

Over and over and over.

I looked up at the sky, the clouds moving across.  Just for a minute a gap opened up, a wee patch of clear blue.

(*Two notes continuing, then fade*)

20   DAVIE:    We better get this place tidied up a bit son.  Folk'll be comin back after the funeral.

(*Moves around as he is talking — ALEC remains static*)

As long as ye keep movin it doesnae hit ye.  Get the fire goin clean the windaes dust the furniture think about somethin for eatin don't stop keep yerself goin.  Sometimes for whole minutes ye can nearly *nearly* forget about it, shove it tae the back ae yer mind.  Then maybe yer lookin for somethin and ye turn round tae ask her where it is an ye wonder for a minute where she's got tae and ye think she's through in the room an ye catch yerself thinkin it and it hits ye and ye think Christ this is it this is me for the rest ae ma days.

25

MARKS

## Questions

5.  Using your own words as far as possible, summarise the situation facing Alec and Davie in this extract.    **2**

6.  During Alec's speech (lines 1–19), there are references to the weather and the setting. By referring closely to the text, explain how **both** of these are important in this context.    **4**

7.  With close reference to **two** examples of the writer's use of language from lines 20–29, explain how Davie is coping with his situation.    **4**

8.  Look closely at the language used by Alec and Davie in this extract.

    Identify **two** key differences between Alec and Davie in their use(s) of language.    **2**

9.  The relationship between father and son is an important theme in the play.

    With close reference to this extract and elsewhere in the play, show how this theme is explored.    **8**

[Turn over

OR

Text 3 — Drama

If you choose this text you may not attempt a question on Drama in Section 2.

Read the extract below and then attempt the following questions.

*Tally's Blood* by Ann Marie di Mambro

*In this scene Rosinella is getting Lucia ready for her Confirmation.*

ROSINELLA:    You look just like a wee bride.  I'm telling you this now, Lucia Ianelli, some day I'll give you a wedding, I'll give you a wedding like nobody here has ever seen before.

LUCIA:    (*Enthusiastic*)  Just like yours?

5 ROSINELLA:    (*Cagey*)  I didn't have much of a wedding, hen.  We were awfy poor in they days.

LUCIA:    (*Sympathetic*)  Oh, Auntie Rosinella.

ROSINELLA:    No, don't get me wrong.  I wouldn't change your Uncle Massimo for any film star.  No for Humphrey Bogart, no for Victor Mature.  My faither
10    wanted me to marry someone else, you know.

LUCIA:    (*Enjoying it*)  He did not.

ROSINELLA:    (*Getting into it*)  He did that.  Ferdinando.  He'd it all fixed up with Ferdinand's faither.  He wasn't very good looking, Ferdinand, but all the girls were after him because he had a beautiful big piece of land.  That's
15    what it's all about over there, you know.  The man's got to have land.  So my daddy was that pleased when his daddy picked me.  It was all set.  Then I met your Uncle Massimo.  I must have met him when he was a wean, before him and his faither moved to Scotland, but I don't remember.  I'm no kidding you, Lucia, I knew the minute I looked at him that he was for
20    me. He was that handsome.

LUCIA:    (*Disbelief*)  My Uncle Massimo?

ROSINELLA:    That was before he put the weight on.  And he'd much more hair then and it was shining black.  Nero.  Nero.  Oh, Massimo!  Swept me off ma feet he did.  Oh hen, I shouldn't be telling you this . . .

25 LUCIA:    (*Desperate to hear the rest*)  Oh no, go on, Auntie Rosinella.

ROSINELLA:    Well, I never married Ferdinand.  I married your Uncle Massimo instead. That's why I didn't have much of a wedding.  (*A beat: she is deciding whether to tell her or not, then does so, with glee.*)  We ran away.

LUCIA:    (*Impressed*)  You did not!

30 ROSINELLA:    (*Enjoying it now*)  We did.  You see, in Italy, where we come from anyway, if a boy and a girl stay out together all night, then they must get married. It's true.  We planned it and we did it.  My faither locked me in my room because I said I wasn't going to marry Ferdinand and your Uncle Massimo came with a ladder and stole me out the window.

MARKS

35  LUCIA:         (*Laughing*) He did not!

    ROSINELLA:   Without a word of a lie, sure as God is my judge standing here.  We just
                 had to spend one night together, on our own.  But we had nowhere to go so
                 we hid up a tree.  And we could hear them out looking for us, all around
                 the village, calling our names and chapping all the doors.  My daddy was
40               screaming and shouting at the top of his voice and calling me for
                 everything.  And the next morning the priest rang the bell — (*She mimics
                 the sound*) "Do-ing, Do-ing, Do-ing" — the way he does when someone has
                 died, to let everyone in the village know I'd disgraced my name and
                 brought shame on my whole family.  Oh it was lovely, so it was.

**Questions**

10.  Using your own words as far as possible, summarise the story that Rosinella tells
     Lucia about her wedding to Massimo.  You should make **four** key points.          4

11.  Referring closely to the extract, explain fully how the stage directions reveal
     Rosinella's changing thoughts about telling Lucia this story.                      4

12.  Identify **one** interesting use of tone created in this extract and explain how it is
     created.                                                                           2

13.  Even though Rosinella is Italian, her speech shows signs of her having lived in
     Scotland.  Find **two** examples from the passage which indicate this.             2

14.  By referring to this extract and to elsewhere in the play, show how the playwright
     explores romantic relationships.                                                  8

[Turn over

## SECTION 1 — SCOTTISH TEXT — 20 marks

### PART B — SCOTTISH TEXT — PROSE

**Text 1 — Prose**

If you choose this text you may not attempt a question on Prose in Section 2.

Read the extract below and then attempt the following questions.

*The Cone-Gatherers* by Robin Jenkins

*In this extract, the brothers are returning to their hut, through the woods. They are being watched by the gamekeeper Duror.*

While his brother was moving away shouting, Calum was kneeling by the rabbit. He had seen it done before: grip the ears firmly, stretch the neck, and strike with the side of the hand: so simple was death. But as he touched the long ears, and felt them warm and pulsating with a life not his own, he realised he could not do the rabbit this peculiar
5 kindness; he must leave it to the callous hand or boot of the gamekeeper.

He rose and ran stumbling and whimpering after his brother.

Hidden among the spruces at the edge of the ride, near enough to catch the smell of larch off the cones and to be struck by some of those thrown, stood Duror the gamekeeper, in an icy sweat of hatred, with his gun aimed all the time at the
10 feebleminded hunchback grovelling over the rabbit. To pull the trigger, requiring far less force than to break a rabbit's neck, and then to hear simultaneously the clean report of the gun and the last obscene squeal of the killed dwarf would have been for him, he thought, release too, from the noose of disgust and despair drawn, these past few days, so much tighter.

15 He had waited for over an hour there to see them pass. Every minute had been a purgatory of humiliation: it was as if he was in their service, forced to wait upon them as upon his masters. Yet he hated and despised them far more powerfully than he had liked and respected Sir Colin and Lady Runcie-Campbell. While waiting, he had imagined them in the darkness missing their footing in the tall tree and coming crashing down through
20 the sea of branches to lie dead on the ground. So passionate had been his visualising of that scene, he seemed himself to be standing on the floor of a fantastic sea, with an owl and a herd of deer flitting by as quiet as fish, while the yellow ferns and bronzen brackens at his feet gleamed like seaweed, and the spruce trees swayed above him like submarine monsters.

25 He could have named, item by item, leaf and fruit and branch, the overspreading tree of revulsion in him; but he could not tell the force which made it grow, any more than he could have explained the life in himself, or in the dying rabbit, or in any of the trees about him.

This wood had always been his stronghold and sanctuary; there were many places secret
30 to him where he had been able to fortify his sanity and hope. But now the wood was invaded and defiled; its cleansing and reviving virtues were gone. Into it had crept this hunchback, himself one of nature's freaks, whose abject acceptance of nature, like the whining prostrations of a heathen in front of an idol, had made acceptance no longer possible for Duror himself.

Questions

**15.** Read lines 1—5.

Using your own words as far as possible, explain what we learn about Calum in the opening lines of this extract.

2

**16.** Read lines 7—14.

How do any **two** examples of the writer's language convey the strength of Duror's feelings towards Calum?

4

**17.** Read lines 18—28.

Choose and comment on any **two** examples of the writer's use of imagery in these lines.

4

**18.** Read lines 29—34.

In your own words, explain how Duror's feelings about the woods have changed since the arrival of the cone-gatherers.

2

**19.** With close reference to this extract and elsewhere in the novel, show how the character of Calum is presented.

8

[Turn over

**OR**

**Text 2 — Prose**

If you choose this text you may not attempt a question on Prose in Section 2.

Read the extract below and then attempt the following questions.

### *The Testament of Gideon Mack* by James Robertson

Nevertheless I continued to lead a double or even triple life for most of my teens.  It suited me to do so.  The fewer people I crossed, the easier life was.  At school — outside the classroom — I could be as coarse-mouthed and broad of accent and disrespectful of authority as any of my peers, although I always remained at the edge of the crowd,
5  careful to avoid serious trouble.  But in classes I kept my head down and worked.  Others, who didn't have my knack of disguise, were mercilessly taunted and assaulted for being good at schoolwork.  I studied hard enough to be successful, so that my teachers had no cause for complaint, but my talent for duplicity enabled me also to avoid being the victim of the bullies.  Some of my more academically challenged fellow pupils even admired my
10  fraudulence:  it was the kind of thing they couldn't get away with, but I could make life easier for them too by helping out with their homework.  I was sleekit and cowardly, even though my name was Gideon.

At home, I maintained an air of piety.  Although within myself I had abandoned my faith, I continued to go to church and be the dutiful son of the manse.  My hair may have grown
15  longer, and I may have slouched in front of the TV watching *Monty Python* — in comparison with which, had he ever seen it, my father would have found *Batman* a beacon of lucidity and common sense — but that was about the extent of my revolutionary activity.  I had hypocrisy down to a fine art.

And so, when my father in his systematic, post-stroke slowness began to instruct me for
20  my first Communion, when I was thirteen, I did not refuse to participate, but went through with the whole business.  This was a rigorous undertaking.  One of my father's jobs was to prepare others for admission to the Kirk, and indeed throughout the year a trickle of young people came to the manse for this purpose.  He didn't let them off easily, I am sure, but turned his fierce eyes on them in search of the light of conviction in theirs;
25  and a few abandoned the process under his interrogation.  This flushing out of the unworthy he would have reckoned almost as much of a victory as bringing the chosen few safely into the Kirk.  But from his own son he required an even greater commitment.

Think of this:  the 107 questions and answers of the Westminster Shorter Catechism, in all their Calvinist glory.  You would have to go a long way west and north of Ochtermill in the
30  1970s to find Presbyterians who learned their Shorter Catechism by heart, but I did.  I was no Calvinist, the Church of Scotland had long since paid only lip-service to the tenets of the Westminster Confession of Faith, and even my father, old-fashioned in so many ways, had moved some distance from a rigid interpretation of such ideas as election and justification.  Yet he used the Catechism to educate me in the Presbyterian faith; and we
35  worked through the questions and answers much as we'd once worked through the detail of our days over the dinner table, as a kind of exercise in pigeon-holing holy information. We dissected and deciphered the nature of God, the nature of mankind, the nature of sin, the nature of faith, the requirements of the ten commandments, the form of the sacraments and the meaning of the Lord's Prayer.  "What is prayer?" he would ask me,
40  and I, who had given it up months before, would say, "Prayer is an offering up of our desires to God, for things agreeable to his will, in the name of Christ, with confession of our sins, and thankful acknowledgement of his mercies," and then we would talk about

MARKS

what that meant, and look at the several texts from the Bible that proved the points. And all the while, the many, many hours that this took, the apostate in me was picking
45 holes in the arguments, but saying nothing, and the voluble hypocrite was mending them. I'll say this:  the grounding for the ministry I would later have at New College was less thorough than the one I had from my father in his stoury study.  We understood each other better then than perhaps we ever did.  I wouldn't say there was warmth between us, but there was something like mutual respect.  And yet, though I was there with him, a
50 part of me was keeping its distance.


**Questions**


**20.** Look at lines 1—18.  Using your own words as far as possible, explain what we learn about Gideon's character from these lines  You should make **four** key points.    4


**21.** Look at lines 19—50.

   (a) Show how **two** examples of the writer's use of word choice makes it clear how difficult it was to learn all that was needed for the first Communion.    4

   (b) Show how **one** example of the writer's use of sentence structure makes it clear how much there was to learn.    2


**22.** Look at lines 44—50.  Explain in your own words the effect that this tutoring has on the relationship between Gideon and his father.    2


**23.** Referring to this extract and elsewhere in the novel, show how the theme of deception is explored.    8


**[Turn over**

**OR**

**Text 3 — Prose**

If you choose this text you may not attempt a question on Prose in Section 2.

Read the extract below and then attempt the following questions.

***Kidnapped*** **by Robert Louis Stevenson**

*In this extract, which is from Chapter 2 of the novel, David Balfour approaches Edinburgh as he seeks out his uncle, Ebenezer Balfour, and the house of Shaws.*

Presently after, I came by a house where a shepherd lived, and got a rough direction for the neighbourhood of Cramond; and so, from one to another, worked my way to the westward of the capital by Colinton, till I came out upon the Glasgow road.  And there, to my great pleasure and wonder, I beheld a regiment marching to the fifes, every foot in
5 time; an old red-faced general on a grey horse at the one end, and at the other the company of Grenadiers, with their Pope's-hats.  The pride of life seemed to mount into my brain at the sight of the redcoats and the hearing of that merry music.

A little farther on, and I was told I was in Cramond parish, and began to substitute in my inquiries the name of the house of Shaws.  It was a word that seemed to surprise those of
10 whom I sought my way.  At first I thought the plainness of my appearance, in my country habit, and that all dusty from the road, consorted ill with the greatness of the place to which I was bound.  But after two, or maybe three, had given me the same look and the same answer, I began to take it in my head there was something strange about the Shaws itself.

15 The better to set this fear at rest, I changed the form of my inquiries; and spying an honest fellow coming along a lane on the shaft of his cart, I asked him if he had ever heard tell of a house they called the house of Shaws.

He stopped his cart and looked at me, like the others.

"Ay," said he.  "What for?"

20 "It's a great house?" I asked.

"Doubtless," says he.  "The house is a big, muckle house."

"Ay," said I, "but the folk that are in it?"

"Folk?" cried he.  "Are ye daft?  There's nae folk there — to call folk."

"What?" say I; "not Mr. Ebenezer?"

25 "Oh, ay," says the man, "there's the laird, to be sure, if it's him you're wanting.  What'll like be your business, mannie?"

"I was led to think that I would get a situation," I said, looking as modest as I could.

"What?" cries the carter, in so sharp a note that his very horse started; and then, "Well, mannie," he added, "it's nane of my affairs; but ye seem a decent-spoken lad; and if ye'll
30 take a word from me, ye'll keep clear of the Shaws."

The next person I came across was a dapper little man in a beautiful white wig, whom I saw to be a barber on his rounds; and knowing well that barbers were great gossips, I asked him plainly what sort of a man was Mr Balfour of the Shaws.

MARKS

"Hoot, hoot, hoot," said the barber, "nae kind of a man, nae kind of a man at all"; and
35 began to ask me very shrewdly what my business was; but I was more than a match for
him at that, and he went on to his next customer no wiser than he came.

I cannot well describe the blow this dealt to my illusions.  The more indistinct the
accusations were, the less I liked them, for they left the wider field to fancy.  What kind
of a great house was this, that all the parish should start and stare to be asked the way to
40 it? or what sort of a gentleman, that his ill-fame should be thus current on the wayside?

**Questions**

24.  Using your own words as far as possible, summarise what happens in this extract
     from the novel.  Make at least **four** key points.                                    4

25.  Look at lines 8—12 ("A little farther on . . . place to which I was bound.").

     Initially, why did David feel he was "surprising" people with his inquiries about
     directions to the house of Shaws?  You should answer in your own words as far as
     possible.                                                                              2

26.  By referring to an example of the writer's language, explain how the writer
     effectively highlights David's mood:

     (a)  at the start of the extract (lines 1—7);                                          3

     (b)  at the end of the extract (lines 37—40).                                          3

27.  By referring to this extract and to elsewhere in the novel, show how the character
     of David Balfour is developed.                                                         8

[Turn over

OR

Text 4 — Prose

If you choose this text you may not attempt a question on Prose in Section 2.

Read the extract below and then attempt the following questions.

*Mother and Son* by Iain Crichton Smith

His mind now seemed gradually to be clearing up, and he was beginning to judge his own actions and hers. Everything was clearing up: it was one of his moments. He turned round on his chair from a sudden impulse and looked at her intensely. He had done this very often before, had tried to cow her into submission: but she had always laughed at
5  him. Now however he was looking at her as if he had never seen her before. Her mouth was open and there were little crumbs upon her lower lip. Her face had sharpened itself into a birdlike quickness: she seemed to be pecking at the bread with a sharp beak in the same way as she pecked cruelly at his defences. He found himself considering her as if she were some kind of animal. Detachedly he thought: how can this thing make my life a
10  hell for me? What is she anyway? She's been ill for ten years: that doesn't excuse her. She's breaking me up so that even if she dies I won't be any good for anyone. But what if she's pretending? What if there is nothing wrong with her? At this a rage shook him so great that he flung his half-consumed cigarette in the direction of the fire in an abrupt, savage gesture. Out of the silence he heard a bus roaring past the window, splashing over
15  the puddles. That would be the boys going to town to enjoy themselves. He shivered inside his loneliness and then rage took hold of him again. How he hated her! This time his gaze concentrated itself on her scraggy neck, rising like a hen's out of her plain white nightgown. He watched her chin wagging up and down: it was stained with jam and flecked with one or two crumbs. His sense of loneliness closed round him, so that he felt
20  as if he were on a boat on the limitless ocean, just as his house was on a limitless moorland. There was a calm, unspeaking silence, while the rain beat like a benediction on the roof. He walked over to the bed, took the tray from her as she held it out to him. He had gone in answer to words which he hadn't heard, so hedged was he in his own thoughts.

25  "Remember to clean the tray tomorrow," she said. He walked back with the tray fighting back the anger that swept over him carrying the rubbish and debris of his mind in its wake. He turned back to the bed. His mind was in a turmoil of hate, so that he wanted to smash the cup, smash the furniture, smash the house. He kept his hands clenched, he the puny and unimaginative. He would show her, avenge her insults with his unintelligent
30  hands. There was the bed, there was his mother. He walked over.

MARKS

## Questions

28. From this extract, summarise in your own words as far as possible, the main reasons for John's anger towards his mother.  You should make at least **four** key points.

    4

29. Look closely at lines 5—14 ("Now however . . . savage gesture.").

    Show how any **two** examples of the writer's use of language contribute to our understanding of John's feelings towards his mother.

    4

30. With close reference to lines 14—24 ("Out of . . . his own thoughts."), show how the writer uses language effectively to emphasise John's feelings of loneliness.

    2

31. Look at lines 25—30.  With reference to **one** example of the writer's use of language, explain how tension is created.

    2

32. With close reference to this extract and at least one other story by Ian Crichton Smith, show how a character comes to realise something of importance.

    8

[Turn over

OR

**Text 5 — Prose**

If you choose this text you may not attempt a question on Prose in Section 2.

Read the extract below and then attempt the following questions.

*All That Glisters* **by Anne Donovan**

The funeral wis on the Wednesday and the days in between were a blur of folk comin an goin, of makin sandwiches an drinkin mugs of stewed tea, sayin rosaries an pourin oot glasses of whisky for men in overcoats.  His body came hame tae the hoose and wis pit in their bedroom.  Ma mammy slept in the bed settee in the livin room wi ma Auntie Pauline.

5      *Are you sure that you want tae see him?*

       Ah wis sure.  Ah couldnae bear the fact we'd never said goodbye and kept goin ower and ower in ma mind whit ah'd have said tae him if ah'd known he wis gonnae die so soon.  Ah wis feart as well, right enough.  Ah'd never seen a deid body afore, and ah didnae know whit tae expect, but he looked as if he wis asleep, better in fact than he'd
10    looked when he wis alive, his face had mair colour, wis less yella lookin an lined.  Ah sat wi him fur a while in the room, no sayin anything, no even thinkin really, just sittin.  Ah felt that his goin wis incomplete and ah wanted tae dae sumpn fur him, but that's daft, whit can you dae when sumbdy's deid?  Ah wondered if ah should ask ma mammy but she wis that withdrawn intae hersel, so busy wi the arrangements that ah didnae like tae.
15    She still smiled at me but it wis a watery far-away smile and when she kissed me goodnight ah felt she wis haudin me away fae her.

       On the Wednesday mornin ah got up early, got dressed and went through tae the kitchen.  Ma Auntie Pauline wis sittin at the table havin a cuppa tea and a fag and when she looked up her face froze over.

20    *Whit the hell dae you think you're daein?  Go and get changed this minute.*

       *But these are ma best claes.*

       *You cannae wear red tae a funeral.  You have tae show respect fur the deid.*

       *But these were ma daddy's favourites.  He said ah looked brilliant in this.*

       Ah mind his face when ah came intae the room a couple of month ago, after ma
25    mammy'd bought me this outfit fur ma birthday; a red skirt and a zip-up jaicket wi red tights tae match.

       *You're a sight fur sore eyes, hen.*

       *That sounds horrible, daddy.*

       He smiled at me.

30    *It disnae mean that, hen, it means you look that nice that you would make sore eyes feel better.  Gie's a twirl, princess.*

       And ah birled roon on wan leg, laughin.

*Page sixteen*

**MARKS**

Questions

33. Using your own words as far as possible, summarise what happens in this extract. You should make **four** key points.     4

34. Look at lines 1—3. Explain how the writer uses language to convey the memory of the days before the funeral. You should refer to **two** examples in your answer.     4

35. Look at lines 6—16. Identify **two** ways in which the writer develops a strong sense of narrative voice at this point in the extract.     2

36. Look at lines 17—23. By referring to **one** example, explain fully how the aunt's reaction is shown.     2

37. By referring closely to this extract and to at least one other story by Donovan, show how the theme of relationships is developed.     8

[Turn over

**SECTION 1 — SCOTTISH TEXT — 20 marks**

**PART C — SCOTTISH TEXT — POETRY**

**Text 1 — Poetry**

If you choose this text you may not attempt a question on Poetry in Section 2.

Read the poem below and then attempt the following questions.

*Valentine* **by Carol Ann Duffy**

Not a red rose or a satin heart.

I give you an onion.
It is a moon wrapped in brown paper.
It promises light
5  like the careful undressing of love.

Here.
It will blind you with tears
like a lover.
It will make your reflection
10  a wobbling photo of grief.

I am trying to be truthful.

Not a cute card or a kissogram.

I give you an onion.
Its fierce kiss will stay on your lips,
15  possessive and faithful
as we are,
for as long as we are.

Take it.
Its platinum loops shrink to a wedding ring,
20  if you like.
Lethal.
Its scent will cling to your fingers,
cling to your knife.

Questions

**38.** In the opening two lines of the poem some of the main ideas and concerns of the poem come across clearly.  Identify **two** of these main ideas or concerns.    **2**

**39.** In lines 3–5, show how **two** examples of the poet's use of language suggest a positive side to love.    **4**

**40.** In lines 7–17, show how **two** examples of the poet's use of language suggest a negative side to love.    **4**

**41.** How effective do you find lines 18–23 as a conclusion to the poem?

Justify your answer with close reference to the text.    **2**

**42.** The theme of relationships is important in this poem.  With close textual reference, show how this theme is explored in this poem and in at least one other poem you have read by Duffy.    **8**

[Turn over

OR

**Text 2 — Poetry**

If you choose this text you may not attempt a question on Poetry in Section 2.

Read the poem below and then attempt the following questions.

*Hyena* **by Edwin Morgan**

I am waiting for you.
I have been travelling all morning through the bush
and not eaten.
I am lying at the edge of the bush
5  on a dusty path that leads from the burnt-out kraal.
I am panting, it is midday, I found no water-hole.
I am very fierce without food and although my eyes
are screwed to slits against the sun
you must believe I am prepared to spring.

10  What do you think of me?
I have a rough coat like Africa.
I am crafty with dark spots
like the bush-tufted plains of Africa.
I sprawl as a shaggy bundle of gathered energy
15  like Africa sprawling in its waters.
I trot, I lope, I slaver, I am a ranger.
I hunch my shoulders.  I eat the dead.

Do you like my song?
When the moon pours hard and cold on the veldt
20  I sing, and I am the slave of darkness.
Over the stone walls and the mud walls and the ruined places
and the owls, the moonlight falls.
I sniff a broken drum.  I bristle.  My pelt is silver.
I howl my song to the moon — up it goes.
25  Would you meet me there in the waste places?

It is said I am a good match
for a dead lion. I put my muzzle
at his golden flanks, and tear. He
is my golden supper, but my tastes are easy.
30  I have a crowd of fangs, and I use them.
Oh and my tongue — do you like me
when it comes lolling out over my jaw
very long, and I am laughing?
I am not laughing.
35  But I am not snarling either, only
panting in the sun, showing you
what I grip
carrion with.

MARKS

I am waiting
40  for the foot to slide,
for the heart to seize,
for the leaping sinews to go slack,
for the fight to the death to be fought to the death,
for a glazing eye and the rumour of blood.
45  I am crouching in my dry shadows
till you are ready for me.
My place is to pick you clean
and leave your bones to the wind.

## Questions

43.  Using your own words as far as possible, identify **two** things which you learn about the hyena in stanza one (lines 1—9).

2

44.  Explain fully how **two** examples of the poet's use of language in stanza two (lines 10—17) increase your understanding of the hyena.

4

45.  By referring closely to **two** examples from stanzas 3 and 4 (lines 18—38), show how the writer uses language to develop a tense, menacing atmosphere.

4

46.  How effective do you find the last stanza (lines 39—48) as a conclusion to the poem? Justify your answer with close reference to the text.

2

47.  By referring closely to this poem, and to at least **one** other poem by Morgan, show how the writer uses word choice and/or imagery effectively to create a striking visual impression, or scene.

8

[Turn over

**OR**

**Text 3 — Poetry**

If you choose this text you may not attempt a question on Poetry in Section 2.

Read the poem below and then attempt the following questions.

*Visiting Hour* **by Norman MacCaig**

The hospital smell
combs my nostrils
as they go bobbing along
green and yellow corridors.

5 What seems a corpse
is trundled into a lift and vanishes
heavenward.

I will not feel, I will not
feel, until
10 I have to.

Nurses walk lightly, swiftly,
here and up and down and there,
their slender waists miraculously
carrying their burden
15 of so much pain, so
many deaths, their eyes
still clear after
so many farewells.

Ward 7.  She lies
20 in a white cave of forgetfulness.
A withered hand
trembles on its stalk.  Eyes move
behind eyelids too heavy
to raise.  Into an arm wasted
25 of colour a glass fang is fixed,
not guzzling but giving.
And between her and me
distance shrinks till there is none left
but the distance of pain that neither she nor I
30 can cross.

She smiles a little at this
black figure in her white cave
who clumsily rises
in the round swimming waves of a bell
35 and dizzily goes off, growing fainter,
not smaller, leaving behind only
books that will not be read
and fruitless fruits.

MARKS

## Questions

48. Look at lines 1—10. Show how MacCaig feels about his hospital visit, referring to **two** examples of language.

4

49. Look at lines 11—18. Referring to **two** examples, explain how MacCaig uses poetic techniques to reveal his attitude towards the nurses.

4

50. Look at lines 19—30. By referring to **two** examples of the poet's use of language, explain how he makes clear the patient's condition.

4

51. MacCaig often uses imagery in his poems. Referring closely to this poem and at least one other poem by MacCaig, show how he uses imagery effectively.

8

[Turn over

**OR**

**Text 4 — Poetry**

If you choose this text you may not attempt a question on Poetry in Section 2.

Read the poem below and then attempt the following questions.

*Divorce* by Jackie Kay

I did not promise
to stay with you til death do us part, or
anything like that,
so part I must, and quickly.  There are things
5  I cannot suffer
any longer:  Mother, you never, ever said
a kind word
or a thank-you for all the tedious chores I have done;
Father, your breath
10  smells like a camel's and gives me the hump;
all you ever say is:
"Are you off in the cream puff, Lady Muck?"
In this day and age?
I would be better off in an orphanage.

15  I want a divorce.
There are parents in the world whose faces turn
up to the light
who speak in the soft murmur of rivers
and never shout.
20  There are parents who stroke their children's cheeks
in the dead of night
and sing in the colourful voices of rainbows,
red to blue.
These parents are not you.  I never chose you.
25  You are rough and wild,
I don't want to be your child.  All you do is shout
And that's not right.
I will file for divorce in the morning at first light.

MARKS

Questions

52. How does the speaker make it clear that she wants to separate herself from her parents in the first sentence of the poem (lines 1—4)? You may refer to language or ideas in your answer.

2

53. Using your own words as far as possible, summarise the impression the speaker gives of her parents in lines 1—14. You should make **three** clear points in your answer.

3

54. Look at lines 16—23. Explain, with reference to **two** examples of the poet's language, how she makes clear how she imagines other parents to be.

4

55. The poet uses different tones throughout the poem. Identify any **one** use of tone and, by making reference to the text, show how the tone is created.

3

56. With close textual reference, show how the theme of family relationships is explored in this poem, and in at least one other poem by Jackie Kay.

8

[END OF SECTION 1]

[Turn over

## SECTION 2 — CRITICAL ESSAY — 20 marks

Attempt ONE question from the following genres — Drama, Prose, Poetry, Film and Television Drama, or Language.

Your answer must be on a different genre from that chosen in Section 1.

You should spend approximately 45 minutes on this Section.

### DRAMA

*Answers to questions on Drama should refer to the text and to such relevant features as characterisation, key scene(s), structure, climax, theme, plot, conflict, setting . . .*

1.  Choose a play in which an important character is in conflict with another character or characters in the play, or with herself or himself.

    Describe the conflict and then, by referring to appropriate techniques, go on to explain why the conflict is important to the development of the play as a whole.

2.  Choose a play where the playwright explores a theme or issue or concern which you feel is important.

    By referring to appropriate techniques, show how effectively the playwright establishes and explores the theme or issue or concern.

### PROSE

*Answers to questions on Prose should refer to the text and to such relevant features as characterisation, setting, language, key incident(s), climax, turning point, plot, structure, narrative technique, theme, ideas, description . . .*

3.  Choose a novel **or** short story in which the writer creates a realistic or convincing character.

    By referring to appropriate techniques, show how the writer creates this character, and say why you find him or her to be realistic or convincing.

4.  Choose a novel **or** short story **or** a work of non-fiction which explores a theme which you find interesting.

    By referring to appropriate techniques, show how the writer explores this theme.

## POETRY

> *Answers to questions on Poetry should refer to the text and to such relevant features as word choice, tone, imagery, structure, content, rhythm, rhyme, theme, sound, ideas . . .*

5. Choose a poem in which setting is an important feature.

   By referring to poetic techniques, show how setting contributes to your appreciation of the poem as a whole.

6. Choose a poem which makes you think more deeply about an aspect of life.

   By referring to poetic techniques, show how the poet explores this aspect of life.

## FILM AND TELEVISION DRAMA

> *Answers to questions on Film and Television Drama should refer to the text and to such relevant features as use of camera, key sequence, characterisation, mise-en-scène, editing, setting, music/sound, special effects, plot, dialogue . . .*

7. Choose a scene or sequence from a film **or** television drama\* which creates a particular feeling or emotion.

   By referring to appropriate techniques, explain how the director leads you to feel this way.

8. Choose a film **or** television drama\* which has a character who is admirable and/or unpleasant.

   By referring to appropriate techniques, explain how the character is presented in the film/television drama\* as a whole.

\* "television drama" includes a single play, a series or a serial.

[Turn over

## LANGUAGE

*Answers to questions on Language should refer to the text and to such relevant features as register, accent, dialect, slang, jargon, vocabulary, tone, abbreviation . . .*

9.  Choose an advertisement which aims to persuade you to buy something or to change your behaviour.

    By referring to specific examples, explain how successful the persuasive language is.

10. Consider the differences in spoken or written language between two groups of people who are from different places, or who are different in significant ways.

    By referring to appropriate techniques, explain and evaluate the differences in language use.

[END OF SECTION 2]

[END OF QUESTION PAPER]

# SQA AND HODDER GIBSON NATIONAL 5 ENGLISH 2015

## NATIONAL 5 ENGLISH
## MODEL PAPER 1

### READING FOR UNDERSTANDING, ANALYSIS AND EVALUATION

1. *Any four of the following for 1 mark each:*
   - tennis players are very superstitious
   - they believe that certain behaviour can affect results
   - research was carried out on pigeons
   - it was discovered that they could be made to believe that certain actions ...
   - ... caused certain outcomes ...
   - ... even though there was no connection.

2. (a) *Any two of the following for 1 mark each:*
   - he believes in the power of superstition
   - he is irrational
   - he is unshakeable/dogmatic
   - he is unaware of his irrational stance.

   (b) *Reference to/explanation of any 2 of the following for one mark each:*
   - use of "even"
   - as a cricketer, he is thought to be more intelligent than other sportspeople
   - use of "even though"
   - "threadbare and smelly" – not what we would expect of a professional sportsman
   - prepared to inconvenience team-mates.

3. *Any four of the following for 1 mark each:*
   - a superstition can be based on a false belief ...
   - ... and therefore can lead to unnecessary behaviour
   - but mostly this causes no damage ...
   - ... provided observing it does not cause huge inconvenience
   - a superstition can be based on a genuine danger/ fear ...
   - ... in which case observing it is beneficial.

4. Key features (*any two from*):
   - repeated/parallel structure, consisting of
   - "some believe/like ..."
   - followed by comma
   - followed by "but"
   - semicolons create list.

   Conveys point by (*any two from*):
   - illustrating just how many different ways people don't let superstition influence them too much
   - showing how similar all these beliefs are
   - showing how easy it is to find examples.

5. (a) It can be seen as either effective or not effective:

   | effective because | just as a spectrum contains a whole range/ variety/scale (of colours) | so there is a (wide) range of superstitions/ (illogical) behaviours/ perceptions/beliefs |
   |---|---|---|
   | not effective because | the (bright) colour imagery implied | is not apt or fitting or helpful to describe/illustrate the (melancholy) subject |

   (b) *Any of the following:*
   - it illustrates his point about the range of "irrationality" by providing an extreme example of superstition
   - it illustrates his point that superstition taken to excess/dogmatically insisted upon has an unhelpful/deleterious effect/outcome
   - he is using reference to a team game to show the influence of superstition on others.

   (c) *Any of the following:*
   - the reference to the elements of help and hindrance recaps the idea of ambivalence explored elsewhere in the passage
   - (metaphor) "kick (the ritual into touch)" reprises references to football/sport used earlier
   - "With a rabbit's foot, obviously" reprises the cynical/sceptical/humorous tone seen elsewhere.

6. *Any two of the following for 2 marks each:*
   - "funny bunch" – slang, off-hand way to describe sportspeople
   - "bring the world collapsing" – exaggeration
   - "poor dears" – mock concern
   - "Yes, really" – suddenly as if speaking directly to reader
   - "feathered fellows" – as if they're human
   - "I know, I know" – pretending to be hearing readers' derision
   - "(pigeons) unavailable for interview" – as if they're human, mocking the standard official response to a difficult question
   - "got up the noses" – slang (plus playful mixing of literal and metaphorical)
   - "abode" – deliberately exaggerated way to describe a cave
   - "scarpers" – (old fashioned) slang sounds out of place for such a threat
   - "his five-a-day" – anachronistic reference to modern nutritional theory.

**7.** *Any four of the following for 1 mark each (may be in bullet point form or in prose):*

- superstitions can been observed in eminent sportspeople
- pigeons can be trained to act as if superstitious
- superstition arises when there is a belief that one action can lead directly to another ...
- ... even when no connection exists
- some/most superstitions are harmless ...
- ... and observing them can bring comfort/hope/peace of mind
- some superstitions lead to damaging behaviour.

# NATIONAL 5 ENGLISH MODEL PAPER 1

## CRITICAL READING

### SECTION 1 — Scottish Text

Generic instructions for the 8 marks questions on all texts.

Candidates may choose to answer in **bullet points** in this final question, or write a number of linked statements. There is **no requirement** to write a "mini essay".

Up to 2 marks can be achieved for identifying elements of **commonality** as identified in the question.

A further 2 marks can be gained for **reference to the extract given**.

4 additional marks can be awarded for similar references to **at least one other text/part of the text** by the writer.

<u>In practice this means:</u>

**Identification of commonality** (e.g.: theme, central relationship, importance of setting, use of imagery, development in characterisation, use of personal experience, sue of narrative style, or any other key element ...)

**from the extract:**

| 1 × relevant reference to technique | 1 × appropriate comment |
|---|---|

**OR**

| 1 × relevant reference to idea | 1 × appropriate comment |
|---|---|

**OR**

| 1 × relevant reference to feature | 1 × appropriate comment |
|---|---|

**OR**

| 1 × relevant reference to text | 1 × appropriate comment |
|---|---|

**(maximum of 2 marks only for discussion of extract)**

from **at least one other/text part of the text:**

as above (× 2) for **up to 4 marks**

### SCOTTISH TEXT — DRAMA

#### Text 1 — Drama — *Bold Girls* by Rona Munro

**1.** Candidates should make general and/or specific points about the way Deirdre's words and/or actions will make the audience see her as strange.
*Possible answers include:*

- the very fact of her intrusion into Marie's home
- she is generally uncommunicative
- she is generally ungrateful for shelter/food
- her blunt opening question/absence of any apology for intrusion
- her ignoring of Nora's remark
- when asked again, merely gestures
- her eventual response is surly, discourteous ("sullen")
- the blunt, monosyllabic "Back of the school there."
- the loud, aggressive repetition of "Back of the school there."
- "nods" and "shrugs" – basic gestures only
- no acknowledgement of/thanks for tea/biscuits
- method of eating ("furtively and ravenously").

2. Candidates should make for each of the three women a general comment about her treatment of Deirdre and support it with appropriate reference to the extract.
*Possible answers include:*

Marie:

- helpful, welcoming, kind
- invites her in/offers tea/doesn't ask questions

Nora:

- inquisitive/a little suspicious/hostile
- asks (and repeats) questions about where she is from, what has happened to her

Cassie:

- suspicious, fearful
- looks away when Deirdre catches her eye.

3. Candidates should show an understanding of what is happening at this moment in the play.
*Possible answers include:*

- As a distraction from the tension/nervousness created by Deirdre's behaviour.

4. Candidates should an awareness of Deirdre's role in this extract and elsewhere in the play as "a catalyst", whose intrusion into the lives of Marie and Cassie has dramatic consequences.

General instructions for marking this question are given on page 158.

### Text 2 – Drama – *Sailmaker* by Alan Spence

5. Candidates should make four separate points for 1 mark each. Quotation is likely but not necessary.
*Possible answers include:*

- Davie tells Billy he has lost his job
- Billy says it's not Davie's fault/not fair/criticises employers
- Davie is very defeatist/thinks he's got nothing going for him
- Billy says he might be able to get him a job
- Davie displays little enthusiasm
- Billy tries to keep Davie's spirits up.

6 Candidates should show how the sentence structure used illustrates Davie's feelings.

*Possible answers include:*

- exclamation shows his feeling of hopelessness, defeat
- use of italics shows how resentful he feels about "them"
- series of short sentences suggests disengaged, depressed, given up
- series of questions suggests at a loss, feels hopeless.

7. Candidates should refer to both characters and quote from or refer to the text.
*Possible answers include:*

- Davie has very little to say/is monosyllabic/sounds defeated
- Bill talks at greater length/offers hope/ encouragement.

8. Candidates should demonstrate an understanding of Davie's personality as it is revealed in these lines.

*Possible answers include:*

- unambitious/never one to get excited – "wouldnae be much"
- feels sort of powerless to affect anything – "*shrugs*"
- takes life as it comes – "better than nothing"
- keen to rationalise/make best of situation – "that was a lousy job anyway"
- mild surprise at something trivial – "Amazin how it gets on top of ye"
- resigned acceptance of everything – "Och aye. No to worry."
- clichéd optimism (or possible ironic repetition of Billy earlier) – "Never died a winter yet"

9. Candidates should show an awareness of how Davie's words and actions here and elsewhere in the play are used to present his character.

General instructions for marking this question are given on page 158.

### Text 3 – Drama – *Tally's Blood* by Ann Marie di Mambro

10. Candidates should make three separate points about Rosinella's character. Quotation is likely but not necessary.
*Possible answers include:*

- Rosinella and Massimo argue (over Rosinella's spoiling of Lucia)
- Massimo admires Lucia's schoolbag
- Lucia refuses to take off her dress
- Massimo suggests a compromise
- the compromise works.

11. Candidates should make two separate points for 1 mark each. Quotation/reference is likely but not necessary.
*Possible answers include:*

- she loves Lucia
- she is generous towards Lucia/is prepared to spoil her
- she is selfless/altruistic
- she is unashamed of her generosity.

12. Candidates should refer to and/or explain the various ways by which Lucia's behaviour is intended to portray her as a five-year-old.
*Possible answers include:*

- the stubbornness implied by repetition (of "No" and/ or "I want to keep it on")
- the quick change(s) of mood from playful to petulant
- starting to shout
- yielding to adult compromise
- perhaps she is aware all along that one of them will weaken …

13. Candidates should quote examples of obviously "Scottish" turns of phrase.
   *Possible answers include:*

   - "see when I …"
   - "wee"
   - "lassie"
   - "wean"
   - "no" (for "not")
   - "tatties"
   - "hen"
   - "I says".

14. Candidates should discuss the portrayal of the relationship between Lucia and her adoptive parents in this extract and elsewhere in the play.

   General instructions for marking this question are given on page 158.

## SCOTTISH TEXT — PROSE

### Text 1 — Prose — *The Cone-Gatherers* by Robin Jenkins

15. Candidates should select two appropriate words or phrases or language features and relate each one to "the violence of the storm".

   Appropriate reference (1 mark). Explanation (1 mark).

   *Possible answers:*

   - "flashed" suggests sudden movement, frightening
   - "crashed" suggests something loud, destructive
   - "shattered" suggests completely broken by a single blow
   - "hurled" suggests that in the brothers' mind the storm has potential to throw them viciously from the tree
   - "fragments" bits of the tree have been reduced to tiny pieces
   - "terrified" the storm has the power to frighten an inanimate object
   - repetition of "every" emphasises dominance, power of the storm
   - "torn its roots" tree seems to have been pulled apart.

16. Candidates should show how two words clarify Neil's impatience.
   *Possible answers:*

   - "flung" suggests as quick, careless movement
   - "snatched up" suggests a quick, unthinking movement
   - "shouted" suggests he is urging Calum to move
   - "gasped" suggests rapid breathing, losing patience
   - "clutched" suggests frantic holding on.

17. Candidates should identify four key points Neil makes, using their own words as far as possible.
   *Possible answers:*

   - for the sake of his (Neil's) health
   - for the sake of Calum's health
   - to avoid danger of lightning
   - the beach hut can be reached quickly
   - not to be afraid of LRC's possible anger

   - they won't cause any damage to the hut
   - no one will know they been there.

18. Candidates should identify and explain at least one feature of these lines which shows Calum's childlike innocence/naivety.

   *Possible answers:*

   - "They'll get all wet, Neil." – rather pathetic statement of the obvious
   - "Aye, that's right" – doesn't realise that Neil's repeating of these words is sarcastic
   - he takes Neil's question about the sun literally
   - murmurs his response as if frightened to disagree with Neil

19. Candidates should discuss the relationship between Calum and Neil in this extract and elsewhere in the novel.

   General instructions for marking this question are given on page 158.

### Text 2 — Prose — *The Testament of Gideon Mack* by James Robertson

20. Candidates should show how Miss Craigie is presented as an intimidating character.
   *Possible answers include:*

   - "Just come in, for heaven's sake" brusque, irritable, impatient
   - *"If locked go away"* the notice is unwelcoming, abrupt
   - "Can't you read?" almost aggressive, demeaning
   - undermines Gideon's attempt to be apologetic with sarcastic response
   - "Oh, it's you" in a clearly unwelcoming tone
   - "distaste" shows her disapproval of Gideon/of the Kirk
   - her reputation as believing Kirk to be "a scabrous outbreak …" sees Kirk/religion as a disease, something that blights society.

21. Candidates should show how the dialogue conveys the friction between the two characters.

   *Possible answers include:*

   - general point: every one of Gideon attempts at politeness is turned against him by her curt responses
   - her immediate contradiction of what he says about the clerical collar
   - her (logical but) rude response when he says he's been reading her book and wants to ask some questions
   - her (understandable but) unnecessary comment about knowing what the word "supplementary" means.

22. Candidates should show how the writer's sentence structure and imagery help to describe the layout of Miss Craigie's hallway.

   *Possible answers include:*

   Sentence structure:

   - the colon (after "location") introduces explanation of what he realises the reason for the layout

- the colon (after "placed") introduces explanation of both the "pre-existing" and the "strategically placed"
- the list beginning "plant-stand" illustrates the large number of objects involved **and/or** creates an imitation of the step-by-step nature of the arrangement

Imagery:

- "a kind of domestic rock-face" just as a rock face can be climbed with the help of pre-planned places to grip hold or to pause so she is able to make a dangerous route less hazardous
- "horizontal climbing-wall" just as a climbing wall is ascended vertically with artificial aids, so she can move along her hallway aided by these objects.

23. Candidates should discuss the relationship between Gideon and Miss Craigie.

    General instructions for marking this question are given on page 158.

**Text 3 — Prose — *Kidnapped* by Robert Louis Stevenson**

24. Candidates should show an understanding of the relationship between Alan's remark and the details in paragraph 1.
    *Possible answers:*
    - James must have gone mad
    - showing so much light
    - will attract the Redcoats.

25. Candidates should make a sensible inference from Alan's introduction.
    *Possible answers:*
    - that David is a man of status "gentleman", "laird"
    - that David is important, notorious, mysterious "give his name the go-by".

26. Candidates should give at least one point for each character for full marks, and should use their own words as far as possible.
    *Possible answers:*
    Alan:
    - not bothered
    - attitude of win-some-lose-some
    - pleased that the Red Fox is dead
    James:
    - thinks it's bad news
    - with dire consequences
    - wishes Red Fox still alive
    - Appin will be blamed, will suffer
    - fears for his family.

27. Candidates should relate specific details and/or language features in these lines to the creation of a sense of panic.
    *Possible answers:*
    - list-like structure of sentence beginning "Some were" suggests extensive, frantic, disorderly activity
    - list of weapons ("guns, swords …") suggests they are all lumped together
    - "no kind of order" – indicates lack of a controlling hand

- "struggled together for the same gun" – shows unruly, disorganised behaviour
- "ran into each other" – almost cartoon-like disorder
- "continually turning about from his talk" – shows his lack of concentration, desperate to get some order into the men's activity
- "orders … never understood" – impression of futile activity, almost anarchic
- "anxious and angry" – clear signs of confusion and panic.

28. Candidates should discuss the characterisation of Alan Breck in this extract and elsewhere in the novel.

    General instructions for marking this question are given on page 158.

**Text 4 — Prose — *Mother and Son* by Iain Crichton Smith**

29. Candidates should show how an unpleasant impression of the mother is created.
    *Possible answers include:*
    - "mouth tightly shut" suggests cruel, harsh, unbending
    - "prim" suggests straitlaced, prissy, moralising
    - "anaemic" suggests cold, pale, lifeless
    - "bitter smile" suggests hostile, nasty
    - comparisons with insurance man suggests smile is insincere, for show only
    - comparison with "witch" suggests evil, wicked, power to harm.

30. Candidates should show how the man's/son's reaction is made clear.
    *Possible answers include:*
    - "cursed vindictively" suggests aggressive, spiteful response
    - "helplessly" suggests the hopelessness he feels
    - "some state of innocence … to which he could not return" suggests resentment at loss of previous, better existence
    - "still and dangerous" suggests something violent, destructive bubbling beneath the surface.

31. Candidates should explain in own words the tone/ delivery of the son's comment.
    *Possible answers include:*
    - flat, unemotional
    - automatic, unthinking
    - detached.

32. Candidates should show how the hostility between the two characters is made clear.
    *Possible answers include:*
    - exclamation mark shows it's not a question but a criticism
    - "snapped" suggests sharp, aggressive tone
    - "pettishly" suggests petulant, irritable, almost childish
    - "sitting there moping while …" direct criticism for neglecting his duties
    - "don't know why we christened you" insulting his very birthname

- "My father was never …" openly demeaning son with comparison
- repetition of "All right, all right" suggests irritable, bad-tempered
- "get a new record for your gramophone" insulting comment, comparing her to a machine
- the added "hundreds of times" emphasises how much it annoys him
- "she wasn't to be stopped" shows her as relentless, persistent
- "mooning about the house" she sees his behaviour as pointless, childish
- "pacing up and down" she sees him as distracted, acting strangely
- "taken to the asylum" open allegation that he is not sane
- "something wrong with their heads" insulting his father's family, shifting blame away from hers
- "in your family but not in ours" insulting one side of the family, defending her own.

33. Candidates should discuss how Crichton Smith explores conflict between characters.

    General instructions for marking this question are given on page 158.

**Text 5 – Prose – *Zimmerobics* by Anne Donovan**

34. Candidates should show how the narrator's physical discomfort is conveyed by two examples of the writer's use of language.

    *Possible answers include:*

    - "jaggy pains" shows she experiences sharp bursts of pain
    - "vertebrae grinding" suggests her bones are crunching, grating against each other
    - onomatopoeic "clicking and clunking" suggests rattling, noisy, malfunctioning
    - simile "like the central heating boiler starting up" suggests (light-heartedly) she is a cumbersome machine.

35. Candidates should identify two aspects of Catherin's personality and support each with reference to the text.

    *Possible answers include:*

    - not interested in aunt – minimal response of "Uh-huh"
    - obsessively tidy – "busy rearranging ornaments on the mantelpiece"
    - unsympathetic – "gave me one of her looks"
    - great believer in virtue of activity – "I should take more interest"
    - persistent – "always trying to get me"
    - brisk, bossy – has organised TV for aunt unasked or her habit of speaking in short, curt sentences.

36. Candidates should show how the contrast between the two women.

    *Possible answers include:*

    - aunt is content to do nothing, while niece has no time for inactivity
      - "daydream"/"lost inside my own head" and
      - "not in her nature to daydream …"

---

- aunt has forgotten about film when Catherine next visits, while it's the first thing niece asks about
- "I was caught off my guard" and
  - "Did you enjoy the film?"
- aunt has no interest in being sociable, while niece thinks meeting people is important
  - "I'd rather just sit here" and
  - "go and meet people"
- aunt is content "inside my own head", while niece criticises her for having no interest in "anything outside yourself"
- aunt is not bothered about order or routine, while niece is like a "stapler", suggesting she is functional, mechanical, controlling
- a good response could be made by comparing the imagery of the stapler with the connotations of the Zimmer.

37. Candidates should discuss the writer's exploration of conflict in "Zimmerobics" and at least one other story.

    General instructions for marking this question are given on page 158.

**SCOTTISH TEXT – POETRY**

**Text 1 – Poetry – *Originally* by Carol Ann Duffy**

38. Candidates should identify key events in the poem. *Possible answers include:*

    - the speaker (and her family) move to a new home/country
    - at first she feels out of place
    - eventually she assimilates
    - by the end she is uncertain of her origins/where she came from.

39. (a) Candidates should provide a simple explanation of what the statement means.
    *Possible answers include:*

    - childhood involves moving from one stage to another
    - nothing remains the same for any child
    - change is normal for any child.

39. (b) Candidates should refer to language/techniques in order to show the distinction the poet makes between "slow" and "sudden" change.

    *Possible answers include:*
    Slow:

    - structure of "leaving you standing, resigned, up an avenue" creates a unhurried pace
    - word choice of "resigned" suggests submissive, inactive
    - "no one you know" suggests loneliness, isolation
    Sudden:
    - structure of "Others are sudden./Your accent wrong." sounds jerky, rushed
    - structure of "Your accent wrong" very compressed/minor sentence like a sudden accusation
    - series of plosive consonants ("Corners … pebble-dashed estates, big boys") creates harsh, rushed, slightly aggressive tone.

40. Candidates should show how the speaker's feelings of uncertainty are conveyed.

    *Possible answers include:*

    - repetition of "or" shows she has no clear memory of when things changed
    - series of questions shows she is unsure/seeking answers
    - "only think" suggests she knows it may not be the case
    - list of things possibly lost ("a river ...") suggests there is a wide range of possibilities/she is unsure exactly what might have been lost
    - her need to clarify strangers' question by asking "Originally?" suggests she is not sure what the question actually means to her
    - word choice of "hesitate" conveys need to pause and think
    - "hesitate" placed crucially as the last word emphasises her inability to answer a straight question.

41. Candidates should discuss similarities and/or differences – in language and/or ideas – between *Originally* and at least one other poem by Duffy.

    General instructions for marking this question are given on page 158.

### Text 2 – Poetry – *Hyena* by Edwin Morgan

42. Candidates should identify specific poetic techniques and link each to the threatening nature of the hyena in these lines
    *Possible answers include:*

    - repetition of "I am" creates dogmatic, arrogant figure
    - direct address to "you" creates sense of reader/ listener being directly targeted
    - alliteration of "fierce without food" focuses attention on the hyena's aggressive nature
    - sibilance in "eyes/screwed/slits/sun" creates hissing, snake-like sound
    - word choice of "You must believe" sounds dogmatic, overbearing.

43. (a) Candidates should suggest why the poet repeats Africa in the similes.
    *Possible answers include:*

    - since the hyena is an African animal
    - shows hyena comparing himself to an entire continent which suggests self-importance
    - the repetition suggests hyena is rigid, inflexible
    - lack of variation suggests hyena is unimaginative.

43. (b) Candidates should identify a specific feature of sentence structure and link it to an element of the poet's description.
    *Possible answers include:*

    - list of verbs suggests range of movements
    - the simplicity of the sentences/statements suggests the single-mindedness of the hyena
    - repetition of "I" + verb suggests self-confidence
    - brutal shortness/simple monosyllabic nature of final sentence highlights the stark conclusion of the hyena's activities.

44. Candidates should explore a number of ways by which the poet conveys the harshness of the hyena's world.
    *Possible answers include:*

    - the slightly menacing tone of "Do you like my song?"
    - description of moon as "hard and cold" makes it seems unwelcoming, hostile
    - reversal of more common romantic, pleasant associations of "moon"
    - "slave of darkness" has connotations of evil, vampire-like
    - "stone walls and the mud walls" suggest (primitive) prison-like conditions
    - "ruined places" suggests desolation, destruction
    - "sniff a broken drum" – imagery of destruction, something with a purpose now ruined
    - "I bristle" – as if prepared for action
    - use of "howl" conveys the reality of the "song" as wild, aggressive
    - "howl my song to the moon" suggests madness, lunacy
    - final question is almost taunting.

45. Candidates should discuss the view of the natural world Morgan presents in "Hyena" and in at least one other poem.

    General instructions for marking this question are given on page 158.

### Text 3 – Poetry – *Assisi* by Norman MacCaig

46. Candidates should choose an appropriate example of the poet's use of language and explain how it adds to the description.

    *Possible answers include:*

    (a) the dwarf:

    - detail of "hands on backwards" suggests deformity, distortion, unable to function properly
    - alliteration/sibilance in "sat, slumped" suggests lifeless, deflated
    - word choice of "slumped" suggests drooping, wilting
    - imagery/simile "like a half-filled sack" suggests incomplete, lacking substance, inhuman, inferior material
    - alliteration "tiny twisted" focuses attention, slightly harsh
    - detail of "tiny twisted legs" emphasises the distortion, out of proportion
    - imagery of "(from which) sawdust (might run)" suggests less than human, left-over material
    - comparison with "ruined temple" elevates him to something holy, magnificent, worthy of worship
    - structure of "eyes wept pus" stark, monosyllabic description emphasises the horror
    - word choice of "pus" associated with ill-health, infection, highly distasteful
    - sound "wept pus" – clash of sounds ("-pt p-") is very harsh, bitter
    - enjambment in "back ... higher/than his head" highlights the dislocation

- word choice of "lopsided" emphasises the distortion, visual difference.

(b) the church:

- "three tiers" – suggests (over)elaborate, like a decorated wedding cake
- plural "churches" – suggests excess, overkill
- "honour of St Francis" – perhaps hints at lack of "honour" to the living.

(c) the tourists:

- word choice of "rush of tourists" – suggests they were not bothering to take much in, over-hasty
- word choice/sound of "clucking" – compares them to hens, lacking individuality, not very bright
- alliteration in "clucking contentedly" – creates an imitative, slightly mocking effect
- word choice of "contentedly" – suggests smugness
- word choice of "fluttered" – suggests light, insubstantial.

47. Candidates should identify an attitude shown by the poet to the priest and support this with at least one appropriate reference.

*Possible answers include:*

Attitude:

- dismissive, scornful, contemptuous, mocking, angry

Support:

- ignores the dwarf
- more interested in the tourists/showing off to them
- patronising tone of "how clever it was"
- unconscious irony in "reveal to the illiterate the goodness/of God", as if only the illiterate need this explained
- rather unctuous "the goodness/of God and the suffering/of His Son", especially since he ignores the suffering of the dwarf before his eyes
- "he scattered/the grain of the Word" – tongue-in-cheek continuation of the "hens" metaphor, suggesting he is like a pompous preacher.

48. Candidates may find these lines effective or not, but for full marks must refer to the lines and to the poem as a whole.

*Possible answers include:*

- despite his physical deformities, the dwarf has an inner beauty (equivalent to that of St Francis)
- his voice is described as "sweet", implying delicate, pleasant  he is compared with a "child," implying innocence  he is compared with a "bird", implying natural beauty, freedom of movement
- the whole poem is about seeing/failing to see the real person  the blindness/hypocrisy of the Church.

49. Candidates should discuss how MacCaig creates sympathy (not necessarily for a person/people) in *Assisi* and in at least one other poem.

General instructions for marking this question are given on page 158.

**Text 4 — Poetry —** *My Grandmother's Houses* **by Jackie Kay**

50. Candidates should identify aspects of personality (not physical attributes).  Quotation/reference is not required. *Possible answers:*

- she is a hard/conscientious worker
- she dominates her granddaughter/is frequently giving orders
- she is subservient to/in awe of/afraid of her "betters"
- she is not well educated/lacks sophistication
- she wants her granddaughter to be seen in a good light
- she is a strict/violent disciplinarian.

51. Candidates should show some ability to deconstruct the chosen image.

*Possible answers:*

- "like an octopus's arms" (to describe the way the rooms lead off the hall)  suggests a large number/ going in all directions/a bit scary
- "a one-winged creature" (to describe the grand piano)  makes to piano seem alive, a little mysterious.

52. Candidates should identify aspects of the woman's personality and support each with an appropriate quotation/reference.

*Possible answers:*

- she is/thinks she is superior/of a higher class "posh"
- she is insincere/putting on a show "all smiles"
- she is (superficially at least) kindly "Would you like …"
- she is (superficially at least) encouraging/friendly "Lovely", "beautiful"
- she is patronising "Lovely", "beautiful"
- she is insensitive, verging on racist "skin the colour of café au lait"
- she is not very p.c. "skin the colour of café au lait"
- she is high-handed, officious, haughty "You just get back to your work".

53. Candidates should show understanding of the presentation of people in the chosen text(s).

General instructions for marking this question are given on page 158.

**SECTION 2 – Critical Essay**

Bands are not grades. The five bands are designed primarily to assist with placing each candidate response at an appropriate point on a continuum of achievement. Assumptions about final grades or association of final grades with particular bands should not be allowed to influence objective assessment.

| | 20–18 | 17–14 | 13–10 | 9–5 | 4–0 |
|---|---|---|---|---|---|
| **The candidate demonstrates:** | • **a high degree of familiarity** with the text as a whole<br>• **very good understanding** of the central concerns of the text<br>• a line of thought that is **consistently** relevant to the task | • **familiarity** with the text as a whole<br>• **good understanding** of the central concerns of the text<br>• a line of thought that is **relevant** to the task | • **some familiarity** with the text as a whole<br>• **some understanding** of the central concerns of the text<br>• a line of thought that is **mostly relevant** to the task | • **familiarity with some aspects** of the text<br>• **attempts** a line of thought **but this may lack relevance to the task** | Although such essays should be rare, in this category, the candidate's essay will demonstrate one or more of the following<br>• it contains numerous errors in spelling/grammar/ punctuation/ sentence construction/ paragraphing<br>• knowledge and understanding of the text(s) are not used to answer the question<br>• any analysis and evaluation attempted are unconvincing<br>• the answer is simply too thin |
| **Analysis of the text demonstrates:** | • **thorough awareness** of the writer's techniques, through analysis, making **confident** use of critical terminology<br>• **very detailed/thoughtful** explanation of stylistic devices supported by a **range of well-chosen** references and/or quotations | • **sound awareness** of the writer's techniques through analysis, making **good** use of critical terminology<br>• **detailed explanation** of stylistic devices supported by **appropriate** references and/ or quotation | • **an awareness** of the writer's techniques through analysis, making **some** use of critical terminology<br>• explanation of stylistic devices supported by **some appropriate** references and/ or quotation | • **some awareness** of **the more obvious** techniques used by the writer<br>• **description of some** stylistic devices followed by limited reference and/or quotation | |
| **Evaluation of the text is shown through:** | • **a well developed** commentary of what has been enjoyed/ gained from the text(s), supported by a **range** of well-chosen references to its relevant features | • **a reasonably developed** commentary of what has been enjoyed/ gained from the text (s), supported by **appropriate** references to its relevant features | • **some** commentary of what has been enjoyed/gained from the text(s), supported by **some appropriate** references to its relevant features | • **brief** commentary of what has been enjoyed/gained from the text(s), followed by **brief** reference to its features | |
| **The candidate:** | • uses language to communicate a line of thought **very clearly**<br>• uses spelling, grammar, sentence construction and punctuation which are **consistently** accurate<br>• structures the essay **effectively to enhance** meaning/ purpose<br>• uses paragraphing which is **accurate and effective** | • uses language to communicate a line of thought **clearly**<br>• uses spelling, grammar, sentence construction and punctuation which are **mainly** accurate<br>• structures the essay **well**<br>• uses paragraphing which is **accurate** | • uses language to communicate a line of thought **at first reading**<br>• uses spelling, grammar, sentence construction and punctuation which are **sufficiently** accurate<br>• attempts to structure the essay **in an appropriate way**<br>• uses paragraphing which is sufficiently accurate | • uses language to communicate a line of thought which may be disorganised and/or difficult to follow<br>• makes significant errors in spelling/grammar/ sentence construction/ punctuation<br>• has not structured the essay well<br>• has made significant errors in paragraphing | |
| **In summary, the candidates essay is:** | thorough and precise | very detailed and shows some insight | fairly detailed and relevant | lacks detail and relevance | superficial and/or technically weak |

## NATIONAL 5 ENGLISH
## MODEL PAPER 2

### READING FOR UNDERSTANDING, ANALYSIS AND EVALUATION

1.  1 mark for selection and one mark for comment.
    *Any two from:*
    - "wrecking" – suggests destruction, violence, etc
    - "vandals" – suggests mindless destruction, etc
    - "Genghis Khan" – associated with uncivilised behaviour, etc
    - "destroying" – suggests demolishing, tearing down, etc
    - "pillaging" – suggests looting, stealing, etc
    - alliteration ("pillaging out punctuation") – adds some weight to the criticism
    - "savaging" – suggests viciously tearing apart, etc
    - alliteration ("savaging our sentences") – adds some weight to the criticism
    - "textese" – suffix "-ese" is pejorative
    - "slanguage" – combines 'language' with 'slang', which is looked down on
    - "virus" – suggests disease, something harmful, etc
    - "bleak" – suggests poverty of language
    - "bald" – suggests plainness of language
    - "shorthand" – suggests superficial, etc
    - "drab" – suggests dreariness, monotony, etc
    - "masks" – suggests concealment, deceit, etc.

2.  (a) • reaction to texting has been both positive and negative
        • reaction to others was negative.
    (b) 1 mark for selection of feature and one mark for comment.
        - use of "ever" ("has there ever been") – suggests he thinks it could be unique
        - list of reactions – shows just how wide-ranging they are
        - use of (rhetorical) question – to make reader think it must be something remarkable.

3.  Any three of the following for 1 mark each:
    - people think it's something entirely new, but it's not
    - people think it's only young people who use it, but it's not
    - people think it impedes reading and writing, but (possibly) it actually improves it
    - people think it will cause lasting harm, but its effect will be slight/short-lived.

4.  1 mark for selection of word and one mark for comment.
    *Any two from:*
    - "hysteria" – suggests critics are in panic, raising irrational objections, etc
    - "swallowed whole" – suggests critics' gullibility, etc
    - "stories"/"reports" – suggests critics are prepared to believe unverified accounts

- "incessantly" – suggests critics are obsessive, won't stop to consider other arguments
- "hoax" – suggests critics are prepared to believe something made up.

5.  *Reference to and/or explanation of the significance of any three of the following for 1 mark each:*
    - historical pedigree (for use of initials)
    - "English literary tradition" – sounds dignified, academic, established, accepted as being of value, etc
    - reference to OED – the most respected dictionary, hallmark of quality, etc
    - reference to four highly respected writers.

6.  1 mark for each of the following explanations:
    - line 55: precedes/introduces an expansion/ explanation of the "extraordinary number of ways ..."
    - line 57: precedes/introduces an expansion/ explanation of what "Professional writers" do
    - line 60: creates pause before adding the most the contentious aspect, the one about which critics blame texting most.

7.  1 mark for selection of word or feature and one for comment.
    *Any two from:*
    - two similar sentences at start – suggests a balance, calmness, nothing to get worked up about
    - "merely" – minimises any negative effect
    - "creative" – suggests something imaginative, positive, worthy, etc
    - "suit the demands" – suggests something helpful, co-operative, etc
    - "no … not … not" – repetition assures us all the bad things will not happen
    - "evolution" – suggests growth, improvement, etc.

8.  Any five of the following for 1 mark each (may be in bullet point form or in prose):
    - features criticised in texting have a long historical pedigree
    - text language is an understandable response to the design of the keypad
    - text language is an understandable way to save time
    - abbreviations are common elsewhere
    - people, especially children, enjoy playing with language
    - playing with language helps develop linguistic skills
    - texters are already skilled in the use of language
    - there is no correct form of English (from which texters are deviating).

# NATIONAL 5 ENGLISH MODEL PAPER 2

## CRITICAL READING

### SECTION 1 — Scottish Text

### SCOTTISH TEXT — DRAMA

#### Text 1 — Drama — *Tally's Blood* by Ann Marie di Mambro

1. (a) 1 mark for acceptable aspect of character and 1 mark for valid textual reference.
   *Possible answers include:*

   - self-centred – ignores Lucia's attempts to speak
   - snobbish/class-conscious – looks up/wants to impress to Palombos; looks down on others (the type who boast "Ma lassie cleaned four chickens.")
   - traditional – determined to marry Lucia to an Italian
   - ambitious for Lucia – wants to marry her into a "good" family
   - fantasist/delusional – convinced Lucia is "daft for" Silvio Palombo.

   (b) *Either of the following:*

   - her repeated "He's okay" – polite but very committal/no enthusiasm at all
   - the repeated "Auntie Rosinella …?" – interrogative tone, trying to change the subject (to her wish to attend the wedding).

2. *Any three of the following for 2 marks each:*
   - she maintains that Italian men work harder than others – but the audience can actually see Hughie working hard ("like a Trojan")
   - she maintains that "Nobody loves their families like the Italians" – but immediately after that Hughie declines to stay for some food, because of a duty he feels to his mother
   - she displays obvious distaste for extra-marital sex (seen as a typical fault of Scottish people), when the audience is in no doubt about what happened between Franco and Bridget
   - she is contemptuous of Scottish men's propensity for alcohol ("Give him two or three days …") – but within seconds we see Hughie declining the offer of a drink from Massimo.

3. Candidates should discuss the role of Hughie in the extract and in the play as a whole.

   General instructions for marking this question are given on page 158.

#### Text 2 — Drama — *Bold Girls* by Rona Munro

4. A contrast clearly defined and suitable textual reference for 2 marks.

   *Any of the following:*
   - Cassie's extroversion versus Marie's shyness
   - Cassie's confidence versus Marie's timidity
   - Cassie's self-centredness versus Marie's obliging nature
   - Cassie's exuberance versus Marie's diffidence.

Reference could be made to any of the following to support any of the contrasts:

Words:
- Marie: "Well, maybe …"
- Marie: the rather feeble meat pie joke – attempted humour
- Cassie "great diet"
- Cassie: "really feel the benefit"
- Cassie: "Let them".

Actions:
- Marie: *"shuffling cautiously"*
- Marie: *"glances round nervously"*
- Cassie: *"dancing … extravagant"*
- Cassie: *"beams, applauding"*.

5. A valid aspect of the relationship and appropriate textual support for 2 marks.

   *Possible answers include:*
   - Marie cares for/is concerned about Cassie ("Cassie, what's wrong?", "Have you had words?")
   - Marie is supportive of Cassie ("It'll be all right Cassie.", "I'll just be across the road, I won't let you go crazy.")
   - Cassie feels she can confide in Marie ("I tell you Marie I can't stand the *smell* of him.")
   - Cassie knows Marie is unshockable, knows she can exaggerate with her ("I'm just bad, Marie, didn't you know?")
   - there is a kind of unspoken understanding between them (*"Slowly Cassie smiles at her."*).

6. *Possible answers include:*
   - the use of italics to emphasise her disgust/contempt
   - "greasy" – suggests unhealthy, slimy, etc
   - "grinning" – suggests leering, unpleasant, etc
   - "beer bellied" – suggests self-indulgence, unpleasant, sloppy appearance
   - "winking away" – suggest lecherous, unsavoury, etc
   - "wriggling" – makes him sound worm-like
   - "fat fingers" – suggests clumsy, distasteful, etc
   - "like I'm a poke of chips" – he treats her as a commodity, something for his own gratification
   - alliteration ("greasy, grinning", "beer bellied", "fat fingers") – harsh sounds emphasise her revulsion
   - climactic structure of the last sentence – builds to the horror of "my *bed*".

7. Answers should focus on the relationship between Marie and Cassie and should take account of the revelations in Scene Four.

   General instructions for marking this question are given on page 158.

## Text 3 — Drama — *Sailmaker* by Alan Spence

8. Any four valid points.

   *Possible answers include:*

   - he is not earning a lot from his job
   - he is gambling heavily
   - he has suffered a significant loss (backing a favourite)
   - he is in debt to the bookie
   - he is paying high interest/not paying off original sum.

9. Any one valid character point and textual support.

   *Possible answers include:*

   - generous – extends loan
   - caring – wants to know what the problem is
   - knows his brother well – suspects drink/knows it's not just the job
   - persistent – doesn't let Davie fob him off
   - nosey/intrusive – keeps asking questions about brother's private life.

10. *Possible answers include:*

    - he knows his brother is (sort of) joking
    - he realises brother is trying to relieve some tension
    - he is amused at the fact brother can bring his sectarianism into anything
    - he realises that the bookie's religion is not going to change anything.

11. The key point is the contrast between Davie's steadfast optimism and Billy's realistic/cynical view of life; identifying this and making reference to at least two different parts of the exchange should gain 4 marks.

    Reference could be made to several occasions when a hopeful comment by Davie is countered by a pessimistic/realistic putdown from his brother, e.g.:

    - the scathing "Whatever that is" showing that Billy lacks Davie's faith
    - the blunt assertions "It's a mug's game. The punter canny win" in response to Davie's rather feeble "Things've got tae get better"
    - the frustrated "Flingin it away!" in response to Davie's dogged "Got tae keep trying"
    - a further contrast can be identified in lines 42–49 where Billy's desire for positive action is met with Davie's passivity ("Ah knew his terms") , culminating in his shoulder-shrugging "Whit a carry on, eh?".

12. Answers should deal with a number of relevant aspects of how money problems and escape are explored, e.g.:

    - Davie's gambling
    - Davie's drinking
    - Billy's move to Aberdeen for work
    - exchanges between Alec and Ian about work prospects
    - the idea of education as a way to betterment
    - football (and sectarianism) as a diversion from poverty
    - religion as an "escape"
    - specific details of Davie's and Alec's situation.

    General instructions for marking this question are given on page 158.

## SCOTTISH TEXT — PROSE

### Text 1 — Prose — *In Church* by Iain Crichton Smith

13. **Before** (any three of):

    - British officer (Colin Macleod) leaves the trenches
    - comes across a ruined church
    - meets a deserter who lives in the crypt
    - the deserter had been studying for the ministry
    - insists on delivering a sermon.

    **After:**

    - he shoots Colin.

14. *Possible answers include:*

    - "forced" – under compulsion, against his will
    - "what they call" – implies he doesn't agree
    - his outlook ("gaze") was different from the army's
    - "despised" – looked down on with contempt
    - "feared" – caused him alarm
    - list of the men's shortcomings – emphasises how many there were
    - "fornicated" – immoral behaviour
    - "spat" – disgusting, unhealthy
    - "filthily" – lack of hygiene, lack of self-respect.

15. *Possible answers include:*

    - contrasts the horrors of war with a friendly/sociable game of football
    - contrasts the horrors of war with the sociable activity of sharing photographs
    - contrasts civilised behaviour of German officer with the bombardment to follow
    - contrasts the banality of looking at watch with horrors to come.

16. *Possible answers include:*

    - used to think God was on the side of the innocent, but no longer
    - believes God is "absent"
    - God has left him alone to suffer
    - God has left the world to suffer
    - God doesn't care
    - God has allowed mankind to engage in the destruction of war.

17. Answers should focus on Crichton Smith's characterisation.

    General instructions for marking this question are given on page 158.

### Text 2 — Prose — *Away in a Manger* by Anne Donovan

18. *Possible answers include:*

    - "shimmerin wi light" – alluring, attractive, etc
    - "brightness sharp against the gloomy street" – contrast to emphasise the appeal of the square
    - "like the plastic jewellery sets wee lassies love" – connotations of precious jewels, bright and shiny, children's enjoyment of play
    - "in a mad rhythm" – uncontrolled, zany, exhilarating, etc

- "ae their ain" – idea of freedom, lack of constraint, etc
- "bells ringin and snow fallin" – association with Christmas fun (plus rhythmical pattern to heighten the sense of involvement)
- "Reindeer and Santas, holly, ivy, robins …" – list to emphasise to the sheer number of attractions
- "bleezin wi light" – as if on fire, extraordinarily bright, etc
- "fillin the air" – the sound is pervasive, dominates the senses
- "like a cracklin heavenly choir" – as if angels are present; suggestions of warmth, comfort, etc.

19. A well-made point for 2 marks and a less assured response for 1 mark.

    *Possible answers include:*

    - to convey the excitement of others around them
    - to give the impression of a babble of disembodied voices everywhere
    - to give a rapid glimpse of some of the attractions (reindeer, star, tree).

20. *Possible answers include:*

    - in the past people on the benches were easily identified as down-and-outs
    - today they looked no different from ordinary shoppers.

21. *Possible answers include:*

    - Amy tugging at mother's arm to attract attention
    - Sandra's "Whit song?" as if she's not been paying attention
    - Sandra's "Do you?" as if struggling to show some interest
    - Amy's gushing detail about school and Mrs Anderson
    - Sandra's very uninterested "Oh."
    - Sandra's "What's no your favourite?" – she hasn't been paying attention at all
    - Amy initiates guessing game
    - Sandra won't play along ("Don't know.")
    - Amy's wheedling "Guess, Mammy, you have tae guess."
    - Sandra joins in to keep the peace (because she knows that's how to get it over with)
    - Amy quickly resorts to "Gie in?"
    - Sandra accepts with alacrity
    - Amy's triumphant "Ah've won!" …
    - … followed almost without a break by a question demanding an explanation.

22. Answers should focus on the development of the parent/child relationship in the extract and in another story. Of the stories on the set list, the most profitable will be: *All That Glisters* or *Dear Santa* or, to a lesser degree, *Virtual Pals*.

    General instructions for marking this question are given on page 158.

## Text 3 — Prose — *The Cone Gatherers* by Robin Jenkins

23. *Possible answers include:*

    - Duror is unable to climb tree
    - Neil is initially polite

- Duror delivers message to Calum and Neil about the deer drive
- Neil protests strongly
- the effect on Duror of being unable to climb the tree is evident.

24. *Possible answers include:*

    - the use of a series of rather threatening sounds – "scrapes", "thumps", "cracked", "barked"
    - the frequency of short sentences – creates a breathless, staccato effect
    - the alternation between sound and silence – creates suspense
    - the references to waiting, once for "three or four minutes" – an agonisingly long time.

25. There should be reference to at least three of the following in order to establish two changes, with each attitude supported by some valid reference to the text:

    - friendly/polite (line 16)
    - helpful (line 19)
    - hopeful/anticipating good news (lines 23 and 25)
    - non-committal/defensive (line 27)
    - angry/slightly aggressive (lines 30–31)
    - disbelieving/indignant (lines 33–35)
    - very assertive (lines 35–37).

26. Clear explanation for 2 marks and 1 mark for a less confident explanation. *A possible answer is:*

    - on the outside he appears normal/healthy, but a malignant force is destroying him from within.

27. Answers should focus on the conflict between Duror and the Cone-Gatherers.

    General instructions for marking this question are given on page 158.

## Text 4 — Prose — *The Testament of Gideon Mack* by James Robertson

28. *Possible answers include:*

    - Gideon is watching TV (on a Sunday)
    - his father returns unexpectedly
    - his father is furious
    - his father forces him to watch rest of programme
    - his father delivers a condemnation of American culture.

29. *Possible answers include:*

    - switches off the TV even though he knows there is no point
    - "jumped to my feet" – sudden action implying nervousness
    - "a flush of shame and fury" – embarrassment and resentment
    - futile action of trying to protect the TV set
    - "bowed my head" – can't look his father in the face
    - fixes eye on crack – trying to shut out the presence of his father
    - "mumbled" suggests he is confused, in a panic.

30. *Possible answers include:*

- use of italics to convey tone of voice
- rhetorical question to express fury at disobedience
- hint of cutting sarcasm in "you have become very skilled at operating that thing"
- "huge right hand descended on my neck" – sense of monstrous threat
- "thumb and fingers gripped" – conveys the tightness, painfulness of the action
- "increased the pressure" – making it even worse
- "thought my head would snap off" – no thought for Gideon's pain
- "breathing was like that of some monstrous creature in its den" – the comparison dehumanises his father, makes him sound like a mythical destroyer
- "If I squirmed ... his grip tightened" – no mercy, prepared to inflict even greater pain
- "he pushed me" – forceful, aggressive action.

31. *Possible answers include:*

- the way he says "What ... is ... that?" as if spitting out the words in disgust
- his refusal to call the programme by it correct name, preferring "Bat ... man" as if the words are disgusting
- "whatever that means" – implying it might mean anything
- "drivel" – he thinks it's worthless, idiotic
- "unutterable garbage" – he considers it to be like rubbish, indescribably useless
- "Garbage from the land of garbage." – repetition/ alliteration – harsh consonant conveys anger, disgust
- "land of garbage" – implying whole country is contaminated.

32. Answers should focus on the relationship between Gideon and his father.

    General instructions for marking this question are given on page 158.

**Text 5 – Prose – *Kidnapped* by Robert Louis Stevenson**

33. Three brief references and comment for 1 mark each.

    *Possible answers include:*

- "steady"/"quiet"/"great stillness" – idea of unnerving peacefulness, calm before the storm, etc
- "muttering voices" – can't be made out, so slightly threatening, etc
- "clash of steel" – sudden sharp noise to break the silence, use of onomatopoeia
- "dealing out the cutlasses" – disturbing idea of dangerous weapons being handed out, an idea of what David and Alan will have to face
- return to "silence" – again nerve-racking, uneasy, etc.

34. *Any two of the following for 1 mark each:*

- uncertainty
- fear
- hopelessness
- anger
- desire for it to be over.

35. Any three valid points with some textual support for 1 mark each.

    *Possible answers include:*

- "all of a sudden" – surprise, frightening
- "a rush of feet" – speed, threat, etc
- "a roar" – aggressive sound
- "and ... and ... and" – structure (list form) gives impression of one action following quickly after another
- "someone crying out as if hurt" – uncertainty
- "I cried" – the exclamation shows his state of alarm
- "Look to your window!" – Alan's response draws attention to more danger
- "pass his sword through the mate's body" – gruesome killing
- "drive the door in" – idea of force, threat
- "But it was now or never" – idea of last chance, resolved to fate
- "shot into their midst" – reckless, desperate action
- "the whole party threw down the yard and ran for it" – sense of victory (albeit short-lived).

36. *Possible answers include:*

- bloodthirsty ("his sword was running blood to the hilt")
- proud ("himself so swelled with triumph")
- impressive appearance ("looked to be invincible")
- believer in cause ("There's one of your Whigs for ye!").

    *A possible answer is:*

- callous ("asked if I had done much execution").

37. What they've experienced so far is nothing much ("but a dram"); much worse, a more substantial battle is yet to come ("meat").

38. Answers should focus on the relationship between David and Alan.

    General instructions for marking this question are given on page 158.

**SCOTTISH TEXT – POETRY**

**Text 1 – Poetry – *Anne Hathaway* by Carol Ann Duffy**

39. *Possible answers include:*

- "a spinning world" – suggests speed, exhilaration, etc
- "castles" – suggests fairy-tale romance, luxury, security, etc
- "torchlight" – suggests carnival atmosphere, brightness, etc
- "clifftops" – suggests dizzy height, dominance, distant horizons, etc
- "forests, castles, torchlight, clifftops, seas" – list suggests profusion of exciting features
- "dive for pearls" – suggests romantic, exotic, etc
- "shooting stars" – suggests brightness, speed, exhilaration, etc
- "kisses/on these lips" – tactile, sensual, etc.

40. *Possible answers include:*

*NB: The comments given below are suggestions only; there will be other, perfectly acceptable, interpretations.*

- "rhyme" – suggesting the lovers' connectedness, sense of belonging together, fulfilling each other
- "assonance" – suggesting they are similar, connected, but retaining some individuality
- "verb dancing in the centre of a noun" – suggesting her lover's ability to bring life, movement, action ... this is a complex image which allows many analyses
- "he'd written me" – as if she is his creation, she owes everything to him
- "a page beneath his writer's hands" – presents her as a passive recipient of his creativity
- "drama (played)" – as if the senses referred to are actors in some greater performance.

41. (a) *Possible answers include:*

- "dozed" – sleeping (with a suggestion of indolence), while the others are more energetically and pleasurably engaged
- "dribbling" – connotations of old age and messiness compared with the others' apparent vitality and clarity of purpose
- "prose" – suggests their lives are dull, ordinary, uninspired, unlike the imaginative "poetry" of the others' love-making.

(b) *Possible answers include:*

- fondness
- respect
- sadness at his death
- devotion.

42. Answers should focus on the development of the theme of love in this poem and another by Duffy. Of the poems on the set list, the most profitable will be: *Valentine* or *Havisham* or, to a lesser degree *Mrs Midas*.

General instructions for marking this question are given on page 158.

**Text 2 – Poetry – *Lucozade* by Jackie Kay**

43. *Possible answers include:*

- refers to the colour of the drink
- it is something associated with childhood/happier times.

44. *Possible answers include:*

- negative: "they only wilt and die", "Don't bring ..."
- passive: "nods off", "fades"
- dismissive: "Orange nostalgia, that's what that is"
- tired of hospital experience: "whole day was a blur, a swarm of eyes"
- distrusting: "Those doctors with their white lies."
- scornful/cutting: "Did you think you could cheer me up with a *Woman's Own*?"

45. *Possible answers include:*

- "grapes have no imagination, they're just green" – shows she has no interest in them, because they are featureless, dull, have nothing to appeal to her ...

**Whereas**

- "the big brandy, the generous gin, the Bloody Mary, the biscuit tin, the chocolate gingers, the dirty big meringue?' – seem livelier, more appealing because of their association with sharp taste, colour, excess, ... (appropriate comment could be made also on the alliteration, the list structure and the self-indulgent glee of "dirty big meringue").

46. *Possible answers include:*

**Mood:**

- happy, upbeat, optimistic, positive, reassured, ...

**References:**

- "clear her cupboard" – hint of a new start, getting rid of the unwanted
- "bags full" – sense of a job well done
- "wave with her flowers" – cheerful gesture
- "My mother ... waves back" – gesture is reciprocated, sense of connection
- "face is light and radiant" – she can see brightness, almost angelic light
- "sheets billow and whirl" – sense of freshness, unrestrained movement
- "She is beautiful" –  a straightforward statement of affection
- "the empty table is divine" – by clearing away all the unwanted things, she has made a simple table seem somehow holy
- "singing an old song" – implying contentedness and connection with her mother.

47. Answers should focus on the way a relationship between generations is presented and explored in *Lucozade* and another poem by Jackie Kay. Any of the poems on the set list would be suitable.

General instructions for marking this question are given on page 158.

**Text 3 – Poetry – *Trio* by Edwin Morgan**

48. *Possible answers include:*

- "Christmas lights" – bright and cheerful, association with festivity, etc
- "the three of them are laughing" – everyone is in a good mood
- "a cloud of happiness" – even their breath is associated with joy
- "Wait till he sees this but!" – sense of anticipation, pleasure in giving.

49. *Possible answers include:*

**The chihuahua:**

- cute, appealing, vulnerable ("tiny")
- colourful, perhaps a little dignified ("Royal Stewart tartan")
- a little ridiculous, incongruous ("coat like a teapot-holder")

**The baby:**

- clean, pure ("white shawl")
- radiant, alert ("all bright eyes")
- like a good luck charm ("mouth like favours")
- sweet, appealing, nourishing ("in a fresh sweet cake")

**The guitar:**

- like something alive, organic ("swells out")
- bright, associated with decoration and with giving ("silver tinsel tape")
- associated with celebration, mystical powers ("brisk sprig of mistletoe").

50. Four basic points for 1 mark each, but some answers will provide a convincing response by dealing with fewer than four points.

    *Possible answers include:*

    - they are objects of wonder/admiration
    - they are a celebration of life
    - they render Christ's birth in a sense irrelevant
    - they have the power to defy death
    - they are united like a conquering army
    - they can overcome any threat.

51. *Possible answers include:*

    - positive ("vanished … yet not vanished")
    - uplifted, inspired ("…they wind/the life of men…")
    - confident, safe ("laughter ringing them round like a guard")
    - saddened, depressed ("vanished … end … winter").

52. Answers should focus on how the poet "transforms the ordinary". Of the poems on the set list, the most profitable will be: "In the Snack-bar" or "Winter" or "Good Friday". It is acceptable in this question to write about a poem by Morgan which is not on the set list.

    General instructions for marking this question are given on page 158.

**Text 4 — Poetry — *Visiting Hour* by Norman MacCaig**

53. *Possible answers include:*

    - "combs my nostrils" – sense of irritation
    - "bobbing along" – uneven movement
    - "green and yellow corridors" – association with sickness, nausea
    - "seems a corpse" – uncertain. disorientated
    - "vanishes" – sense of mystery
    - "I will not feel, I will not/feel, until/I have to" – jerky rhythm conveys tension, disorientation.

54. *Possible answers include:*

    - admiration of their calmness
    - respect for their ability to cope with death/suffering
    - appreciation of their bright, uncomplaining approach/attitude.

55. *Possible answers include:*

    - "white cave of forgetfulness" – comparison of room to a "cave" conveys idea of seclusion, isolation from rest of world
    - "trembles on its stalk" – comparison of arm to "stalk" conveys its thinness, fragility
    - "a glass fang is fixed,/not guzzling but giving" – comparison of drip to a "fang" creates ghoulish/slightly amusing idea of vampire in reverse
    - "the distance of pain" – suggests that pain can in some way be measured and that he is aware of how much she is suffering.

56. There are many possible responses and each has to be judged on its merits. Better answers will explore the oxymoron of "fruitless fruits" and/or the futility of "books that will not be read" and/or the impact of "only". Some sense of the speaker's mood/feelings should be included.

57. Answers should focus on the way strong emotion is presented and explored in *Visiting Hour* and another poem by MacCaig. Of the poems on the set list, the most profitable will be: *Aunt Julia* or *Memorial* or *Sounds of the Day* or, to a lesser degree, *Assisi*.

    General instructions for marking this question are given on page 158.

**SECTION 2 – Critical Essay**

Please see the assessment criteria for the Critical Essay on page 165.

## NATIONAL 5 ENGLISH
## MODEL PAPER 3

### READING FOR UNDERSTANDING, ANALYSIS AND EVALUATION

1.  *Any two of the following:*
    - the bluntness/brevity/content of the opening sentence
    - "hundreds of others" is emphasised by use of parenthesis
    - the use of the colon isolates or enforces the pause before "Soweto"
    - the positioning of "Soweto" gives a climactic effect.

2.  *Any three of the following for 1 mark each:*
    - because of the law/rule enforcing/requiring use of Afrikaans in schools
    - because they saw this as offensive/demeaning
    - because this came on top of other examples of poor treatment
    - because loss of language means loss of free thought
    - because they were generally being downtrodden, denied freedom.

3.  *Any four of the following for 1 mark each:*
    - he stood up to authority
    - although he was weak, he showed he was not afraid
    - his story illustrated that there is suffering/hardship everywhere
    - he gave inspiration to young black South Africans
    - they were amazed that the book/story had not been prohibited
    - his creator seemed to understand human suffering.

4.  1 mark for selection of word and 1 for comment. *Any two of the following:*
    - "frail" – suggests undernourished, etc
    - "courageous" – suggests he was willing to stand up for himself, etc
    - "oppression" – suggests he suffered severely at the hands of his masters
    - "slave labour" – suggests he was treated cruelly, unfairly, inhumanely, etc
    - "thin rations" – suggests the extreme meagreness of his food
    - "cruel" – suggests vindictive, spiteful nature of his enemies
    - "taunts" – suggests the malicious, aggressive behaviour of his enemies.

5.  It introduces an explanation of the way in which they "took Oliver to heart".

6.  *Any four of the following for 1 mark each (may be in bullet point form or in prose):*
    - his books were shared among many people
    - there was a waiting list for his books
    - he inspired the formation of a committee dedicated to improving conditions among young black people
    - his characters were known well, referred to by name

- he connected people to the great books of the world
- he was chosen as favourite by Hugh Masakela on *Desert Island Discs*.

7.  *Any two of the following for 1 mark each:*
    - they were not interested in black people improving themselves
    - they were actively opposed to black people improving themselves
    - they were tyrannical, vicious, over-severe in punishment
    - they were ruthless
    - they were dishonest/corrupt (the charge of "violence" for a non-violent act.

8.  (a) • (first) the idea of grandparents carrying out initial education then strongly encouraging as much learning as possible
    - (second) the idea of encouraging isolated/primitive peoples to understand/have control over their own world/environment
    - (third) the idea of using your own language to learn about your own world.

    (b) 1 mark for selection of word or feature and 1 mark for comment.
    *Any two of the following:*
    - "love" – shows books were treated with respect, passion, devotion, etc
    - "inspire" – suggests leading towards something uplifting, etc
    - "mentor" – idea of helpful, inspirational teacher
    - "spent a lifetime" – idea of dedication, devotion to a worthy cause
    - "future" – suggests hope, improvement, etc
    - short sentence "And they got it." – triumphant tone
    - "sacrifices" – suggests a worthwhile, if costly, course of action, done for the benefit of others
    - "applaud" – idea of approval, support, etc.

### SECTION 2 – Critical Essay

Please see the assessment criteria for the Critical Essay on page 165.

## NATIONAL 5 ENGLISH 2014

### READING FOR UNDERSTANDING, ANALYSIS AND EVALUATION

1. Candidates should paraphrase "wretchedly indulgent".

   - eg appallingly/dreadfully/extremely/shamefully – ie appreciation of the intensifying function of "wretchedly"

   - eg (over-) tolerant/libertarian/lenient/non-disciplinarian (accept colloquial "soft")

   - 1 mark for reference to "revisiting one's own childhood" (eg comparing one's own childhood).

2. Candidates should identify the structural link, but may do so in either direction

   Selection and identified reference from examples below – no "mix and match"

   **or**

   Selection identified as looking back

   Selection identified as looking forward

   - "When I was little" looks back to (idea of)"one's own childhood"

   - "given no choices" looks forward to (list of words suggesting) idea of compulsion/(comparative) deprivation

   - "I could only choose what to read" looks forward to "we had all the books we could read".

3. Candidates should draw inferences from the writer's use of language to show appreciation of this important idea

   **Word choice**

   - "only once" suggests rarity of eating out

   - "motorway café" implies moderately-priced venue

   - "wincing" suggests pained reaction to perceived expense

   - "wincing" or "stomach-churning" suggests repellent nature of comestibles

   - "spag bol" suggests cheap option

   - "From the children's menu" suggests limitation of choice

   - "mainly spent "wooding" for winter fuel" suggests lack of facilities/choice/spartan nature of activity

   - "on rainswept hillsides" suggests spartan nature of activity

   - "(father would invariably book) cheap (overnight ferry crossings)" suggests thrift/parsimony

   - "He would never shell out for a cabin" suggests thrift/parsimony

   - "there was nothing to do for weeks on end except rake leaves" suggests lack of facilities/choice/spartan nature of activity.

   **Sentence structure**

   - (idea of) minor sentence or brevity of "From the children's menu" complements idea of lack of choice/adds emphasis

   - (idea of parenthetical) insertion of "mainly spent "wooding" for winter fuel on rainswept hillsides" illustrates/develops/exemplifies idea of lack of facilities/choice.

4. Candidates should offer a gloss of both words and a correct analytic comment

   - "benign" (eg kind/caring/compassionate/well-meant)

   - "neglect (eg ignoring/leaving alone/not paying attention to, but synonym should not have critical connotation);

   - (idea of) paradox/oxymoron/contrast.

5. Candidates will make selections and offer correct explanations of their effect – these require the drawing of inferences from connotations and/or nuances

   - "manic (mum)" suggests/indicates excess/(near-) insanity

   - "(calls herself a) Tiger Mother" suggests excessive competitiveness/ambition

   - "produce" suggests parenthood being analogous to a manufacturing process

   - Any part of "straight-A ...superkids" suggests excessive ambition

   - "pushy" suggests assertiveness/forcefulness

   - "anxious" suggests over-concern/worry/angst

   - "helicopter parents" or "hover" suggests excessive proximity/involvement

   - "mothers pulled out their sons because the weather forecast was 'rainy'" suggests over-protectiveness/feather-bedding

   - "traumatic" suggests deleterious effect of parental involvement

   - "over-involvement" states excess/inappropriateness of parental attachment

   - "mummies and daddies" allows the inference that (eg) parental view of relationship is inappropriate.

6. Comment may express approval or disapproval.

   Candidates may comment on expression of

   - diversity

   - high achievement

   - preternatural quality

   - hyphenation

   - the effect of a list.

7. Candidates have to select and comment upon aspects of the writer's use of language, to show (inferred) understanding of the father's attitude.

   Apparent attitude:

   - Uses the word "great" **or** an exclamation mark **or** "cried" to suggest enthusiasm.

   Actual attitude:

   - did not miss a beat" suggests calmness

   - "astutely" suggests wisdom

   - "if he approved the plan, I would never carry it out" shows (inferable) disapproval.

8. Candidates have to identify two similarities, either by specific reference or expression of more generalised comparisons.

    *Possible examples include:*

    - undergoing training/going on courses/taking classes in it
    - childcare vouchers
    - aims imposed by government/rules
    - professional advice/support eg online
    - sources of advice
    - idea of multiplicity of activities
    - idea of diversity of activities
    - idea of constantly being on duty
    - idea of bureaucratic vigilance.

9. Candidates have to recognise and restate key points.

    *Any five points from:*

    **Then**

    Glosses of

    - "we were given no choices" eg children were not given options/consulted
    - "There was not so much stuff" eg children had fewer possessions
    - "we made our own fun" eg children entertained themselves
    - "Our parents provided us with the essentials" eg care was basic , parents were not so generous
    - "then got on with their own lives" eg parents were more remote/hands-off
    - "there was not the expectation of having every wish granted" eg children did not anticipate being given everything they wanted
    - "My parents were so hard-up" eg reference to spartan holiday travel and activities
    - "Keeping children busy and happy was not a parental priority" eg parents' first concern was not their children's pleasure
    - Lack of school "involvement" eg skimpy attention paid to reports, non-attendance at meetings
    - "It was the complete opposite in my day" eg lack of involvement pre-tertiary education
    - "Becoming a mother or father is no longer something you just are" eg people discovered what to do as they went along.

    **Now**

    Glosses of

    - "wretchedly indulgent state of modern parenting" eg parents are excessively lenient/lax/soft
    - "many of my son's 15-year-old friends have iPods, iPads, MacBooks ... Pay Pal, eBay and iTunes accounts" eg children have many/a variety of modern devices
    - "unlimited access to their parents' credit cards" eg children are given a great deal of/excessive financial extravagance
    - "I can't repeat this sensible regime ..." eg parents are unable to be as removed as hers were

    - "examples of 'wet parenting' abound" eg there are many instances of excessive/over-indulgent/over-protective behaviour
    - "(traumatic level of) parental over-involvement just at the exact moment that mummies and daddies are supposed to be letting go" eg parents are too concerned/interfering/hands-on when their children are older
    - "Parenting is something you do ... has become subsidised and professionalised" eg parents now are more rule-bound/have more people telling them what to do.

## CRITICAL READING

### SECTION 1 — Scottish Text

### SCOTTISH TEXT — DRAMA

### Text 1 — Drama — *Bold Girls* by Rona Munro

1. Candidates should show how the word choice and/or sentence structure create the impression that Marie's daily life is demanding.

   (The volume/range of work she has to do and the general lack of resources is likely to be commented upon.)

   1 mark for selection of relevant quotation about **word choice**.

   1 mark for appropriate comment. 1 mark for selection of relevant reference to **sentence structure**.

   1 mark for appropriate comment.

   **Examples of word choice include:**

   - use of plural on "irons" and "boards" suggests volume of work
   - "piles" suggests the scale of the work to be undertaken
   - "waiting to be smoothed" (personification) suggests demanding nature of house work
   - Description of toys in different states of repair suggests the never ending cycle of pace of life
   - "swallowed up the year's savings" suggests money is tight
   - "pots and pans and steam..." suggests the multiplicity of the tasks to be done
   - "always hot" suggests the relentlessness of the chores
   - "furniture bald with age" suggests lack of money
   - "gleaming clean" suggests how hard Marie works/ house proud
   - "never deserted" suggests little peace
   - "too stuffed" suggests it is cramped
   - "clutter of housework" suggests she never gets to the end of her work
   - "picture of the virgin" suggests she is religious
   - "blown-up photo" suggests sentimentality.

   **Examples of sentence structure include:**

   - repeated use of "It's" suggests immediacy of domestic life
   - use of complex sentences suggests the scale of the work she does
   - use of semi-colons for expansion of detail intensifies demanding nature of Marie's remit.

2. Deirdre's words and actions create a bleak mood/ atmosphere. Candidates should demonstrate understanding of this through reference to and comment upon one aspect of the **stage directions** and one aspect of her dialogue.

   1 mark for selection of relevant quotation about stage directions.

   1 mark for appropriate comment.

   1 mark for selection of relevant quotation about **dialogue**.

   1 mark for appropriate comment.

   **Examples of stage directions include:**

   - "not in this room" suggests she is an outsider (not part of community)
   - "crouching on all fours" suggests she is afraid/or in a hostile environment
   - "darkness" suggests bleakness
   - "only her face is visible" suggests mystery/ concealment
   - "wary" suggests suspicion/danger
   - "black-out" at the end of her speech suggests she is an outsider/builds tension.

   **Examples of dialogue include:**

   - "sun going down" suggests literally lack of light/ metaphorically lack of hope
   - "sky is grey" suggests bleakness/dullness/lack of interest
   - "hills...green" suggests a contrasting brighter setting
   - "I can't hardly see them..." suggests she is cut off from (more) appealing setting
   - "stones" suggests coldness/harshness
   - repetition of "grey" suggests drabness/hopelessness
   - "Somewhere a bird is singing" suggests her environment lacks natural beauty/suggests she knows there is something better elsewhere.
   - "ice cream van" suggests a nostalgia for the past
   - "helicopter overhead" suggests military action/ urban policing/crime
   - "I hear the ice cream van... and the helicopter overhead" suggests the contrast between daily life and extreme circumstances...

3. (a) Candidates must identify Marie's attitude, eg. she treats him kindly **or** is willing to discipline him.

   Candidates might provide an example of her kindness and an example of discipline.

   **Examples of kindness include:**

   - asks him about the flavour of the crisps he wanted
   - tells him he can swap them
   - deals with him immediately ("hurls the bag")
   - she explains her decisions to him.

   **Examples of discipline include:**

   - she restricts the intake of his food
   - she tells him to pick up the crisps
   - she tells him not to be "so bold".

   (b) 1 mark for identification of/comment on Marie's attitude – eg. she accepts that she has a lot of work to do/tries to do all her chores speedily/successfully.

   Candidates should quote and comment on any one aspect of Marie's efficiency.

   1 mark for identification/comment and one mark for relevant quotation.

   **or**

   Relevant summary of Marie's attitude (without quotation) towards her daily routine – up to 2 marks.

Examples of Marie's efficiency include:

- "starts two jobs simultaneously" suggests competence/skill
- "First...then" suggests a logical approach to her tasks/running order
- "needs ironing and what doesn't" suggests an economy of effort/doesn't do needless jobs
- "sorts a few items then starts peeling potatoes" suggests the range of tasks to be undertaken
- "all her movements have a frenetic efficiency" suggests her competence in all respects.

4. Candidates should identify areas of difficulty in the characters' lives from this extract and elsewhere in the play.

*Possible areas for comment are:*

- the setting of the play is bleak and there is the constant threat of violence
- the women do not have a lot of money and struggle to make ends meet
- the women do not have a male figure at home to help them with family life
- the community in which they live is intrusive and there is a lack of privacy
- the women have committed immoral acts which they hide from others
- the women have dreams and aspirations beyond what they can secure.

Candidates may choose to answer in **bullet points** in this final question, or write a number of linked statements. There is **no requirement** to write a 'mini essay'.

Up to 2 marks can be achieved for identifying elements of **commonality** as identified in the question.

A further 2 marks can be achieved for **reference to the extract given.**

4 additional marks can be awarded for similar references to **at least one other part of the text** by the writer.

In practice this means:

**Identification of commonality** (eg: theme, central relationship, importance of setting, use of imagery, development in characterisation, use of personal experience, use of narrative style, or any other key element...)

**from the extract:**

1 × relevant reference to technique

1 × appropriate comment

**or**

1 × relevant reference to idea

1 × appropriate comment

**or**

1 × relevant reference to feature

1 × appropriate comment

**or**

1 × relevant reference to text

1 × appropriate comment

**(maximum of 2 marks only for discussion of extract)**

from **at least one other part of the text:**

as above (× 2) for **up to 4 marks**

**Text 2 — Drama — *Sailmaker* by Alan Spence**

5. Any two key points.

Candidates are expected to use their own words.

*Possible answers include:*

- Davie comes home drunk
- Alec is worried
- Alec is annoyed
- Alec complains about the state of the house
- Davie tries to defend the way things are
- Alec becomes frustrated that his father will not move on with his life and challenges him
- Davie will not admit his interest in the woman he has met in the pub
- Davie slaps Alec for his rudeness/directness ...
- Alec is left reflecting on the way his relationship with his father has changed/broken down
- Alec is trying to remember something but is unsure what it is.

6. (a) Candidates should identify or comment on an appropriate feeling.

This feeling should be supported by an appropriate quotation or reference.

*Possible answers include:*

Alec is feeling angry/frustrated/let down ...

*Evidence might include:*

- Alec criticises the untidy/unclean house – "Look at the state ae us"/"livin like bloody Steptoe and Son"/"Place is like a midden"/"When did we last gie it a good clean?"/"Needs gutted"
- Alec is annoyed that the electricity has been cut off – "Nae light"
- Alec criticises Davie for going to the pub instead of taking responsibility – "ye go an get bevvied"
- Alec is frustrated that Davie seems to like women but won't commit to a relationship – "That was no lady, that was a really nice person"
- Alec's sarcastic tone conveys his frustration – stage direction
- Alec's question reflects his frustration – "Why don't ye just admit that ye fancy her?".

(b) Candidates should identify at least two appropriate feelings

One quotation or reference to language technique (1 mark)

Appropriate comment about feeling (1 mark)

*Possible answers include:*

Davie is feeling upset/resigned/defensive/fleetingly positive or cheerful/ultimately angry ...

*Evidence might include:*

- defends his lack of cleaning – "It's hard son"/"It's no easy on yer own"
- defensive with Alec when he mentions going to the pub – "Ye'd think ah came in steamin every night"
- feels he is entitled to a night out – "Nae harm in it"
- emphasises that by repeating it in lines 7 and 15

- cheerful when he remembers the evening and the singing – "Wee sing song"/"That lassie's a rare singer"
- angry with Alec at the end (perhaps because Alec's challenge is uncomfortable for him) – stage directions – "slaps him, exits".

7. Alec's state of mind should be justified with reference to an example of word-choice

**and**

appropriate comment

**and**

Alec's state of mind should be justified with identification of a feature of sentence structure and appropriate comment

Both word-choice and sentence structure should be justified for full marks.

*Possible answers include:*

Alec is confused/regretful

**Word-choice:**

- repetition of "somethin"/"something" vagueness suggest he is confused/seeking answers
- "sometimes" again suggests lack of pattern in his life /confusion
- "lost"/"looking for" suggests he is confused /seeking answers …
- language is mostly English – he has moved on/ changed and doesn't understand this/thinks he no longer belongs …

**Sentence Structure:**

- three questions suggests he is looking for answers
- use of ellipsis struggling to find the words to finish the sentence
- short/abrupt sentence – "God knows" suggests he cannot work out what has gone wrong
- series of short sentences/questions thoughts are not flowing well/confused ideas.

8. Candidates should identify the way in which Alec has changed with reference to this extract and to elsewhere in the play.

Both sides of the change (eg. working class to middle class/using Scots to English/school to university) should be identified for 1 mark.

Supporting evidence /comment for each side can be rewarded with 1 mark each.

- Alec has become more (openly) critical of his father/ has lost respect for him.
- he becomes increasingly more responsible and mature
- Alec becomes more distant from his father and more of a contrast to him
- ultimately, the roles reverse and Alec becomes more like the father in the relationship
- however, Alec still feels something is missing in his life.

**Extract:** Alec is critical of his father

**Elsewhere:**
At start of play Alec shows a lot of respect and admiration for his father especially in his conversations with Ian in Act 1 where he boasts of his dad's sailmaking skills and shows off his dad's tools. He also has faith in his father that he will fix the yacht that he also shows to Ian.

**Extract:** Alec criticises his father's drinking

**Elsewhere:**
Earlier in Act 1 Alec says to Davie 'You've been drinkin. I can smell it.' But that is all he says – he simply makes a statement; he does not criticise or antagonise Davie further about it.

**Extract:** relationship is at its lowest point as Alec is very critical and Davie ends up slapping him

**Elsewhere:**
Earlier in Act 2 – Alec criticises his dad's cooking so there are signs of this side of Alec before now

End of play – Alec finally questions Davie about why he gambles which he always just accepted before

End of play – Alec tells Davie he plans to move out

Prior to this event in the extract, Alec tells of a time Davie teased him about a girl to the extent Alec was so angry he hit his father; the complete opposite of what has happened here highlighting the role reversal

**Extract:** it is Alec who criticises the state of the house

**Elsewhere:**
Twice in Act 1 – at start and later on – it is Davie who comments on the state of the house – not Alec and Alec never responds showing he had no interest/this wasn't his concern before

Alec also shows his maturity and sense of responsibility when he offers Davie the money for the electricity bill.

It is also Alec who suggests burning the furniture at the end of the play to keep warm, showing his ability to present solutions to problems

**Extract:** Alec still questions what he has lost, what is missing from his life

**Elsewhere:**
Earlier, Alec has similar thoughts after the argument with Davie about his cooking

Also, earlier in the play, Alec turns to religion to try to fill a gap in his life and has doubts about his reasons for his interest in the church

Candidates may choose to answer in **bullet points** in this final question, or write a number of linked statements. There is **no requirement** to write a 'mini essay'.

Up to 2 marks can be achieved for identifying elements of **commonality** as identified in the question.

A further 2 marks can be achieved for **reference to the extract given.**

4 additional marks can be awarded for similar references to **at least one other part of the text** by the writer.

In practice this means:

**Identification of commonality** (eg: theme, central relationship, importance of setting, use of imagery, development in characterisation, use of personal experience, use of narrative style, or any other key element…)

**from the extract:**

1 × relevant reference to technique

1 × appropriate comment

**or**

1 × relevant reference to idea

1 × appropriate comment

**or**

1 × relevant reference to feature

1 × appropriate comment

**or**

1 × relevant reference to text

1 × appropriate comment

**(maximum of 2 marks only for discussion of extract)**

from **at least one other part of the text:**

as above (× 2) for **up to 4 marks**

**Text 3 — Drama —** *Tally's Blood* **by Ann Marie de Mambro**

9.  (a) Candidates should identify two stereotypes then explain how they are shown to be false.

    - Rosinella says Italian men are willing to work hard/no one works as hard as them
    - but Hughie is shown to be working hard/Hughie is described as "working like a trojan"
    - Rosinella says that "Nobody loves their families like the Italians"
    - but Hughie is shown to love his mum by going home to sit with her **or** Bridget is willing to help her brother out with his wedding preparations because his mum can't
    - Rosinella criticises Hughie's brother (and in effect all Scottish men) for drinking
    - but then Massimo reaches for the wine **or** Hughie refuses a drink.

    (b) Identification of reaction (1 mark)

    Explanation/justification (1 mark)

    - think it is funny
    - think it is ironic
    - think Rosinella is stupid/prejudiced for saying it
    - they might be angry
    - any other appropriate audience reaction accepted with explanation.

10. (a) Identify two examples of Rosinella's kindness/caring

    - offers Hughie food
    - knows Rigatoni is Hughie's favourite
    - gives Hughie money for a present for his brother
    - is interested in/asks about Hughie's family
    - calls Hughie "son".

    (b) Identify two examples of Rosinella's unkindness/unpleasantness.

    - suggests Hughie's brother has got his fiancée pregnant
    - assumes Bridget is going out to see a man but calls it 'winching' to cheapen it
    - Lucia is too scared to ask her something (to go to the wedding)

    - suggests that Bridget will never get married
    - suggests that Hughie's brother will be out drinking days after his wedding
    - doesn't realise that neither Massimo or Lucia are interested in her conversation
    - keeps insisting that she is 'right' in the things she is saying
    - Rosinella makes prejudiced statements.

11. Candidates are asked to identify two examples:

    'wee bit'/'up the road'/'winching'/'up to it'/'amn't'/'poke'/'wee'/'pals'/'son'/'mammy'/'give's a hand'/'Hang on a minute'/'Help them out'/'shooshes'

12. Candidates should discuss how racism is explored in this extract and elsewhere in the play.

    *Possible answers may include:*

    - Rosinella's comments from elsewhere about Italians (always positive) eg makes you special, makes you more attractive, etc
    - Rosinella's comments from elsewhere about Scots (usually negative) eg can't look after their children properly, allow their girls to go out unsupervised, have looser moral standards, etc
    - Rosinella's racism towards Bridget when she is dating Franco
    - Rosinella's racism towards Hughie when he is in love with Lucia
    - the treatment of Massimo by the public at the outbreak of war/when his shop is attacked
    - the treatment of the Italian people who were taken during the war
    - Rosinella's refusal to let go of what happened to them during the war
    - Lucia's mimicry of the school teacher showing the racism she has suffered
    - there may be valid comments about the war itself as an example of Nationalism becoming racism.

    Candidates may choose to answer in **bullet points** in this final question, or write a number of linked statements. There is **no requirement** to write a 'mini essay'.

    Up to 2 marks can be achieved for identifying elements of **commonality** as identified in the question.

    A further 2 marks can be achieved for **reference to the extract given**.

    4 additional marks can be awarded for similar references to **at least one other part of the text** by the writer.

    In practice this means:

    **Identification of commonality** (eg: theme, central relationship, importance of setting, use of imagery, development in characterisation, use of personal experience, use of narrative style, or any other key element…)

    **from the extract:**

    1 × relevant reference to technique

    1 × appropriate comment

    **or**

    1 × relevant reference to idea

    1 × appropriate comment

or

1 × relevant reference to feature

1 × appropriate comment

or

1 × relevant reference to text

1 × appropriate comment

**(maximum of 2 marks only for discussion of extract)**

from **at least one other part of the text:**

as above (× 2) for **up to 4 marks**

## SCOTTISH TEXT — PROSE

### Text 1 — Prose — *The Cone Gatherers* by Robin Jenkins

13. Both emotions for full marks.
    - at first delight/happiness
    - then fear for the animals

14. Can have either aspect for full marks or implied recognition of contrast.

    "marvellous grace and agility" plus comment

    or

    "flew for the doom ahead" plus comment

    or

    Accept grace/doom. Accept a gloss on: they were very beautiful, but they were going to be killed anyway.

15. *Any two from:*
    - "Moaning"
    - "gasping"
    - "Impulse"
    - "Not … so swift and sure of foot"
    - "He fell and rose again"
    - "avoided one tree (only to collide with another close to it)".

16. Two quotations with references and associated comments:
    - "Wails of lament" distress being loudly expressed
    - "Dashed on at demented speed" dashed suggests speed of his movement; demented as though he is mad
    - "A deer screaming" suggests the terror of the animal
    - "Scrabbling around on its hindquarters" the struggle of the wounded animal to escape
    - "Calum saw no one else" unheeding of anything but the animal
    - "Screaming in sympathy" loud distress shared by Calum
    - "Terrified more than ever" implies losing control through fear
    - "It dragged him about with it" creature in its agony instinctively trying to escape, even with Calum holding it.
    - "In mortal agony" unaware of anything but its death throes.
    - "heedless of the danger of being shot" emphasising that he is in such a panic that his personal safety is not important to him.

17. We would expect him to be angry but instead he seems to be enjoying what he is seeing.

    or

    The others are horrified but he is laughing.

    or

    He has planned this so is pleased.

18. Candidates should discuss the portrayal of Duror in this extract and elsewhere in the novel.

    This passage is a culmination of Duror's plot to get rid of the cone gathering brothers, Callum and Neil. The passage holds a great deal of information but we will focus on the parts specifically pertaining to Duror.

    Throughout the novel there is an irrational animosity towards Callum and Neil, but mainly Callum displayed by the gamekeeper, Duror and this passage is the watershed which signals his descent into madness.

    His intention had been to use the deer hunt as a means to cause Callum harm or distress resulting in a more overt obsession.

    He has an obsessive hatred for Callum because he has detested anything misshapen since his younger days and this has manifested itself in his disgust of his bedridden wife whom he cannot even touch.

    He is embittered because of the situation he finds himself in including his relationships with his mother in law, his repeated rejection by the army as this is set during the war and his sense of frustration towards his employer Lady Runcie-Campbell whom he desires but it is a one sided desire.

    **L5 Duror caught sight of them and rushed in pursuit** this is a literal pursuit in the extract but is also the pursuit of his goal to get rid of the brothers throughout the novel, an irrational pursuit.

    **L17 The dogs barked fiercely** and **Duror fired his gun** the word choice of barked fiercely and fired contrasts with words to describe Callum in this extract such as **silent** and **desperate**.

    **L22 Duror bawled to his dogs** a line filled with hard sounding consonants and plosives

    By his would be attack on the brother, it is as if he is simultaneously acting unnaturally and attacking nature itself. This is evident through the word choice of **screaming** to describe the noise made by both Callum and the deer.

    Not only is Callum associated with animal symbolism, Duror himself latterly in the novel can be seen as embodying evil and darkness and in this rural setting can be seen to represent the serpent from the Garden of Eden. It is paradoxical in that his role within the novel is as a gamekeeper on a large estate who should maintain control of the animals.

    At the end of this extract, Duror **came leaping out of the wood** and **seemed to be laughing in some kind of berserk joy.** This overt display of madness contrasts with the reactions of the other witnesses to this event, Captain Forgan, Young Roderick and Lady Runcie-Campbell who are standing **petrified.**

    His abnormal reaction foreshadows his descent into madness and irrational behaviour which leads ultimately to the tragic ending, the murder of Callum and his own suicide.

Candidates may choose to answer in **bullet points** in this final question, or write a number of linked statements. There is **no requirement** to write a 'mini essay'.

Up to 2 marks can be achieved for identifying elements of **commonality** as identified in the question.

A further 2 marks can be achieved for **reference to the extract given.**

4 additional marks can be awarded for similar references to **at least one other part of the text** by the writer.

In practice this means:

**Identification of commonality** (eg: theme, central relationship, importance of setting, use of imagery, development in characterisation, use of personal experience, use of narrative style, or any other key element…)

**from the extract:**

1 × relevant reference to technique

1 × appropriate comment

**or**

1 × relevant reference to idea

1 × appropriate comment

**or**

1 × relevant reference to feature

1 × appropriate comment

**or**

1 × relevant reference to text

1 × appropriate comment

**(maximum of 2 marks only for discussion of extract)**

from **at least one other part of the text:**

as above (× 2) for **up to 4 marks**

### Text 2 — Prose — *The Testament of Gideon Mack* by James Robertson

**19.** Full marks can be obtained in a variety of ways – by making four brief points or by making fewer, more developed points for multiple marks, adding up to 4.

*Possible answers include:*

- freedom ('took me out of myself'/'minister off the leash') with supplementary points about forgetting about job and wider world problems
- released energy inside him , perhaps with explanation of the candidate's understanding of what that means
- rebellion against his disapproving parishioners
- vanity, as he thinks he looks good or runs well
- loses himself in it to the point that he notices the different sounds his trainers make on different surfaces
- increased awareness and appreciation of surroundings
- sense of living life to the full.

**20.** 1 mark for attitude and 1 mark for appropriate evidence

Attitude identified is likely to be negative eg not committed, even interested/sees it as a burden/sees himself as a hypocrite etc.

Plus appropriate evidence.

**21.** (a) Example (1 mark)

NB 1 mark for each example given

**or**

One well developed explanation could gain all 3 marks at once.

*Possible answers include:*

- **extended sentence** in first paragraph **giving** all the alternative reasons for running
- using the **repetition** of 'not'/**parenthesis** adding weight to each point
- **simple sentence** to emphasise his real reason for running
- the word 'but' indicates a change in direction
- **italics** for emphasis of the word 'needed'
- **repetition** (of the sentence starter 'I ran') to emphasise how much/how freely he ran
- **use of semicolons** to separate the things he can ignore when running to emphasise the freedom from worry.

(b) Identification of image (1 mark)

Brief comment on image (1 mark)

Relation of image to running (1 mark)

*Possible answers include:*

- 'as if the fire blazing away in there was my fuel' suggests that the energy/heat he refers to is what is propelling him when he runs just as petrol/fuel propels a car/machinery /feels he has to run/is able to run because of this energy.
- 'emptied my head of work, the Kirk, the world' suggests that running is removing his worries from his head Mack feels free when running.
- 'difficult issues and awkward individuals were' suggests the issues and people were pushed back which removes his worries /allows him to feel free when he is running.
- 'their ghosts faded into the trees' suggests his problems disappeared from his mind when running. Mack feels free and relaxed when running.

**22.** Candidates should discuss one aspect of Gideon Mack's character with reference to this extract and elsewhere in the novel.

*Possible answers may include:*

**Need to escape**
Extract: *When I set off…I could feel the disapproval of some of my parishioners*
Elsewhere in novel: mountains/B and B…

**Reluctance to conform**
Extract: *there was something just no richt about a minister in shorts*
Elsewhere in novel: references could include wanting to be a school teacher not a minister; funeral for Catherine Craigie; didn't believe in God; Having sex on his marital bed with Elsie…

**Hypocrite**
Extract: *an escapee from my professional hypocrisy, a minister off the leash*
Elsewhere in novel: *Although within I had abandoned my faith, I still attended church and remained the dutiful son of the manse*; Gideon joins the Church as a minister despite his lack of belief…

### Outsider

Extract: *The loneliness of the long distance runner*; references to film.

Elsewhere in novel:  References could include when he met the boys in his new school in the 1970s; dual existence – pretending to be one person to satisfy his parents while being someone else to satisfy classmates.

### Represses memories/feelings

Extract: *Running emptied my head of work, the Kirk, the world*

Elsewhere in novel:  references to hiding feelings; Elsie says "terrible childhood which strangled love at every turn"...

### Frustrated by others

Extract: *Difficult issues and awkward individuals were repelled by the force of my energy...*

Elsewhere in novel:  References to relationship with father; Peter Macmurray and his dislike of Gideon.

Candidates may choose to answer in **bullet points** in this final question, or write a number of linked statements. There is **no requirement** to write a 'mini essay'.

Up to 2 marks can be achieved for identifying elements of **commonality** as identified in the question.

A further 2 marks can be achieved for **reference to the extract given**.

4 additional marks can be awarded for similar references to **at least one other part of the text** by the writer.

In practice this means:

Identification of commonality (eg:  theme, central relationship, importance of setting, use of imagery, development in characterisation, use of personal experience, use of narrative style, or any other key element...)

**from the extract:**

1 × relevant reference to technique

1 × appropriate comment

**or**

1 × relevant reference to idea

1 × appropriate comment

**or**

1 × relevant reference to feature

1 × appropriate comment

**or**

1 × relevant reference to text

1 × appropriate comment

**(maximum of 2 marks only for discussion of extract)**

from **at least one other part of the text:**

as above (× 2) for **up to 4 marks**

## Text 3 – Prose – *Kidnapped* by Robert Lewis Stevenson

23. Four points to be made.

    1 mark for each point.

    *Possible answers include:*

    - it is foggy
    - Alan's boat is struck by the *Covenant*
    - Alan's boat is split in half
    - Alan's boat sinks
    - the whole crew die except Alan

- Alan grabs hold of the *Covenant*'s bowspirit
- Alan is saved and brought on to the *Covenant*.

24. 1 mark for each individual point about his physical appearance and his character.

    Candidates must deal with both physical appearance and character for full marks but not necessarily in equal proportion.

*Possible answers include:*

A gloss of **physical characteristics**:

- "smallish in stature"
- "well set"
- "nimble as a goat"
- "open expression"
- "sunburnt very dark"
- "heavily freckled"
- "pitted with the small-pox"
- "eyes were unusually light"
- (eyes had) "dancing madness"

A gloss on his **character**:

- "His manners … were elegant"
- "he pledged the captain handsomely"
- "engaging"
- "alarming"
- "rather call my friend than my enemy".

25. Candidates should show an awareness of the friction between Alan and Hoseason.

    Full marks for two examples with detailed comments.

    *Possible answers include:*

    **Word choice:**

    - "still (watching him)" emphasis of the fact that Hoseason has possibly been wary of Alan
    - "(still) watching (him)" watching with connotations of careful inspection emphasising possible concern
    - "Oho!" exclamatory interjection of surprise and realisation indicates friction in this context
    - "(laid his hand) quickly" emphasises the suddenness of Alan's response in reaching for his pistols/ emphasises Alan's concern for his situation/action could also be seen as a response to a slight by Hoseason.
    - "(Don't be) hasty" emphasises Hoseason's attempt to quell Alan, or shows his concern about what Alan may do with the pistols.

    **Metaphor:**

    - "is that how the wind sets?" emphasises Alan's perception of Hoseason's now clear antagonistic attitude towards him.

    **Sentence structure:**

    - "Oho!" exclamatory nature of the interjection
    - Rhetorical question – "…is that how the wind sets?" emphasis on the fact that Alan feels he knows Hoseason's antagonistic view of him.
    - Repetition of "Don't be …" emphasises Hoseason's attempt to quell Alan, or shows his concern about what Alan may do with the pistols

26. Candidates should discuss the development of David and Alan's relationship with reference to this extract and to elsewhere in the novel.

*Possible references:*

The idea of 'commonality' is one which may be established in several ways. It could be made explicit in the candidate response or it could be implicitly delivered through the overall answer of the candidate for this question.

Some possible aspects of the developing relationship between David and Alan which candidates may discuss are:

- the contradictory/contrasting natures of the characters as developed throughout the text;

- tensions in the relationship as it develops throughout the text;

- the theme of duality established by looking at the relationship throughout the text;

- the admiration the characters have for each other at points throughout the texts;

- the developing movement from uncertainty towards true friendship and understanding which is developed throughout the text;

- a mixture of elements from some or all of the above.

The points above could be seen as the more accepted ideas about the relationship between David and Alan in this text. Be open to accepting well-argued points which are not included within the points above.

Candidates may choose to answer in **bullet points** in this final question, or write a number of linked statements. There is **no requirement** to write a 'mini essay'.

Up to 2 marks can be achieved for identifying elements of **commonality** as identified in the question.

A further 2 marks can be achieved f**or reference to the extract given.**

4 additional marks can be awarded for similar references to **at least one other part of the text** by the writer.

In practice this means:

**Identification of commonality** (eg: theme, central relationship, importance of setting, use of imagery, development in characterisation, use of personal experience, use of narrative style, or any other key element...)

**from the extract:**

1 × relevant reference to technique

1 × appropriate comment

or

1 × relevant reference to idea

1 × appropriate comment

or

1 × relevant reference to feature

1 × appropriate comment

or

1 × relevant reference to text

1 × appropriate comment

**(maximum of 2 marks only for discussion of extract)**

from **at least one other part of the text:**

as above (× 2) for **up to 4 marks**

**Text 4 – Prose – *The Telegram* by Iain Crichton Smith**

27. Example/reference to language feature with comment

Suggested examples include:

**Short sentences** build up the pace

**Sentence structure:** sentence beginning 'She had dreamt...' climactic effect

**Repetitive sentence structure**/'She had dreamt'; 'She could see'; 'She could never..' emphasis on the rising panic of the fat woman

**Word choice:** we are shown fat woman's thoughts 'Oh pray God...' etc helps us to understand her rising fear/tension/panic

**Repetition** of 'God'/repeated references to religion like she is praying/becoming hysterical

28. (a) Example with comment

*Possible examples/explanations:*

- 'lips...white and bloodless' emphasises her state of shock

- 'dreaded' emphasises the worry/panic she feels that her son may be dead.

(b) Example with comment

*Possible examples/explanations:*

- 'lips pressed closely together' emphasises her attempt to hold back her emotion/expression

- 'wasn't crying or shaking' not showing her emotions

- 'firm voice' does not shake with emotion.

29. Candidates should give four relevant points for 4 marks.

Must be an attempt to use own words.

*Suggested answers include:*

- she is poor

- struggles to feed herself and her son

- she is a widow/no husband to support her/single parent

- gloss of 'bringing up a son in a village not her own' eg an outsider

- people have been unkind/unsupportive.

30. Candidates should discuss how the writer creates sympathy for a character/characters in this story and in at least one other story by Iain Crichton Smith.

*Possible references:*

**"Mother And Son"**
John, central character – Aggression of mother (may be expressed by reference to speech, "she snapped pettishly"); sustained denigration; low self-esteem (because of being butt of others' humour); joblessness; word choice such as his life being "hell", his "loneliness" ...

**"The Red Door"**
Murdo, central character – His unmarried status (reluctance to enter/fear of entering a relationship); his fear of breaching convention despite desire to expand horizons; lack of academic success and clumsiness at school; he has "never been [himself]"; loneliness; unhappiness at lifestyle (repetition of "he didn't like"); the difference of the red door symbolising everything that he was not

**"The Painter"**
William Murray, focus of account – Ill health; incongruity of this character in a conventional, inward-looking village; the fact that the painting was destroyed by the narrator; ostracisation and banishment of painter

**"The Crater"**
Lt Robert Mackinnon, central character – Context of war; danger of raid, hazards of No Man's Land; responsibilities of leadership; expression of fear (emphasised by repetition); the awful appearance of the victim in the crater (eg emphasis on colour green); implication of stress shown by (unusual) swearing; irony of victim dying

**"In Church"**
Lt Colin Macleod, central character – General context of war; specific perception that fate is indifferent to him and his comrades; discomfiting character of (lunatic) "priest"; ending where (defenceless) central character is murdered

Candidates may choose to answer in **bullet points** in this final question, or write a number of linked statements. There is **no requirement** to write a 'mini essay'.

Up to 2 marks can be achieved for identifying elements of **commonality** as identified in the question.

A further 2 marks can be achieved for **reference to the extract given.**

4 additional marks can be awarded for similar references to **at least one other short story** by the writer.

<u>In practice this means:</u>

**Identification of commonality** (eg: theme, central relationship, importance of setting, use of imagery, development in characterisation, use of personal experience, use of narrative style, or any other key element...)

**from the extract:**

1 × relevant reference to technique

1 × appropriate comment

**or**

1 × relevant reference to idea

1 × appropriate comment

**or**

1 × relevant reference to feature

1 × appropriate comment

**or**

1 × relevant reference to text

1 × appropriate comment

(maximum of 2 marks only for discussion of extract)

from **at least one other short story by the writer:**

as above (× 2) for **up to 4 marks**

**Text 5 – Prose –** *Away in a Manger* by Anne Donovan

31. Candidates should make two clear points

Must make an attempt to use own words.

- the family go to see the nativity
- in George Square
- the mother explains the scene
- a homeless man has climbed inside the crib to escape the cold
- they think he is an angel.

32. Identification or exemplification of technique with comment

*Possible answers could include:*

- **Personification**/'staunin' suggests bronze statues are brought to life/which makes them seem more like ordinary human beings.
- **Metaphor**/the straw is described as a carpet as something familiar (we would see in the home).
- **Simile**/'what looked like a hoose made of glass'. The manger/crib is surrounded by a glass screen. This is compared again to the ordinary or familiar, the 'hoose' again making it seem less unusual.

Candidate may refer to Amy from lines 11–29.

Possible answers could include:

- questions show that she does not know who they are
- use of dash in line 12 or 14 indicates pause for recognition
- italics (in line 15) for emphasis
- statements followed by question
- exclamation marks (in line 29) for emotion/recognition.

33. Identification of language feature (1 mark)

Comment on its effect (1 mark)

- Omission of capital letters/full stops creates the impression of changes of mind.
- Use of commas (creates pauses), giving us the impression of an idea being challenged/altered/thought through.
- Sentence structures suggest/sound like someone speaking (out loud).
- Opening statement 'Sandra wisnae very religious' is then qualified with, 'no religious at all,' then a second time in, 'really'. The final part of the sentence then acts as explanation (that, despite her lack of religious conviction, 'it was nice for wee ones tae have a crib').
- Parenthesis (line 7) – indication of thinking.

34. Two identifications of word choice with comment on effect

*Possible examples of word choice include:*

- "Huddled" cold/insecure/protecting himself
- "Hidden" doesn't want to be seen/hiding
- "a man" no idea of age
- "Slightly built" unhealthy/underfed
- "Auld jeans" poverty/lack of money
- "Thin jaicket" not suited to winter, therefore he is poor/unemployed
- "Worn trainin shoe" poor/doesn't have a lot of money
- "Cheapest kind" poverty
- "Quite young" engages our sympathy/surprise
- "Pointed face" thin/undernourished
- "Longish dark hair" uncut as he can't afford it/reminds us of Jesus
- "Stubbly growth covered his chin" reminds us of Jesus.
- "Sound asleep" exhausted/tired/engages our sympathy.

35. Candidates should discuss any one theme explored in this story and in at least one other story by Donovan.

*Possible references to theme:*

**"Away in a Manger"**
Family relationships, childhood, naiveté, parent/child relationships, misunderstanding, love, generational differences, growing up, Christmas

**"All that Glisters"**
Family relationships, childhood, naiveté, parent/child relationships, misunderstanding, love, generational differences, growing up

**"Dear Santa"**
Family relationships, childhood, parent/child relationships, misunderstanding, love, growing up, Christmas

**"Virtual Pals"**
Childhood, naiveté, misunderstanding, growing up, love, relationships

**"A Chitterin Bite"**
Childhood, growing up, relationships, love

**"Zimmerobics"**
Relationships, generational differences

Candidates may choose to answer in **bullet points** in this final question, or write a number of linked statements. There is **no requirement** to write a 'mini essay'.

Up to 2 marks can be achieved for identifying elements of **commonality** as identified in the question.

A further 2 marks can be achieved for **reference to the extract given**.

4 additional marks can be awarded for similar references to **at least one other short story** by the writer.

Un practice this means:

**Identification of commonality** (eg: theme, central relationship, importance of setting, use of imagery, development in characterisation, use of personal experience, use of narrative style, or any other key element...)

**from the extract:**

1 × relevant reference to technique

1 × appropriate comment

**or**

1 × relevant reference to idea

1 × appropriate comment

**or**

1 × relevant reference to feature

1 × appropriate comment

**or**

1 × relevant reference to text

1 × appropriate comment

**(maximum of 2 marks only for discussion of extract)**

from **at least one other short story by the writer:**

as above (× 2) for **up to 4 marks**

**SCOTTISH TEXT — POETRY**

**Text 1 — Poetry — *War Photographs* by Carol Ann Duffy**

36. 2 marks can be awarded for two main ideas or concerns shown in stanza one.

The war photographer:

- has from become isolated from other people/needs to be alone
- has been exposed to the pain and suffering of others
- is very methodical
- feels he has a duty to inform the public about the pain he has witnessed
- has travelled to many war zones (needs more than just he is well travelled)
- has developed a pessimistic world view.

37. 4 marks can be awarded for two examples of language helping to bring out his attitude.

Example (1 mark) plus comment (1 mark) – any two will gain 4 marks.

Other examples from stanza are acceptable.

- the position of the short emphatic sentence "He has a job to do"
- suggests the photographer's professionalism/matter of fact view of his work.

**or**

- the need to adopt this attitude as a coping strategy given the horror of his work.
- the word choice of "... did not tremble then" suggests his need to control/suppress his feelings/ focused on his job while in the war zone
- the contrast in "though seem to now" suggests the long term emotional effect of what he witnessed abroad/having an impact on him now
- the word choice of "explode"/"nightmare heat" suggests the threat/danger
- the contrast of "Rural England" and "explode"/"nightmare heat" highlights the danger he became accustomed to in the war zone.

**or**

- the difficulty of re-adjusting to home
- "ordinary pain" suggests his awareness of how trivial the problems faced by people in Britain are (compared to those in the war zones)
- the word choice of "dispel" suggests how shallow/ easily addressed he feels the problems faced by people in Britain are.

38. 2 marks can be awarded for one example of dramatic language.

Example (1 mark) plus comment (1 mark)

- the positioning of the abrupt sentence "Something is happening" suggests sudden activity
- the word choice of "twist" suggests violent activity/ distorted in pain
- the ambiguity of "twist before his eyes" suggests the image being revealed but also the distressing nature of the image

- the word choice of "half formed ghost" suggests being haunted by memories/idea of memories being slowly revealed

- the word choice of "cries" suggests the anguish of the man's wife

- the use of sense words such as "blood stained"/"cries" suggests the vivacity of the memory.

39. Candidates should show an understanding of how the content of the last stanza continues ideas and/or language from the first three stanzas.

    - "A hundred agonies" refers to scenes of pain and suffering mentioned earlier

    - the word choice of "black and white" continues the references to the development of photographs/suggests a truthful representation of the suffering

    - the contrast in numbers – "hundred" with "five or six" continues the process of trivialising suffering/callousness to suffering in the war zones

    - the word choice of "prick with tears" is another example of the limited emotional response to the suffering in the war zone

    - the juxtaposition/alliteration of "between the bath and the pre-lunch beers" suggests the brief period of concern for the suffering/suggests a contrast between the safety and comfort of life in Britain and the dangers of life in the war zone

    - the word choice of "impassively" suggests the beginning of his coping strategy as he flies out to his next assignment

    - the word choice of "earns his living" suggests a return of the matter of fact way of viewing his job/beginning of his coping strategy as he returns to the war zone

    - "they do not care" emphasises the indifference of people in Britain to the suffering in the war zones.

40. Candidates should show awareness of the presentation of a main character through ideas and/or language in this poem and at least one other poem by Duffy.

    Candidates may refer to how the war photographer has endured an upsetting/difficult experience that has profoundly affected his view of society. This is a theme which emerges in **"Havisham"** and **"Mrs. Midas"** in which the main character has also endured such an experience.

    In **"Valentine"**, the speaker is the main character. The speaker gives an account of the experience of sharing valentine's gifts.

    In **"Anne Hathaway"**, the speaker is the main character. Here, she reflects on her life with her husband following his death.

    In **"Originally"**, the speaker is the main character. Here she reflects on the difficulties she endured when moving from one place to another.

    Candidates may choose to answer in **bullet points** in this final question, or write a number of linked statements. There is **no requirement** to write a 'mini essay'.

    Up to 2 marks can be achieved for identifying elements of **commonality** as identified in the question.

    A further 2 marks can be achieved for **reference to the extract given**

    4 additional marks can be awarded for similar references to **at least one other poem** by the writer.

In practice this means:

**Identification of commonality** (eg: theme, central relationship, importance of setting, use of imagery, development in characterisation, use of personal experience, use of narrative style, or any other key element...)

**from the extract:**

1 × relevant reference to technique

1 × appropriate comment

or

1 × relevant reference to idea

1 × appropriate comment

or

1 × relevant reference to feature

1 × appropriate comment

or

1 × relevant reference to text

1 × appropriate comment

**(maximum of 2 marks only for discussion of extract)**

from **at least one poem by the writer:**

as above (× 2) for **up to 4 marks**

**Text 2 – Poetry – In the Snack-bar by Edwin Morgan**

41. (a) Candidates should identify two of the poem's main ideas or central concerns that are introduced in this extract.

    *Possible answers:*

    - how the less fortunate are treated in society

    - appearance and reality

    - isolation/loneliness

    - society's selfishness/lack of interest in helping others

    - for some disabled people tasks that might seem to be straightforward to us can involve many potential hazards

    - public places can be full of difficulties for some disabled people

    - society fears what looks strange

    - some disabled people have no choice but to rely on strangers to help them.

    (b) Examples of use of language with comment on how it clarifies a central concern

    *Possible answers:*

    - use of alliteration/"cup capsizes along the formica".

    **and/or**

    - use of onomatopoeia/"with a dull clatter"

    - to highlight the loudness of the sound made by the old man/the fact that other customers in the snack bar would have definitely heard his attempts to stand (but do nothing to help)

    - use of contrast/"a few heads turn in the crowded evening snack bar" to highlight that though the café was full very few people were prepared to show even the slightest interest in the old man's plight.

- use of simile/"like a monstrous animal caught in a tent"
- to highlight that the old man is seen by others as a terrifying creature
- use of direct speech/"I want – to go to the – toilet" to emphasise that the old man must ask strangers to help with the necessities of life
- use of dashes/"I want – to go to the – toilet" to highlight his uncertainty/anxiety.

42. Candidates should identify the change in the poet's role between stanzas 1 and 2.

In stanza 1 the poet is a mere observer – ( his only reference to himself is when he writes "I notice now his stick")

In stanza 2 the poet is a participant – (he is involved in what is going on and experiences first hand the old man's plight)

43. Candidates should comment on two ways in which the poet uses language to emphasise the difficulty of the start of the journey to the toilet.

*Possible answers:*

- he uses direct speech/"Give me – your arm – it's better" to emphasise the awkwardness of movement
- he says they move "Inch by inch"/reference to repetition which emphasises how slowly they move "a few yards of floor are like a landscape to be negotiated" shows how far it feels they have to travel/difficult crossing the floor is for them
- "drift"/"slow setting out"/"slow dangerous inches" suggests unfocused movement/limited progress/threat .
- he creates a long list of all the obstacles the old man has to cope with which highlights the many everyday objects that are challenging and/or dangerous to the old man
- "concentrate my life to his" emphasises understanding of the challenges faced by the old man.

44. Candidates should show their ability to analyse the poet's characterisation by referring closely and relevantly to the text of this poem and at least one other Morgan poem.

*Possible references:*

In Morgan's **"In the Snack-bar"** the poet creates an interesting character – a vulnerable blind man who relies on the poet's assistance.

Other interesting characters are presented in **"Trio"** where three individuals, who embody the spirit of Christmas, are walking up Buchanan Street.

In the opening line of **"Hyena"**, Morgan creates an interesting character. "I am waiting for you" establishes the intimidating nature of the persona. Through Morgan giving the hyena a voice, he brings the character to life by directly addressing the reader.

"Wait till he sees this but!" – Morgan's use of direct speech in **"Trio"** allows the reader to hear the excitement in the boy's voice as he anticipates the joy he will bring through his gift.

In **"Good Friday"** the drunk man is an interesting character because he openly acknowledges to a complete stranger his own lack of knowledge about Easter. This allows Morgan to explore the idea of the value of religion in modern society.

In **"Trio"** all three characters are interesting because through them Morgan explores the central idea of love. He details the objects they carry and celebrates the happiness they radiate.

Candidates may choose to answer in **bullet points** in this final question, or write a number of linked statements. There is **no requirement** to write a "mini essay".

Up to 2 marks can be achieved for identifying elements of **commonality** as identified in the question.

A further 2 marks can be achieved for **reference to the extract given**.

4 additional marks can be awarded for similar references to **at least one other poem** by the writer.

Underline: In practice this means:

**Identification of commonality** (eg: theme, central relationship, importance of setting, use of imagery, development in characterisation, use of personal experience, use of narrative style, or any other key element…)

**from the extract:**

1 × relevant reference to technique

1 × appropriate comment

**or**

1 × relevant reference to idea

1 × appropriate comment

**or**

1 × relevant reference to feature

1 × appropriate comment

**or**

1 × relevant reference to text

1 × appropriate comment

**(maximum of 2 marks only for discussion of extract)**

from **at least one other poem by the writer:**

as above (× 2) for **up to 4 marks**

**Text 3 — Poetry —** *Basking Shark* **by Norman MacCaig**

45. Incident (1 mark)

Relevant reference to text (1 mark)

Reaction (1 mark)

At sea/rowing/sticks oar in water/disturbs/hits a shark/shark rises up

**and**

disorientated "a rock where none should be"

**or**

threatened "rise with a slounge"

46. Two references (1 mark) with comment (1 mark)

"not too often though enough" rare occurrence but still prompted reflection

**and/or**

"I count as gain" valuable/thought-provoking experience

**and/or**

"roomsized monster with a/matchbox brain" humorous/not that frightening/insulting

47. Upset/changed/questioned MacCaig's certainty/
perspective/view of evolution

    **and**

    "he shoggled me centuries back" use of humour/made
MacCaig think about origins/evolution/life

    **or**

    "this decadent townee" thinks of his own position
culturally

    **or**

    "Shook on a branch of his family tree" evolution/that
they are different/same origin

48. *Possible answers:*

    "Swish up the dirt" disturbance of the water and
disturbance of MacCaig's thoughts/views

    **or**

    "a spring is all the clearer" once water settles, it is
clearer as are MacCaig's thoughts/views

    **or**

    "I saw me in one fling, emerging from the slime
of everything" makes him reflect on his own
origins/"slime" – primordial, viscous

49. Candidates should discuss how MacCaig uses personal
experience in this poem and in at least one other poem
to explore wider themes.

    Themes explored through experience:

    - the temporariness/insignificance of man
    - the relationship between man and other species, man
and nature
    - the randomness of the process of evolution
    - the scale of human evolution vs species which have
remained unchanged/unevolved.

    *Possible references:*

    **"Assissi"** The hypocrisy of the church/desensitization to
poverty and suffering.

    **"Aunt Julia"** – How lack of common language prevents
can be frustrating/prevent communication BUT despite
this a real bond between speaker and Aunt is clear. On
a wider level, this experience is a comment on the loss
of some traditional aspects of Scottish heritage that is in
danger of being lost.

    **"Memorial"** – Grief/Permanence, lack of relief from
sense of loss/Impact on death and grief on the artistic
process.

    **"Sounds of the Day"** – Impact of love and loss on the
psyche/Whether experience of relationship worth the
pain.

    **"Visiting Hour"** – Death and loss and our own attitudes
towards mortality.

    Candidates may choose to answer in **bullet points** in this
final question, or write a number of linked statements.
There is **no requirement** to write a 'mini essay'.

    Up to 2 marks can be achieved for identifying elements
of **commonality** as identified in the question.

    A further 2 marks can be achieved for **reference to the
extract given**.

    4 additional marks can be awarded for similar references
to **at least one other poem** by the writer.

    Un practice this means:

    **Identification of commonality** (eg: theme, central
relationship, importance of setting, use of imagery,
development in characterisation, use of personal
experience, use of narrative style, or any other key
element…)

    **from the extract:**

    1 × relevant reference to technique

    1 × appropriate comment

    **or**

    1 × relevant reference to idea

    1 × appropriate comment

    **or**

    1 × relevant reference to feature

    1 × appropriate comment

    **or**

    1 × relevant reference to text

    1 × appropriate comment

    **(maximum of 2 marks only for discussion of extract)**

    from **at least one other poem by the writer:**

    as above (× 2) for **up to 4 marks**

## Text 4 — Poetry — *Lucozade* by Jackie Kay

50. Two points for 2 marks:

    - Flowers wilt/die. This reminds her of illness/death/
being in hospital.
    - Ref to "sad chrysanthemums". Flowers don't make
her happy/she thinks they are pointless.
    - Lucozade reminds her of past. This brings thoughts of
possibility of death.

51. Two references with comment:

    - ref to "doctors with their white lies" she doesn't
trust doctors/like being in hospital
    - ref to "Don't bring magazines, too much about size"
she doesn't like media images of women/approve of
diets etc
    - ref. to "groggy and low" she is down/depressed
    - ref to any of "Big brandy … meringue" doesn't
approve of diets/she is unconventional/not a
stereotypical mother/likes to live for moment/has
her own opinions etc
    - ref to "luxury" she likes indulgence
    - ref to "grapes" she's not keen on conventions/
healthy eating
    - ref to "stop the neighbours coming" she is bored/
irritated by neighbours/small talk etc.

52. To be awarded full marks, candidates should identify
through references and comments some change – eg
sadness to celebration, negative to positive.

    Any three references plus acceptable comments for 6
marks.

    To gain 6 marks, both sides of change must be dealt
with.

    - "sad (chrysanthemums)" she is upset
    - "weighted (down)" she is burdened/full of negative
thoughts
    CHANGES TO
    - "high hospital bed" girl sees that mother is raised
up/not low (connotations of being elevated)

- "light"/"radiant"  positive connotations/optimistic
- "billow and whirl"  full of life/energy
- "beautiful"  admiration, pleasure
- "divine"  elevated etc
- "(singing) an old song"  good memories of the past

53. Candidates should identify a theme or themes from the poetry of Kay, and be able to show how it is explored in this poem and in at least one other poem by Kay.

Candidates are probably likely to identify one of the following themes:

Illness/death, Family Relationships, Parent/Child relationships

Possible references:

**"Bed"** – themes of **illness/infirmity/impending death AND/OR mother – daughter relationships**

**"Gap Year"** – Closeness of parent/child bond.

Candidates may also make reference to the CONTRAST between the obvious bond between the mother and daughter in **"Lucozade"** with the very different exploration of the parent/child relationships considered in **"Divorce"**, **"Keeping Orchids"** and to a lesser extent also in **"Bed"**

Candidates may choose to answer in **bullet points** in this final question, or write a number of linked statements. There is **no requirement** to write a 'mini essay'.

Up to 2 marks can be achieved for identifying elements of **commonality** as identified in the question.

A further 2 marks can be achieved for **reference to the extract given**.

4 additional marks can be awarded for similar references to **at least one other poem** by the writer.

<u>In practice this means:</u>

**Identification of commonality** (eg: theme, central relationship, importance of setting, use of imagery, development in characterisation, use of personal experience, use of narrative style, or any other key element…)

**from the extract:**

1 × relevant reference to technique

1 × appropriate comment

**or**

1 × relevant reference to idea

1 × appropriate comment

**or**

1 × relevant reference to feature

1 × appropriate comment

**or**

1 × relevant reference to text

1 × appropriate comment

**(maximum of 2 marks only for discussion of extract)**

from **at least one other poem by the writer:**

as above (× 2) for **up to 4 marks**

## SECTION 2 – Critical Essay

Please see the assessment criteria for the Critical Essay on page 165.

# NATIONAL 5 ENGLISH 2015

## READING FOR UNDERSTANDING, ANALYSIS AND EVALUATION

1.  Candidates should explain why the first paragraph is an effective opening for the passage.

    *Any three points from:*

    - It shows/introduces/explains/describes/connects to
    - the idea (fight-flight-freeze)/theme/focus of the text/the rat
    - creates interest/shock/pathos/drama.

    *Also accept:*

    - reference to second person/"you"
    - with chatty/informal tone
    - single word/minor sentence/short sentence/"Ferociously!"
    - series of short sentences.

2.  **Glosses of both words:**

    - "deeply" eg very/completely/profoundly
    - "ingrained" eg embedded/fixed/rooted/established/intuitive/natural/instinctive/in a long standing fashion.

3.  Candidates should explain in their own words two aspects of "danger" or "threat" for two past experiences and two present experiences, from lines 14–21.

    **Past – glosses of two:**

    - "head-on" eg direct/face to face
    - "regularly" eg frequent
    - "predators ...animal" eg creatures (which wanted to harm/kill us)
    - "predators ...human kind" eg others like us (wanted to harm/kill us, eg through wars)
    - accept example of predator
    - "to life or limb" eg real physical harm.

    **Present – glosses of two:**

    - "artificial" eg non-physical/psychological
    - "to ego" eg to pride/self-esteem/vanity
    - "to livelihood" eg to job/earnings
    - "(consequences of) messing up" eg doing it wrong
    - gloss of "taking exam"
    - gloss of "giving a speech"
    - gloss of "taking a penalty".

4.  Referring to lines 22–37, candidate should summarise using their own words some of the changes in the body which occur with the response.

    **Changes – glosses of:**

    - "acceleration of heart ... function" eg the heart beats more quickly
    - "acceleration of ... lung function" eg breath comes faster
    - "there is paling and flushing" eg the skin changes colour
    - "there is an inhibition of stomach action, such that

    digestion almost completely ceases" eg the intestines work less
    - "there is a constriction (of blood vessels)" eg (blood vessels) narrow
    - "there is a freeing up of metabolic energy sources (fat and glycogen)" eg feel more energetic
    - "there is a dilation (of the pupils)" eg the eyes widen/expand/enlarge
    - "a relaxation of the bladder" eg waterworks loosen
    - "perception narrows" eg concentration is (more) focused
    - "shaking"/"trembling" eg shuddering or quaking or similar
    - "prime (the muscles)" eg prepare/ready (the muscles)
    - "increase body strength" eg become stronger
    - "increase ... blood pressure" eg higher (blood pressure)
    - "(become) hyper-vigilant" eg more alert/pay more attention
    - "(adrenalin) pumping like crazy" eg increase (in adrenalin)
    - "taut" eg tense/tightened
    - "pumped" eg ready.

5.  The candidate must offer an explanation on how the sentence "How to deal with these responses?" in line 44 provides an appropriate link at this point of the passage.

    - "These responses" looks back
    - "How"/"to deal" or question (mark) looks forward

    or

    - "These responses" looks back
    - to actions of team-mates or inner dialogue

    or

    - "How"/"to deal" or question (mark) looks forward
    - to identification of strategy (may quote "reflection")

    or

    - reference to the ideas in the text before the link
    - reference to the ideas in the text after the link.

6.  By referring to lines 50–54, the candidate must explain **two** examples of the writer's word choice which demonstrate the "benefit" of the response.

    *Any two points from:*

    - "huge" eg considerable
    - "therapeutic" eg it helps
    - "It takes the edge off" eg it makes us calmer
    - "(It makes a ... bewildering reaction) into a comprehensible one" eg (it turns a baffling/puzzling reaction) into one which we understand
    - "liberation" eg freeing
    - "(liberation) from tyranny" eg from oppression
    - "pressure" eg stress.

7. The candidate should explain the attitude of top athletes to pressure, and how two examples of the language used make this attitude clear with reference to lines 55–61.

Identification of attitude, eg pressure can be positive/beneficial.

*Possible answers include:*

- "paradoxical" /reference to paradox eg emphasises that expectation is worse than reality

- "Pressure is not a problem" eg bluntly states attitude

- "privilege" eg shows that this is something positive

- colon to introduce motto/mantra

- reference to alliteration eg accentuates the positive

- semi-colon after "problem" complements the balance

- balance/(idea of) antithesis of "Pressure ... privilege" draws attention to the bilateral nature

- example(s) cited of famous sportsmen suggests agreement

- "perfectly open" suggests acceptance

- reference to "but" starting sentence emphasises the contrast

- "great pride" emphasises how good they feel

- "facing up to them" shows positive attitude to confronting them

- "they didn't see these ... as signs of weakness" provides a clear statement

- "They created mechanisms" suggests coping strategies

- "grow" emphasises a chance to develop

- "seized (every opportunity)" shows they are keen

- repetition of "They" at the start of a sentence/parallel structure shows affirmative nature of the attitude.

8. The candidate should fully explain using their own words why the advice to "grab" the opportunity might at first seem strange by referring to lines 62–67.

*Any three points from:*

**Then**

**Glosses of:**

- "you will feel uncomfortable" eg you will find it awkward/unpleasant/unnerving

- "your stomach will knot" eg you will feel physically stressed

- "at the moment of truth, you will wish to be anywhere else in the world" eg at the critical/vital time you would wish you were not doing it

- "a nation's expectations on their shoulders" eg much is being hoped for you/pressure is applied/your patriotism is under test.

9. The candidate should pick an expression from the final paragraph (lines 68–71) and show how it helps to contribute to an effective conclusion to the passage.

Reference to an expression from earlier in the article should be made.

*Possible answers include:*

- "paradoxical" eg repeats word used earlier (line 55)

- "you will grow, learn and mature" eg revisits actual words "grow" (line 56) or "learnt" (line 57) or ideas of athletes profiting from the experience

- "on the football pitch" eg refers back to lines 9–12 or the title

- "in the office" eg refers back to "job interview" (line 45) or "at work" (lines 19–20)

- "fluff your lines" eg refers back to "giving a speech" (line 17)

- "if you miss" eg refers back to "taking a penalty" (line 17).

## NATIONAL 5 ENGLISH 2015

### CRITICAL READING

### SECTION 1 — Scottish Text

### SCOTTISH TEXT — DRAMA

### Text 1 — Drama — *Bold Girls* by Rona Munro

1. Candidates should show an understanding of the key events in this scene. Although the scene is short, many points are revealed here.

   Candidates should deal with four separate points.

   *Possible answers include:*
   - Marie says she does not know how Cassie coped with Joe's affairs
   - Marie displays an idealised view of her relationship with Michael
   - Cassie seems to be preparing herself to confess her affair to Marie
   - Cassie reacts against her environment
   - Marie assures her there are things to look forward to
   - Cassie says she is leaving
   - Marie is shocked
   - Cassie talks about her mother's idealised treatment of the men-folk in prison
   - Cassie admits to stealing money from Nora by exploiting her lack of knowledge re the price of fruit
   - Cassie shows humour/sarcasm in describing her predicament
   - Cassie shows realism
   - Marie shows her concern.

2. Candidates should show understanding of the attitudes of Marie.

   Marie feels that men can be untrustworthy.

   Marie has a romantic/idealised view of her relationship with Michael.

   Candidates should refer to the dialogue and quotation is expected to support the argument.

   1 mark for relevant quotation selected.

   1 mark for appropriate comment about the attitude it reveals.

   *Possible answers include:*
   - "I don't know how you coped with all Joe's carry on." plus comment
   - "You were the martyr there, Cassie" plus comment
   - "I couldn't have stood that, just the lying to you" plus comment
   - "It'll tear the heart out of me but tell me, just tell me the truth 'cause I'd want to know." plus comment
   - "I never worried." plus comment
   - "he was like my best friend" plus comment
   - "that's what I miss most. The crack. The sharing." plus comment.

3. Candidates should demonstrate understanding of at least two aspects of Cassie's mood.

   1 mark for selection of relevant reference.

   1 mark for appropriate comment.

Cassie is in a reflective mood at the start of the extract. Her replies are short and monosyllabic/"It gave me peace."

She becomes more hesitant/regretful as indicated by the ellipsis/"Marie…"

She becomes angry and kicks the ground she stands on/"Aw Jesus I hate this place!"/she uses an exclamation

She makes a stand/she becomes defiant "I'm leaving"

She is sullen/belligerent She does not elaborate/"Cassie says nothing"

She complains at length about the way Joe and Martin are treated by Nora. She becomes sarcastic/"…she can spoil them with fruit…"

Sarcastic/bitter "I'll bring her home something that looks and smells like the Botanic Gardens…"

She becomes emphatic (about her plans to leave) "I've two hundred pounds saved. I'm going."

She then criticises herself (for stealing from Nora) "It's desperate isn't it? Thirty-five years old and she's stealing from her mummy's purse."

4. Candidates should discuss the treatment of gender in this extract and in at least one other scene from the play.

   **Points likely to be made about women include:**
   - Women take care of domestic work
   - They struggle to make ends meet
   - They support their friends
   - They look after the children
   - They do not have the same "social" freedom as men
   - They support their men in prison
   - They live with the threat of paramilitary/domestic violence.

   **Points likely to be made about men include:**
   - Men are more likely to be imprisoned
   - Men imprisoned for paramilitary activities are highly regarded by their community
   - Men have more "social freedom"
   - Men "con" each other
   - Men do not carry out domestic chores
   - Men are more likely to commit acts of domestic violence.

   Candidates may choose to answer in **bullet points** in this final question, or write a number of linked statements. There is **no requirement** to write a "mini essay".

   Up to 2 marks can be achieved for identifying elements of **commonality** as identified in the question.

   A further 2 marks can be achieved for **reference to the extract given**.

   4 additional marks can be awarded for similar references to **at least one other text/part of the text** by the writer.

   In practice this means:

   **Identification of commonality** (eg: theme, central relationship, importance of setting, use of imagery, development in characterisation, use of personal experience, use of narrative style, or any other key element…)

**from the extract:**

1 × relevant reference to technique

1 × appropriate comment

**or**

1 × relevant reference to idea

1 × appropriate comment

**or**

1 × relevant reference to feature

1 × appropriate comment

**or**

1 × relevant reference to text

1 × appropriate comment

**(maximum of 2 marks only for discussion of extract)**

from **at least one other text/part of the text:**

as above (× 2) for **up to 4 marks**

**Text 2 – Drama – *Sailmaker* by Alan Spence**

5. Any two points to summarise the situation for one mark each.

*Possible answers include:*

- Alec's mother/Davie's wife has died
- Alec is beginning to come to terms with his mother's death
- Davie is struggling to cope with his grief/the death of his wife
- They are getting the house ready for visitors after the funeral.

6. Candidates should refer to **both** the weather and the setting for full marks.

1 mark for reference.

1 mark for comment.

*Possible answers include:*

**Weather**

- "breeze was warm"/"the breeze touched my cheek"/"sun shone"/"glinted"/"clouds moving across"
- Reflects Alec's feeling that his mother has gone to heaven/is safe
- "wee patch of clear blue"
- Patch of blue symbolises his mother going to heaven/a sign from her to reassure him.

**Setting**

- "ordinary"/"Nothing had changed" in contrast to the enormity of their loss
- "grey tenements"/"middens ... dustbins ... spilled ashes"/"broken glass"
- Setting is drab/miserable reflects their feelings of despair/depression/bereavement/poverty
- Evidence of rubbish/vandalism suggests lack of care his mother is now in a better place away from here
- "wee boy playing mouth organ"
- Notes on the mouth-organ sound like a bugle call as his mother leaves this world and enters heaven/ reflects feelings of sadness.

7. Candidates should clearly identify how Davie is coping with his current situation.

Candidates should support their responses with quotation and/or reference.

1 mark for reference.

1 mark for comment.

*Possible answers include:*

**Supporting evidence:**

- Short sentence(s) to start speech  Davie is trying to keep busy to avoid thinking
- Long sentence with no punctuation  reflects Davie's mind – he is trying to do lots of things to avoid stopping and thinking
- Repetition of "nearly"/2nd time with italics for emphasis suggests he can never actually manage to forget
- "Christ" use of blasphemy suggests the strength of his feeling
- Use of 2nd  person pronoun  "ye"/"you" – to distance himself from situation/make it more general rather than face up to it
- List of things Davie does reflects him carrying out a number of tasks to avoid thinking
- "whole minutes" emphasises how often he is thinking about his wife
- "hit(s) ye" – suggests the almost physical nature of his pain.

8. Candidates should focus on the language used by the characters.

2 marks for identification of two differences.

*Possible answers include:*

- Alec speaks in English, Davie speaks in Scots
- Alec's words are in the past tense, Davie's words are in the present tense
- Alec's words are in sentences, Davie's sentences lack punctuation
- Alec's sentences are short(er), Davie's are long(er)
- Alec's sentences are (more) structured, Davie's are (more) unstructured/chaotic
- Alec's words are more descriptive/poetic, Davie's words are more matter of fact/down to earth
- Alec's words act as narration, Davie's words act as the speech of a character.

9. Candidates should identify the way the father-son relationship is developed in this extract and elsewhere in the play.

*Possible comments from elsewhere include:*

- Admiration at start of play
- Spending the bursary money
- Drinking/gambling issues
- Lack of trust
- Neglect/physical abuse
- Acceptance of going separate ways
- Burning yacht etc a resolution/more positive
- Contrast with Billy and Ian's relationship.

Candidates may choose to answer in **bullet points** in this final question, or write a number of linked statements. There is **no requirement** to write a 'mini essay'.

Up to 2 marks can be achieved for identifying elements of **commonality** as identified in the question.

A further 2 marks can be achieved for **reference to the extract** given.

4 additional marks can be awarded for similar references to **at least one other text/part of the text** by the writer.

In practice this means:

**Identification of commonality** (eg: theme, central relationship, importance of setting, use of imagery, development in characterisation, use of personal experience, use of narrative style, or any other key element...)

**from the extract:**

1 × relevant reference to technique

1 × appropriate comment

**or**

1 × relevant reference to idea

1 × appropriate comment

**or**

1 × relevant reference to feature

1 × appropriate comment

**or**

1 × relevant reference to text

1 × appropriate comment

**(maximum of 2 marks only for discussion of extract)**

from **at least one other text/part of the text:**

as above (× 2) for **up to 4 marks**

**Text 3 – Drama – *Tally's Blood* by Ann Marie de Mambro**

10. Candidates need to cover four separate points to achieve full marks.

    *Possible answers include:*

    - Her father had arranged for her to marry someone else (Ferdinando, who had a lot of land)
    - Then she met Massimo and fell in love at first sight/very quickly
    - Her father wouldn't allow it and locked her in a room
    - Massimo climbed up to rescue her
    - They spent the evening together hiding up a tree
    - To deliberately cause a scandal
    - So they would have to be allowed to get married.

11. Candidates should deal with four of the points suggested. For full marks they must show some **change** in Rosinella's thoughts.

    1 mark for reference.

    1 mark for comment.

    *Possible answers include:*

    - At first she is "*Cagey*" suggesting she is reluctant initially
    - Then she starts "*Getting into it*" suggesting she is starting to take some pleasure in it

- She is "*Undecided about whether or not to tell*" suggesting she is unsure about what to do
- "*but then does so with glee*" suggesting that she is taking delight in it
- "*Enjoying it now*" suggests she is taking pleasure from it
- "*Mimics the sound*" suggests she is telling the story with some conviction
- By the end she is "*Moved by her story*" suggesting she is completely involved.

12. 1 mark for identification of tone.

    1 mark for comment.

    *Possible tones might include:*

    nostalgic, romantic, reflective, wistful, humorous, etc.

    Any reasonable justification for answer.

13. Candidates are only being asked to identify examples from the extract.

    *Possible examples include:*

    "wee", "awfy", "they" (instead of those), "no" (instead of not), "faither", "wean", "hen", "ma" (instead of my).

    Any two for 1 mark each.

14. Candidates should discuss how romantic relationships are developed in this extract and elsewhere in the play.

    *Possible comments from elsewhere include:*

    - Comment on forbidden relationships
    - Lucia and Hughie are childhood friends who end up in a relationship
    - Franco and Bridget's difficult relationship
    - Rosinella and Massimo's elopement and enduring relationship.

Candidates may choose to answer in **bullet points** in this final question, or write a number of linked statements. There is **no requirement** to write a "mini essay".

Up to 2 marks can be achieved for identifying elements of **commonality** as identified in the question.

A further 2 marks can be achieved for **reference to the extract given.**

4 additional marks can be awarded for similar references to **at least one other text/part of the text** by the writer.

In practice this means:

**Identification of commonality** (eg: theme, central relationship, importance of setting, use of imagery, development in characterisation, use of personal experience, use of narrative style, or any other key element...)

**from the extract:**

1 × relevant reference to technique

1 × appropriate comment

**or**

1 × relevant reference to idea

1 × appropriate comment

**or**

1 × relevant reference to feature

1 × appropriate comment

**or**

1 × relevant reference to text

1 × appropriate comment

**(maximum of 2 marks only for discussion of extract)**

from **at least one other text/part of the text:**

as above (× 2) for **up to 4 marks**

**Text 1 – Prose – *The Cone-Gatherers* by Robin Jenkins**

**15.** Any two for one mark each.

*Possible answers include:*

- sensitive
- gentle
- empathy with animals
- clumsy in his movements (when not in the trees)
- upset.

**16.** 1 mark for identification.

1 mark for comment.

*Possible answers include:*

- "Icy sweat of hatred" plus comment
- "His gun aimed at the (feebleminded) hunchback" plus comment
- "The obscene squeal of the killed dwarf" plus comment
- "Noose of disgust and despair" plus comment.

**17.** 1 mark for any one quotation.

1 mark for comment.

*Possible answers include:*

- Sea imagery – "sea of branches"/"fantastic sea"/"quiet as fish"/"seaweed"/"submarine monsters" plus comment
- "bronzen brackens" plus comment
- "the overspreading tree of revulsion" plus comment.

**18.** Candidates must show Duror's feelings before and after.

Before the arrival he felt safe/happy/secure/peaceful/calm, etc there.

After the arrival he felt it had been spoiled/ruined, etc for him.

**19.** Candidates should discuss how the character of Calum is presented in this extract and elsewhere in the novel.

*Possible answers from elsewhere include:*

- Calum's gentleness
- Examples of descriptions of Calum's gentleness
- References to Calum's clumsiness when he is not in the trees
- Detailed description of nature (and how it relates to Calum) which occurs throughout the novel.

Candidates may choose to answer in **bullet points** in this final question, or write a number of linked statements. There is **no requirement** to write a "mini essay".

Up to 2 marks can be achieved for identifying elements of **commonality** as identified in the question.

A further 2 marks can be achieved for **reference to the extract given.**

4 additional marks can be awarded for similar references to **at least one other text/part of the text** by the writer.

In practice this means:

**Identification of commonality** (eg: theme, central relationship, importance of setting, use of imagery, development in characterisation, use of personal experience, use of narrative style, or any other key element...)

**from the extract:**

1 × relevant reference to technique

1 × appropriate comment

or

1 × relevant reference to idea

1 × appropriate comment

or

1 × relevant reference to feature

1 × appropriate comment

or

1 × relevant reference to text (1)

1 × appropriate comment (1)

**(maximum of 2 marks only for discussion of extract)**

from **at least one other text/part of the text:**

as above (× 2) for **up to 4 marks**

**Text 2 – Prose – *The Testament of Gideon Mack* by James Robertson**

**20.** 1 mark for each identification of aspect.

*Possible answers include:*

- Two faced/duplicitous
- rebellious
- made himself inconspicuous
- clever/crafty.

**21. (a)** 1 mark for reference.

1 mark for comment.

*Possible answers include:*

- "went through with the whole business" suggesting difficulty or hardship or lack of enjoyment
- "a rigorous undertaking" suggesting difficulty or hardship
- "an even greater commitment" suggesting a lot is being asked of him
- "you would have to go a long way...but I did" suggesting his task was harder or that he achieved more than others
- "dissected and deciphered" suggesting the in-depth nature of the work.

**(b)** 1 mark for reference.

1 mark for comment.

*Possible answers include:*

- "think of this" – use of command to get the reader's attention/force the reader to consider the task
- repetition of "the nature of" to emphasise the full extent of the task
- listing to emphasise the sheer number of topics covered
- repetition in "many, many hours" to emphasise the time spent on this.

**22.** 1 mark for comment on the relationship.

1 mark for supporting evidence.

*Possible answers include:*

- grudging admiration – "respect"
- understanding from Mack – "I was there with him"
- still a lack of closeness between them – "a part of me was keeping its distance".

**23.** Candidates should discuss how the theme of deception is explored in this extract and elsewhere in the novel.

*Possible comments from elsewhere include:*

- he became a minister although he doesn't believe in God
- he continues to be hypocritical within his profession
- the first person narration allows the reader to see the inner thoughts versus the outward appearance
- various individual scenes of duplicity throughout the novel, any two examples.

Candidates may choose to answer in **bullet points** in this final question, or write a number of linked statements. There is **no requirement** to write a "mini essay".

Up to 2 marks can be achieved for identifying elements of **commonality** as identified in the question.

A further 2 marks can be achieved for **reference to the extract given.**

4 additional marks can be awarded for similar references to **at least one other text/part of the text** by the writer.

In practice this means:

**Identification of commonality** (eg: theme, central relationship, importance of setting, use of imagery, development in characterisation, use of personal experience, use of narrative style, or any other key element...)

**from the extract:**

1 × relevant reference to technique

1 × appropriate comment

or

1 × relevant reference to idea

1 × appropriate comment

or

1 × relevant reference to feature

1 × appropriate comment

or

1 × relevant reference to text

1 × appropriate comment

**(maximum of 2 marks only for discussion of extract)**

from **at least one other text/part of the text:**

as above (× 2) for **up to 4 marks**

**Text 3 – Prose –** *Kidnapped* **by Robert Louis Stevenson**

**24.** Four points to be made.

One mark for each point.

*Possible answers include:*

- David arrives in/near Edinburgh
- David asks for directions to Cramond
- David sees/hears the redcoats
- David asks/talks to a man with a cart about the house of Shaws
- David receives negative response from the carter
- David asks/talks to a barber about the house of Shaws
- David receives negative response from the barber
- David is left concerned.

**25.** There should be an understanding that David believes that it is the juxtaposition between his simple, grubby clothes which jarred with his asking about – what he thought was – a grand house such as the Shaws.

**A gloss of:**

"At first I thought the plainness of my appearance, in my country habit, and that all dusty from the road," (1 mark)

"consorted ill with the greatness of the place to which I was bound." (1 mark)

**26. (a)** 1 mark for statement of mood in opening paragraph.

1 mark for example of writer's use of language in opening paragraph.

1 mark for comment on language.

*Possible answers include:*

- mood – optimistic, happy, content, etc.

**Word choice:**

- "pleasure" have a great liking/desire
- "wonder" – as to marvel at a great spectacle
- "beheld" – to observe something of great impact
- "pride" delight/joy at the sight
- "merry (music)" – joyful/happy.

**Metaphor:**

- "the pride of life seemed to mount into my brain" to be at the forefront of the mind/to be directly connected to the mind in a powerful way.

**Alliteration:**

- "merry music" repeated "m" sound has a length which pleasant, soft, jaunty and childlike in its alliterative use.

**(b)** 1 mark for statement of mood in final paragraph.

1 mark for example of writer's use of language in final paragraph.

1 mark for comment on language.

*Possible answers include:*

- mood – pessimistic, confused, perturbed, etc.

**Word choice:**

- "illusions" – deceptive/misconception
- "indistinct" – unclear
- "accusations" – negative connotations of illegal actions
- "fancy" imagination not reality
- "start and stare" showing shock at the mention of Shaws (also could award marks for the sharp alliterative effect of the sibilance)
- "ill-fame" – of poor reputation.

Metaphor:

- "the blow this dealt to my illusions" – affected almost physically/violently as with a blow.

Sentence structure:

- use of two questions/placement of questions at end of paragraph emphasising doubt and confusion/climactic nature.

27. Candidates should discuss the development of David Balfour's character in this extract and elsewhere in the novel.

    *Possible comments from elsewhere include:*

    - becomes more adventurous
    - becomes more experienced
    - becomes more confident
    - any two specific points in the novel which show his development.

    Candidates may choose to answer in **bullet points** in this final question, or write a number of linked statements. There is **no requirement** to write a "mini essay".

    Up to 2 marks can be achieved for identifying elements of **commonality** as identified in the question.

    A further 2 marks can be achieved for **reference to the extract given.**

    4 additional marks can be awarded for similar references to **at least one other text/part of the text** by the writer.

    In practice this means:

    **Identification of commonality** (eg: theme, central relationship, importance of setting, use of imagery, development in characterisation, use of personal experience, use of narrative style, or any other key element…)

    **from the extract:**

    1 × relevant reference to technique

    1 × appropriate comment

    **or**

    1 × relevant reference to idea

    1 × appropriate comment

    **or**

    1 × relevant reference to feature

    1 × appropriate comment

    **or**

    1 × relevant reference to text

    1 × appropriate comment

    **(maximum of 2 marks only for discussion of extract)**

    from **at least one other text/part of the text:**

    as above (× 2) for **up to 4 marks**

**Text 4 – Prose – *Mother and Son* by Iain Crichton Smith**

28. Candidates should give 4 relevant points for 1 mark each.

    *Possible answers include:*

    - Constantly ridicules him – "always laughed at him"
    - Picks on him/highlights his faults persistently – "pecked cruelly at his defences"

- Hates the power she has over him despite her frailty – "What is she anyway?"/"How can this thing….?"
- Anger that she uses illness as a reason to behave as she does – "She's been ill…doesn't excuse her"
- Anger that she is destroying his life – "she's breaking me up"
- Also his chances of a life in the future – "if she dies…good for anyone."
- Blames her for his loneliness/isolation from his peers – "shivered inside his loneliness"/"That would be the boys…".

29. 1 mark for reference.

    1 mark for comment.

    *Possible examples/explanations:*

    - "face had sharpened itself… quickness"/"pecking at….cruelly at his defences" – emphasises her sharpness/although small and frail like a bird has the capacity to destroy him
    - "some kind of animal"/"this thing" – makes her seem less than human
    - "breaking me up" – idea that she is destroying him
    - Description of his angry actions shows his feelings
    - "abrupt"/"savage"/shaking with anger towards her/"rage shook him" shows how angry he is
    - Use of questions/"How can this thing…"/"What is she anyway?" Emphasise the hateful thoughts he has towards her.

30. 1 mark for reference.

    1 mark for comment.

    *Possible examples/explanations:*

    - (sense of loneliness) "closed around him" feels engulfed by loneliness
    - "on a boat on the limitless ocean" feels adrift and alone in an endless sea
    - (compares this to his own home) "just as his house was on a limitless moorland" – gives sense of isolation.

31. 1 mark for reference.

    1 mark for comment.

    *Possible answers include:*

    - "Remember to clean the tray tomorrow"/mother's words are seen as provocative
    - "fighting back the anger" suggests rising emotion
    - "swept over him" overwhelming feelings
    - "He turned back to the bed." – it's a dramatic moment
    - (Repetition of) "smash" suggestion of potential violence
    - (Repetition of) "there was" creation of drama
    - Final short sentence makes for dramatic ending.

32. Candidates should discuss a character's realisation in this extract as well as at least one other character's realisation from at least one other story.

    *Possible comments from other stories include:*

    **'The Telegram'** – true destination of telegram, more understanding between the two women

'**The Red Door**' – realisation of sense of freedom for main character

'**In Church**' – realisation of futility of war

'**The Painter**' – realisation of unpleasantness of community.

Candidates may choose to answer in **bullet points** in this final question, or write a number of linked statements. There is **no requirement** to write a "mini essay".

Up to 2 marks can be achieved for identifying elements of **commonality** as identified in the question.

A further 2 marks can be achieved for **reference to the extract given.**

4 additional marks can be awarded for similar references to **at least one other text/part of the text** by the writer.

<u>In practice this means:</u>

**Identification of commonality (2)** (eg: theme, central relationship, importance of setting, use of imagery, development in characterisation, use of personal experience, use of narrative style, or any other key element…)

**from the extract:**

1 × relevant reference to technique

1 × appropriate comment

**or**

1 × relevant reference to idea

1 × appropriate comment

**or**

1 × relevant reference to feature

1 × appropriate comment

**or**

1 × relevant reference to text

1 × appropriate comment

**(maximum of 2 marks only for discussion of extract)**

from **at least one other text/part of the text:**

as above (× 2) for **up to 4 marks**

**Text 5 – Prose –** *All That Glisters* **by Anne Donovan**

33. Four separate points for one mark each.

    *Possible answers include:*
    - The family prepare for the funeral
    - Father's body put in parents' bedroom
    - Girl asked if she wants to see body
    - Girl has mixed feelings about seeing the body
    - Girl feels her mother is acting aloof
    - Girl gets dressed for funeral
    - Auntie Pauline reacts badly to girl's choice of outfit
    - Memory of wearing dress for father
    - Memory of father's approval.

34. 1 mark for reference.

    1 mark for comment.

    *Possible answers include:*
    - "blur" unclear/many things happening/movement
    - Movement of people "comin and goin" busy/confusing

    - ("makin sandwiches" and "pourin oot glasses of whisky") for "men in overcoats" whom she doesn't recognise, perhaps distant or seldom seen relatives
    - "makin sandwiches"/"pourin oot glasses of whisky" suggests endless hospitality
    - reference to listing or use of commas suggests confusion of events or lack of clarity.

35. 1 mark for identification of feature.

    *Possible answers include:*
    - (Repeated) use of first person
    - Use of parenthesis
    - Use of question
    - Use of Scots
    - Use of colloquial language
    - Long/rambling sentences.

36. 1 mark for reference.

    1 mark for comment.

    *Possible answers include:*
    - "her face froze over" shows her disgust/astonishment
    - Use of (rhetorical) question/"Whit the hell do you think you're daein?" shows shock/disapproval
    - Use of (expletive)/"hell" shows anger
    - Use of imperatives/"Go…get changed" shows her disapproval of the outfit
    - Instructions/commands/insistence show her disapproval.

37. Candidates should discuss how the theme of relationships is explored in this extract and in at least one other story by Donovan.

    *Possible comments from other stories include:*

    '**A Chitterin' Bite**' – breakdown of two relationships, loss of friendship etc

    '**Zimmerobics**' – relationships across generations

    '**Dear Santa**'/'**Away in a Manger**' – mother-daughter relationships

    Candidates may choose to answer in **bullet points** in this final question, or write a number of linked statements. There is **no requirement** to write a "mini essay".

    Up to 2 marks can be achieved for identifying elements of **commonality** as identified in the question.

    A further 2 marks can be achieved for **reference to the extract given.**

    4 additional marks can be awarded for similar references to **at least one other text/part of the text** by the writer.

    <u>In practice this means:</u>

    **Identification of commonality** (eg: theme, central relationship, importance of setting, use of imagery, development in characterisation, use of personal experience, use of narrative style, or any other key element…)

    **from the extract:**

    1 × relevant reference to technique

    1 × appropriate comment

    **or**

1 × relevant reference to idea

1 × appropriate comment

**or**

1 × relevant reference to feature

1 × appropriate comment

**or**

1 × relevant reference to text

1 × appropriate comment

**(maximum of 2 marks only for discussion of extract)**

from **at least one other text/part of the text:**

as above (× 2) for **up to 4 marks**

**Text 1 – Poetry – *Valentine* by Carol Ann Duffy**

38. Two marks can be awarded for two main ideas or concerns shown in first two lines.

    Only one mark should be awarded for one main idea or concern.

    *Possible answers include:*

    - (The unsatisfactory nature of) traditional Valentine gifts
    - The rejection of a clichéd/conventional view of love
    - Offering of an alternative
    - The need to be honest/truthful about love
    - The importance of recognising the mundane/ unpleasant aspects of love.

39. Four marks can be awarded for two examples of language used to create a positive view of love.

    1 mark for example.

    1 mark for comment.

    *Possible answers include:*

    - The word choice of "moon" suggests romance/is a conventional romantic symbol
    - The word choice of "promised" suggests commitment/guarantee that love will flourish
    - The word choice of "light" links to "moon" to reinforce romantic associations/has positive connotations linked to goodness or truth
    - The word choice of "careful" has connotations of tenderness
    - The comparison of removing the skin of an onion to "undressing" adds seductive/sexual element.

40. Two marks can be awarded for one example of language used to create a negative view of love.

    1 mark for example.

    1 mark for comment.

    *Possible answers include:*

    - "blind you with tears" suggests upset/pain
    - "blind" suggests the distortion/lack of clarity cc
    - "a wobbling photo of grief" suggests unsettling/ distorting nature of love Accept comments on "photo" or "grief" itself
    - The personification of "kiss" as "fierce"/word choice of "fierce" suggests danger/threat/aggression

    - "will stay on your lips" (to suggest the lingering taste of the onion) suggests the difficulty of escaping a relationship
    - The word choice of "possessive" suggests jealousy/ desire to control
    - The juxtaposition of "possessive" and "faithful" undermines the normally positive view of commitment
    - The inclusion/qualification of "for as long" suggests that the commitment will not last.

41. Candidates should show understanding of the term "conclusion" and how the content of the last stanza continues ideas and/or language from the earlier stanzas.

    2 marks for reference to the final stanza referring back to earlier in the poem.

    *Possible answers include:*

    - (The imperative) "Take it" continues the portrayal of the speaker as commanding/insistent
    - (The imperative) "Take it" concludes a series of imperatives to suggest the listener's reluctance to accept the gift
    - "platinum" suggests the enduring value of love (despite the negative features highlighted)
    - "loops" suggests never ending commitment/ constraint/control highlighted earlier
    - "shrink" reinforces the claustrophobic/constraining nature of marriage
    - The comparison of the inner rings of the onion to a "wedding ring" continues the subverting of conventional symbols of love/reinforces the constraining nature of marriage
    - The parody of a wedding proposal in " if you like "continues the subverting of conventional romantic symbols
    - The positioning of "Lethal" in a line of its own/the word choice of "Lethal" develops/reinforces previous examples of aggression
    - "cling"/repetition of "cling" links back to the "possessive" nature of love mentioned earlier
    - "knife" reinforces love as menacing or dangerous.

42. Candidates should show awareness of the ideas and/or language of this poem and at least one other poem by Duffy.

    *Possible comments from other poems include:*

    **"Havisham"** – pain of relationship breaking down

    **"Originally"** – relationship with environment/identity/ self-knowledge

    **"Ann Hathaway"** – sexual relationship

    **"War Photographer"** – photographer's relationship with work/material

    **"Mrs Midas"** – breakdown in relationship/memories of good times.

    Candidates may choose to answer in **bullet points** in this final question, or write a number of linked statements. There is **no requirement** to write a "mini essay".

    Up to 2 marks can be achieved for identifying elements of **commonality** as identified in the question.

A further 2 marks can be achieved for **reference to the extract given.**

4 additional marks can be awarded for similar references to **at least one other text/part of the text** by the writer.

<u>In practice this means:</u>

**Identification of commonality** (eg: theme, central relationship, importance of setting, use of imagery, development in characterisation, use of personal experience, use of narrative style, or any other key element...)

**from the extract:**

1 × relevant reference to technique

1 × appropriate comment

**or**

1 × relevant reference to idea

1 × appropriate comment

**or**

1 × relevant reference to feature

1 × appropriate comment

**or**

1 × relevant reference to text

1 × appropriate comment

**(maximum of 2 marks only for discussion of extract)**

from **at least one other text/part of the text:**

as above (× 2) for **up to 4 marks**

**Text 2 – Poetry – *Hyena* by Edwin Morgan**

43. For full marks answers should make two clear points.

One mark for each point. Own words required.

*Possible answers include:*

- Hyena is patient
- Hyena is dangerous/threatening
- Hyena is self-obsessed
- Hyena is hungry and thirsty
- Hunger makes hyena more threatening
- Hyena must not be underestimated
- Hyena may appear to be asleep but can pounce at any time.

44. Two references plus comments on two features used by the writer in these lines.

1 mark for reference.

1 mark for comment.

*Possible answers include:*

- "I have a rough coat" **or** "with dark spots like the bush-tufted plains of Africa" **or** "a shaggy bundle" – he is inelegant/scruffy
- "crafty" he is sly/clever
- "I sprawl ... of gathered energy" eg he appears to be relaxed but is ready to pounce
- "I lope, I slaver" – he is ungainly/clumsy
- The list describes the hyena's movement, etc
- "I am a ranger" he scans the landscape for dead animals

- Reference to "I eat the dead" eg he profits by feeding on creatures already dead/lacks the dignity or skill of a hunter, etc
- Use of short sentences suggests threatening nature of hyena/his grim certainty, etc
- Use of repetition suggests threatening nature, etc
- Use of question suggests apparent confidence of hyena, etc.

45. 1 mark for reference to feature.

1 mark for comment relating to tense, menacing atmosphere.

*Possible answers include:*

- Use of questions to emphasise the hyena's slyness or power
- Use of euphemism as the hyena calls his howl his "song"
- Reference to aspects of setting/background, eg "moon pours hard and cold" suggests eerie place
- Use of short sentences to increase tension
- Conversational tone eg "Would you meet me there in the waste places?" creating false sense of friendliness
- "my golden supper" is a macabre image
- "I am not laughing" is a chilling statement
- "crowd of fangs" is threatening/dangerous
- "I am not laughing" could be seen as a threat/warning.

46. For 2 marks, candidates should refer to a feature of the last stanza and show how it effectively continues an idea/language feature from earlier in the poem.

*Possible answers include:*

- "I am waiting" repeats opening line/reiterates that the hyena is always ready to feed on carrion/gives the poem a cyclical structure
- "I am crouching ... till you are ready for me" recalls the hyena lying in wait in stanza one
- "My place is to pick you clean and leave your bones to the wind" brings the references to "you" throughout the poem to a macabre climax.

47. Candidates should show understanding of how Morgan uses word choice and/or imagery effectively to create a striking visual impression or scene in this poem and in at least one other poem.

*Possible comments on other poems include:*

**"Good Friday"** – clear sense of scene comes across with several visual references to the journey of the bus ("brakes violently," "lurches round into the sun," etc)

**"In the snack bar"** – many references to place/scene throughout the poem

**"Trio"** – winter/Christmas scene established through expressions such as "sharp winter evening," "under the Christmas lights," etc

**"Winter"** – many references to place/scene throughout the poem

**"Slate"** – many references to place/scene throughout the poem.

Candidates may choose to answer in **bullet points** in this final question, or write a number of linked statements. There is **no requirement** to write a "mini essay".

Up to 2 marks can be achieved for identifying elements of **commonality** as identified in the question.

A further 2 marks can be achieved for **reference to the extract given.**

4 additional marks can be awarded for similar references to **at least one other text/part of the text** by the writer.

<u>In practice this means:</u>

**Identification of commonality** (eg: theme, central relationship, importance of setting, use of imagery, development in characterisation, use of personal experience, use of narrative style, or any other key element…)

**from the extract:**

1 × relevant reference to technique

1 × appropriate comment

or

1 × relevant reference to idea

1 × appropriate comment

or

1 × relevant reference to feature

1 × appropriate comment

or

1 × relevant reference to text

1 × appropriate comment

**(maximum of 2 marks only for discussion of extract)**

from **at least one other text/part of the text:**

as above (× 2) for **up to 4 marks**

**Text 3 – Poetry – *Visiting Hour* by Norman MacCaig**

**48.** 1 mark for reference.

1 mark for comment.

*Possible answers include:*

- "The hospital smell combs my nostrils" suggests visit is familiar/unpleasant/overpowering smell/vivid sensory image
- "green and yellow corridors" suggests he finds visit unpleasant – connotations of colours/vivid sensory image
- "What seems a corpse" suggests he feels uncertainty/anxiety about visit
- "trundled" suggests he feels the patient is being treated impersonally/dehumanised
- "vanishes" suggests he is very aware of death as absolute/final
- "heavenward" suggests he is very aware of finality of death/religious questions
- "I will not feel, I will not feel, until I have to"/repetition here tries to delay/avoid emotions.

**49.** 1 mark for technique.

1 mark for comment.

*Possible answers include:*

- "walk lightly, swiftly" – repetition of adverbs admires nurses' ability to deal with stresses of nursing

- "here and up and down and there" – unusual word order lightens mood/emphasises number/activity of nurses
- "their slender waists miraculously carrying their burden" – word-choice/metaphor admires nurses' ability to deal with stresses/burden despite being small/light
- "miraculously" – word choice – religious connotations poet thinks nurses are angelic/have magical powers
- "so much pain, so/many deaths …/so many farewells" – Repetition of "so" suggests admiration for nurses who have to deal with pain and death frequently.

**50.** 1 mark for reference.

1 mark for comment.

*Possible answers include:*

- "white cave of forgetfulness" or gloss suggests curtains or sheets are impenetrable/patient is isolated or ignored/poet is excluded/patient herself cannot remember things
- "withered hand/trembles on its stalk" or gloss woman's body is dying/frail/weak
- "Eyes move behind eyelids too heavy to raise" or gloss impersonal description/suggests how ill/weak patient is
- "Arm wasted of colour" or gloss arm is pale, lifeless, useless, no longer functioning
- "glass fang" or gloss suggests vampire-like IV, emphasising the poet's grief and distress
- "not guzzling but giving" or gloss alliteration suggests poet first sees the transfusion as pointless but then realises it is keeping patient alive.

**51.** Candidates should discuss MacCaig's use of imagery in this poem and in at least one other poem.

*Possible comments from other poems include:*

**"Assisi"** – appropriate comments on eg "half-filled sack"; "clucking contentedly", etc

**"Memorial"** – appropriate comments on eg "carousel of language"; "sad music", etc

**"Basking Shark"** – appropriate comments on eg "tin-tacked with rain"; "roomsized monster with a matchbox brain", etc

**"Sounds of the Day"** – "black drums rolled"; "bangle of ice round your wrist", etc

**"Aunt Julia"** – "she was buckets"; "with a seagull's voice", etc.

Candidates may choose to answer in **bullet points** in this final question, or write a number of linked statements. There is **no requirement** to write a "mini essay".

Up to 2 marks can be achieved for identifying elements of **commonality** as identified in the question.

A further 2 marks can be achieved for **reference to the extract given.**

4 additional marks can be awarded for similar references to **at least one other text/part of the text** by the writer.

In practice this means:

**Identification of commonality** (eg: theme, central relationship, importance of setting, use of imagery, development in characterisation, use of personal experience, use of narrative style, or any other key element…)

**from the extract:**

1 × relevant reference to technique

1 × appropriate comment

or

1 × relevant reference to idea

1 × appropriate comment

or

1 × relevant reference to feature

1 × appropriate comment

or

1 × relevant reference to text

1 × appropriate comment

**(maximum of 2 marks only for discussion of extract)**

from **at least one other text/part of the text:**

as above (× 2) for **up to 4 marks**

**Text 4 – Poetry –** *Divorce* by Jackie Kay

52. Candidates can refer to meaning or to techniques.

Two references to meaning 1 mark each.

1 mark for reference to technique.

1 mark for comment.

*Possible answers include:*

- She did not make a vow to stay together
- As her parents had done
- She wants out now
- She uses an emphatic tone
- She uses monosyllabic words
- She uses enjambment
- She uses a cliché
- She uses an ironic tone
- She uses negative language.

53. Candidates should make 3 distinct points for 3 marks.

*Possible answers include:*

- Gloss of "you never, ever said/a kind word" – mother was not positive/encouraging to her
- Gloss of "or a thank-you" – mother was ungrateful
- "tedious chores" – parents made the persona do hard/demanding housework
- "your breath smells like a camel," etc – father was (personally) repulsive
- "Are you in the cream puff," etc – father made sarcastic comments
- "Lady muck" – father put her down
- "I'd be better off in an orphanage" – emphasises how bad they are.

54. 1 mark for reference.

1 mark for comment.

*Possible answers include:*

- "faces turn up to the light"  "(turn) up" **or** "light" suggest positivity, enlightenment
- "who speak in the soft murmur of rivers" suggests calmness/quiet
- "and never shout" suggests calm, quiet approach
- "stroke their children's cheeks" suggests love/ gentleness/caring
- "sing in the colourful voices of rainbows, red to blue" suggests brightness/enjoyment/happiness/beauty/ varied approach, etc.

55. 1 mark for identification of tone.

1 mark for reference.

1 mark for comment.

*Possible answers include:*

**Humour:**

- "and quickly" – persona can't wait to get away from parents
- "your breath smells like a camel" humorously unappealing/exaggeration/further reference to "gives me the hump"
- "I would be better off in an orphanage" – humorous exaggeration.

**Despair:**

- reference to "there are things I cannot suffer any longer" – persona is at end of tether.

**Anger:**

- "I never chose you" – persona is angry with parents/ fact that she is trapped.

**Dismissive:**

- reference to "I don't want to be your child"/"These parents are not you"/"not you"  persona rejects parents.

**Admiration:**

- reference to "There are parents whose faces turn up to the light"/"There are parents who stroke their children's cheeks"/"sing in the colourful voices of rainbows", etc, the persona admires these parents and wishes hers could be more like them.

Any other reasonable identification of a tone, plus reference, plus comment.

56. Candidates should discuss the theme of family relationships in this poem and at least one other poem by Jackie Kay.

*Possible comments on other poems include:*

**"My Grandmother's Houses"** – girl/grandmother

**"Lucozade"** – mother/daughter

**"Gap Year"** – mother/daughter

**"Bed"** – mother/daughter

**"Keeping Orchids"** – mother/daughter

Candidates may choose to answer in **bullet points** in this final question, or write a number of linked statements. There is **no requirement** to write a "mini essay".

Up to 2 marks can be achieved for identifying elements of **commonality** as identified in the question.

A further 2 marks can be achieved for **reference to the extract given.**

4 additional marks can be awarded for similar references to **at least one other text/part of the text** by the writer.

<u>In practice this means:</u>

Identification of commonality (eg: theme, central relationship, importance of setting, use of imagery, development in characterisation, use of personal experience, use of narrative style, or any other key element...)

**from the extract:**

1 × relevant reference to technique

1 × appropriate comment

**or**

1 × relevant reference to idea

1 × appropriate comment

**or**

1 × relevant reference to feature

1 × appropriate comment

**or**

1 × relevant reference to text

1 × appropriate comment

**(maximum of 2 marks only for discussion of extract)**

from **at least one other text/part of the text:**

as above (× 2) for **up to 4 marks**

### SECTION 2 – Critical Essay

Please see the assessment criteria for the Critical Essay on page 165.

# Acknowledgements

Permission has been sought from all relevant copyright holders and Hodder Gibson is grateful for the use of the following:

The article 'Superstition' by Matthew Syed © The Times/News Syndication, 1st July 2009 (Model Paper 1 Reading for Understanding, Analysis and Evaluation pages 2 to 3);
An extract from 'Bold Girls' copyright © 1991 Rona Munro. Excerpted with permission of Nick Hern Books Ltd: www.nickhernbooks.co.uk (Model Paper 1 Critical Reading pages 2 to 3);
An extract from 'Sailmaker' by Alan Spence. Reproduced by permission of Hodder Education (Model Paper 1 Critical Reading pages 4 to 5);
An extract from 'Tally's Blood' by Ann Marie di Mambro, published by Education Scotland. Reprinted by permission of Ann Marie di Mambro/MacFarlane Chard Associates (Model Paper 1 Critical Reading pages 6 to 7);
An extract from 'The Cone Gatherers' by Robin Jenkins published by Canongate Books Ltd. (Model Paper 1 Critical Reading page 8);
An extract from 'The Testament Of Gideon Mack' (Hamish Hamilton 2006, Penguin Books 2007). Copyright © James Robertson, 2006. Reproduced by permission of Penguin Books Ltd. (Model Paper 1 Critical Reading page 10);
An extract from 'Kidnapped' by Robert Louis Stevenson, published by Cassell and Company Ltd 1886. Public domain. (Model Paper 1 Critical Reading page 12);
An extract from 'Mother and Son' by Iain Crichton Smith, taken from 'The Red Door: The Complete English Stories 1949-76', published by Birlinn. Reproduced by permission of Birlinn Ltd. www.birlinn.co.uk (Model Paper 1 Critical Reading page 14);
An extract from 'Zimmerobics' by Anne Donovan, taken from 'Hieroglyphics and Other Stories' published by Canongate Books Ltd. (Model Paper 1 Critical Reading page 16);
The poem 'Originally' by Carol Ann Duffy from 'The Other Country' (Anvil, 1990). Reproduced by permission of the author c/o Rogers, Coleridge & White Ltd., 20 Powis Mews, London W11 1JN (Model Paper 1 Critical Reading page 18);
The poem 'Hyena' by Edwin Morgan, from 'From Glasgow to Saturn' published by Carcanet Press Limited 1973 (Model Paper 1 Critical Reading page 20);
The poem 'Assisi' by Norman MacCaig from 'The Many Days: Selected Poems of Norman MacCaig' published by Polygon. Reproduced by permission of Birlinn Ltd. www.birlinn.co.uk (Model Paper 1 Critical Reading page 22);
The poem 'My Grandmother's Houses' by Jackie Kay, from 'Darling: New & Selected Poems' (Bloodaxe Books, 2007). Reprinted with permission of Bloodaxe Books, on behalf of the author. www.bloodaxebooks.com (Model Paper 1 Critical Reading page 24);
An extract from the article '2b or not 2b' by David Crystal from 'The Guardian' 5 June 2008. Originally from 'txtng: the gr8 db8' published by Oxford University Press, 2008 © David Crystal (Model Paper 2 Reading for Understanding, Analysis and Evaluation pages 2 to 3);
An extract from 'Tally's Blood' by Ann Marie di Mambro, published by Education Scotland. Reprinted by permission of Ann Marie di Mambro/MacFarlane Chard Associates (Model Paper 2 Critical Reading pages 2 to 3);
An extract from Bold Girls copyright © 1991 Rona Munro. Excerpted with permission of Nick Hern Books Ltd: www.nickhernbooks.co.uk (Model Paper 2 Critical Reading pages 5 to 6);
An extract from 'Sailmaker' by Alan Spence. Reproduced by permission of Hodder Education (Model Paper 2 Critical Reading pages 7 to 8);
An extract from the story 'In Church' by Iain Crichton Smith, taken from 'The Red Door: The Complete English Stories 1949-76', published by Birlinn. Reproduced by permission of Birlinn Ltd. www.birlinn.co.uk (Model Paper 2 Critical Reading page 10);
An extract from 'Away In A Manger' by Anne Donovan, taken from 'Hieroglyphics and Other Stories' published by Canongate Books Ltd. (Model Paper 2 Critical Reading pages 12 to 13);
An extract from 'The Cone Gatherers' by Robin Jenkins published by Canongate Books Ltd. (Model Paper 2 Critical Reading pages 14 to 15);
An extract from 'The Testament Of Gideon Mack' (Hamish Hamilton 2006, Penguin Books 2007). Copyright © James Robertson, 2006. Reproduced by permission of Penguin Books Ltd. (Model Paper 2 Critical Reading pages 16 to 17);
An extract from 'Kidnapped' by Robert Louis Stevenson, published by Cassell and Company Ltd 1886. Public domain. (Model Paper 2 Critical Reading page 18);
The poem 'Anne Hathaway' by Carol Anne Duffy, taken from 'The World's Wife', published by Picador 1999. Reproduced by permission of Pan Macmillan © Carol Ann Duffy 1999 (Model Paper 2 Critical Reading page 20);
The poem, 'Lucozade' by Jackie Kay, from 'Darling: New & Selected Poems' (Bloodaxe Books, 2007) Reprinted with permission of Bloodaxe Books, on behalf of the author. www.bloodaxebooks.com (Model Paper 2 Critical Reading page 21);
The poem 'Trio' by Edwin Morgan, from 'New Selected Poems' published by Carcanet Press Limited 2000 (Model Paper 2 Critical Reading page 23);
An extract from the poem 'Visiting Hour' by Norman MacCaig, taken from 'Three Scottish Poets', published by Canongate Books. Reproduced by permission of Birlinn Ltd. www.birlinn.co.uk (Model Paper 2 Critical Reading pages 25 to 26);